FORGING GODLY MEN

A Discipleship Manual For Dads and Their Teenage Sons

MIKE CURTIS

Forging Godly Men

Published by Powerline Productions
Lake Mary, FL. U.S.A.
www.powerlineprod.com

All inquiries may be made to the author, Mike Curtis, through email:
Pastormike@powerlinecc.com

Unless otherwise noted, all Scripture quotations taken from the New American Standard Bible®, Copyright © 1960, 1962, 1963, 1968, 1971, 1972, 1973, 1975, 1977, 1995 by The Lockman Foundation
Used by permission. (www.Lockman.org)

Other Scripture quotations, where noted, taken from The Holy Bible, New International Version®, Copyright © 1973, 1978, 1984 by International Bible Society.

ISBN 979-8-9864664-9-1

Acknowledgements

Thank you to my supportive wife, Meredith, whose patience and understanding have been limitless as my heavenly Father has had to first form the truths in this book in my own life,

To my son, Jimmy, who was the first victim of experiment with this discipleship manual—and daily walks its principles out,

To Laura Nolette for her countless hours in format editing,

To Meredith, Jenny Rose, Julianna, Tim, Steve, Scott, Cole, Jim, and Josh for their invaluable editorial comments and corrections,

And to numerous dads who have used this book to help carry out their God-given mandate to make Christ-impassioned disciples of their sons.

Table of Contents

Introduction

Our boat had stalled in deep water.

It was loaded to the hilt with camping gear we were trying to get to the other end of the lake where our rented cabin was. My mother and brothers were settling into it while my dad and I were attempting to bring the last load in a rented boat. What happened that late summer afternoon has served to define for me what a man is and remind me of what men do when faced with insurmountable odds.

We were struggling to keep the rented boat's old motor running. This was not a place I wanted to be stranded—in the middle of a large lake facing my fears of deep water. I was always terrified of the unknown as a child. Whatever lurked down there was none of my business, and I definitely wanted to keep it that way.

As evening was settling in, a friendly neighboring camper approached us in his large-engine boat and asked if we needed help. My dad was eager to accept after numerous struggles with our stalling motor, so we tossed him our tow rope, and he secured it to the stern. After we climbed aboard his boat, he started off slowly, tapping only slightly into the engine's 80hp. I sat in the back keeping a watchful eye on our tiny boat that sat low in the water.

What happened next caught me completely by surprise. As our neighborly camper picked up speed, the water displaced by the bow of our disabled boat crested the brow and within seconds it plummeted straight into the deep waters. I yelled frantically to stop. All our gear had gone down. What were we going to do? My fears stifled any answer. I froze. My world stood still. Everything in it but my dad, of course! Within seconds he had quickly pulled his shirt and shoes off and dove in where our boat's contents had suddenly emptied. Though the boat soon resurfaced, my dad was nowhere to be found. My fears intensified. Had he gotten entangled in the weeds below or had some unknown creature gotten the best of him? Ten-year-old boys have vivid imaginations. My fears forbade me to dive in after him. I felt cowardly as the waters grew still.

Suddenly, my dad's head popped out of the water. But after two gasps of breath, he disappeared into the murky depths again. A few items had resurfaced, and I began to pull them into the boat. A calm settled over the waters once again while my fears were stirred up more. "Dad? Dad!" I began to call. By now I was kneeling down, leaning over the boat's edge, peering into nothingness, not even a reflection. Soon, long, metal poles broke the stillness of the water's surface as my dad overturned our capsized boat and tossed our tent poles into it. He said he couldn't reach the bottom where our tent no doubt had settled, so we salvaged the remaining equipment that had managed to resurface and placed it into our little boat. Needless to say, the tow the rest of the way to our rented cabin was slow and uneventful.

In the space of about five minutes that day, I was impacted by a stark contrast that was both humbling and admirable. A sense of shame that hung over me concerning my fears and cowardly inaction was soon displaced by a sense of pride. My dad responded to a crisis situation with reflex action, braved the depths of the unknown and rescued all he could from the demise of our upended boat. He was a hero that day. Courage had taken the helm. Fear was tossed to the backseat (where I was!). There was something in the midst of all this that helped define for me what it meant to be a man.

Our "Local Vertical"

Have you ever asked yourself the question: What does it mean to be a man? As you try to define it, does it feel like oil slipping through your fingers? You can't quite grasp it? If so, join the countless others who fumble with the concept of manhood. After I had given a talk on "Raising Godly Men in a Feminist Culture," a dad of six pulled me aside and confessed he had never been taught as a boy or a young man what it meant to be a man. It was elusive. I felt his frustration. So, where are we to get our measure of a man?

Before answering that question, let me first illustrate our predicament, men (and by "men," I especially mean every dad, every young man with no father as a model, and every son aspiring to be that godly hero). Some time ago, five men entered a space capsule for eighty days to test their limits on disorientation. This capsule was not in space but was a terrestrial biosphere. It simulated weightlessness. There was no "local vertical," no indicators of right-side-up, and upside down. They didn't walk, they floated. They took no baths, because the water would not stay in the tub. No showers, because the water floated. Pills drifted out of their uncapped bottles. Shaving kits were opened, and razors were plucked from the air. Food refused to remain on spoons or plates. Should one try to turn a screw with a

screwdriver, good luck—he turned! The sun rose and set sixteen times every 24 hours. This created complete and total disorientation, affecting their ability to cope.

Today, we live in a society of cultural relativism with similar disorientation. We are told that there are no moral absolutes except what each culture determines, that God is an archaic concept defined by superstitions, and that the only difference between male and female are the obvious biological ones that determine reproduction. Period. But even this is in dispute. Male/female roles are culturally defined and, therefore, relative. Dress and mannerisms? The same. Even sexual orientation is a flip of the coin. Basically, masculine/feminine concepts are to be discarded as a new unisex model takes center stage.

In short, our society has lost its "local vertical." Feminist anthropologists express contempt for the genetic disparity between men and women. The Y chromosome is held in disdain, mocked as the main contributor to high crime rates. Maleness is viewed as an undesirable trait, a genetic mutation. Truth has been bent, twisted, and distorted beyond recognition, shaped into what we want it to be. "We define it," they demand, "not God!" Even many who belong to the Church (or at least they say) have sought to blur the line between men and women, masculine and feminine. They hold in their hands Jack Sparrow's broken moral compass, leading them where their heart desires.

The question "what is a man?" must initially be answered biologically, regardless of our culture's contentions. The "culprit" is indeed the Y chromosome. It is the distinctive difference between you and your sister. The SRY gene on it triggers the formation of a boy's testes while in his mother's womb, which then will produce testosterone. Among other things, this will produce more aggressive behavior and larger muscles in general (certain conditioning, or training, will affect these as well). As much as our generation may want to deny it, there is a significant difference between boys and girls that will impact numerous factors in their lives, not the least of which will be certain callings of God, including biblical roles they will perform.

What about the Scriptures though? Does it offer us a "local vertical," a clear picture of maleness that as men we can embrace? I believe so. One clue is found in I Corinthians 16:13, where it says, *"Be men of courage"* (*NIV*, 1978). Paul's command here is the single Greek word *andrízomai*, based on the word for "man, male or husband" (*aner*) as opposed to "man or mankind in general" (*anthropos*). A literal translation of the Greek command would then read: "Be a man!"

Throughout this study book you will discover specific ways you can effectively walk in your manhood according to Scripture. As you do the lessons, allow me (and your mentor) to call out the man in you, that the Spirit of God would stir you to live out these traits courageously as a Godly Man.

Masculinity is not a strictly culturally defined word. It is biblically grounded. We are not left with a best-guess solution to the question, "What is a man?" Scripture is quite clear. Let's discover that together!

The Need for Forging Godly Men Today

Needless to say, our society struggles with the concepts of masculinity and manhood. It even has difficulty defining a man. And whatever men do that suggests strength is usually labeled "toxic masculinity." Jesus' overturning the money changers tables in the temple to defend the honor of His heavenly Father is discarded as such and discouraged. The feminizing of men has become epidemic. Now more than ever we must train our young men to be strong, to stand up to evil, and to boldly emulate the life of Jesus. Do not be mistaken, however, "toxic masculinity" is indeed a deep-rooted problem in our culture. But most men have no proper plumbline for what it means to be a man. There is a much-needed balance between steel and velvet, firmness and compassion. But extremes rule.

This workbook will help you find that biblical balance and avoid the extremes that are truly toxic and not just touted as such by society. God's truth must be your "local vertical," guiding you to become the man He created you to be. He will take you through a forging process that will mold you, sharpen you, and strengthen you to this end. It is neither easy nor brief. Consider the forging process of a sword. Though it will be explained in more detail later in the book, know that when the steel blade is heated, its molecular structure is changed, rearranging the iron and carbon atoms,

making it stronger—less breakable and retaining its sharp edge longer. The Scriptural principles in this book will call you to a similar radical change. So, learn to embrace this process bravely. It is necessary, and there is no substitute. Much is at stake.

How to Use This Book

This book comprises ten of the thirty qualities of manhood that I walked my son through, and, I believe, you will want to walk in as well. Most of these ten character traits are specific for men, though women may hold them to a lesser degree. Other traits are equally shared by our female counterparts but are necessary for us men to possess if we are to be the godly men this world needs, that our family needs, and that God longs for us to be in order to lead and change this world for His purposes and His glory.

Now allow me to share with you how to get the most from this book. Each chapter is divided into three sections: "**DIG IN!**", a Bible study that focuses on observations and interpretations of the relevant Scriptures; "**THINK ABOUT IT!**", a teaching on the particular subject; and "**BRING IT HOME!**", several questions that focus on the application of the biblical principles discussed.

Make sure you answer all questions fully and thoughtfully, not settling for quick, short answers. As you read the "**THINK ABOUT IT!**" section, be sure to underline or highlight those points you find to be significant or helpful to you. Drawing upon them during your discussions will facilitate deeper and more personal reflection upon the topic. Dads/mentors, you will want to walk your son/mentee through the first and last set of questions. For my son and me, this took two (and occasionally three) one-hour, weekly sessions per chapter. We covered the introduction and "**DIG IN!**" sections the first week and the "**THINK ABOUT IT!**" and "**BRING IT HOME!**" sections the second week. Should the Bible study portion need to be divided up due to time constraints, each "**DIG IN!**" has two sections with a brief wrap up concluding them. Dads/mentors, interject some of your own life examples and insights into your discussion of the "**THINK ABOUT IT!**" teaching. This will help personalize the sessions with your son/mentee. To do this, you will need to complete the chapter yourself and make personal notes, drawing upon them in your time together.

The enclosed Bible studies, teachings, and personally reflective questions are challenging, regardless of your age. They are topics we all must deeply consider and grow in. Many, however, under thirteen or fourteen may find them a bit beyond their grasp (though I began to teach them to my son in pared down form when he was twelve). Each dad and mentor will need to assess their son's/mentee's maturity to determine their readiness for this material. The content is also quite relevant for any young man in his twenties and perhaps beyond. Regardless, the principles taught are much needed in this generation of young men whom I believe are eager to learn them.

We live in a day in which God's Word *must* be our "local vertical." So, guys, "Be a man!"—one who is a hero to his son and a godly example of masculinity to the world. Take the risk. Dive in. And salvage the contents of this sinking boat called "Godly Manhood"!

Godly Men
Are Passionate for God

My older brother tossed me a small pamphlet which on the cover read, "Am I Going to Heaven? Find out inside."

"Seriously?" I thought to myself with a quick but discreet roll of the eyes. Little did I realize in the midst of my annoyance that what followed would challenge and change me from a superficial, religious "Christian" to a young, impassioned follower of Jesus Christ, who was going to invite me on a journey to discover what it really meant to be a godly man.

I knew my brother had recently been going through some unusual changes in his life. At least from my perspective they were unusual. He seemed to enjoy "religious things" more those days, attending Bible studies without being asked to, playing Scripture songs on his new guitar constantly, and reading the Bible every day. This just seemed way too religious to me. Don't get me wrong, my family went to church every Sunday. My dad was the choir director, so we had to. But that was pretty much it. My brother was really getting into the "church stuff," and he seemed genuinely excited about it. I guess he felt it was my turn to dive in, but I was far more hesitant. "It's only Friday, please! Why the heaven lecture now?" I groaned to myself.

Admittedly, I was very resistant as I began to read: "I'm going to heaven, because…" (check one)

- ❏ "I go to church."

- ❏ "I tithe."

- ❏ "I've been baptized."

- ❏ "I keep holy unction."

"Wait a minute," I thought to myself, "'Holy unction'? What's that?" It sounded pretty religious, so I checked it off like I had the others. I was doing well going through the list, checking each square as I went. "This is easy. I've got heaven in the bag!" I said as I came to the last box:

- ❏ "Other," it read.

I checked that one just to cover all my bases. What I read next, however, challenged me to the core. It began to explain what it meant to be a *real* Christian. I began to realize that I'd been riding on my parents' coattails. I knew about Jesus without really knowing *Him*. The resistance in my heart began to fade. I grew hungry. I began to want this new life my brother had. I was fourteen and already tired of my lifestyle. I knew something was wrong. My sin felt like dirt clinging to me. I truly began to hate it at that moment, but I felt trapped like a prisoner in it. I looked up at my brother and asked, "Okay, so what do I do?"

He shared a cute anecdote that has stuck with me since: "Michael, going to church doesn't make you a Christian any more than standing in a garage makes you a car."

Honestly, it was a little silly and fairly obvious, but it hit home for me. I did see myself as a Christian because I went to church. I did believe I was going to heaven because I had done some good things. He continued: "You see, you have to surrender your life to Him, Michael. Believe *in* Him. Follow *Him*! Honestly, you haven't." It was a little forward, but I let him say it. I knew he was right.

That day I discovered what real faith was, my need to repent, and what it meant to really give my heart to Jesus. As I did these things, my life was changed. That's what this chapter will help you understand. But it will go further to challenge you to live wholeheartedly for Christ, to be His impassioned follower. Remember to answer the questions thoroughly. Give considerable thought to them. Mark any questions or passages of Scripture you don't understand and have your dad or mentor explain them more thoroughly.

DIG IN!

Study Section 1

READ Romans 3:23.

What is sin?

God's glory is the majesty of all of His perfections. List some ways God is perfect.

READ Galatians 5:19-21, Romans 1:28-32, and II Timothy 3:1-5.

List some ways we can sin and miss God's perfection.

List some ways *you* have sinned.

READ Isaiah 59:1-2.

What is the consequence, or result, of our sins?

REREAD Romans 1:32 and Romans 6:23.

What is another consequence of our sins?

READ Ephesians 2:1.

Describe the type of death this passage is referring to.

What is *"the gift of God"* in Romans 6:23?

What is a gift? Is it earned by something we do?

READ Isaiah 53:6 and Romans 5:8.

The Isaiah passage is a prophecy. That means it predicts what will happen in the future. It was written sometime around 700 B.C. and speaks of Jesus the Messiah. What did the Lord do to Jesus according to this verse?

What part does the Cross play in this?

What is God's heart towards us?

READ John 3:16.

How did God demonstrate His love for us?

How are we to respond to this display of love?

READ John 8:30-34.

John divides those who eagerly listened to Him into two groups: those who "believed in Him" and those who "believed Him."

How is *"believed in him"* different from *"believed him"*?

How did the latter group respond to Jesus?

READ Luke 14: 27, 33.

What is a disciple? (You may need to look this word up in the dictionary or a Bible dictionary)

What does a disciple of Jesus do?

Please note that Scripture makes clear that being a believer in Jesus and a disciple of Jesus is the same thing and not two different levels of Christianity. Since faith is required to become a disciple, it is fair to say that true faith is expressed in those ways just listed. Words such as "surrender" and "wholehearted commitment" help summarize these and give us a deeper understanding of faith. So, by faith we surrender to Jesus as Savior and Lord. What is it that we need to surrender to Christ?

Understand that our initial surrender to Christ (saving faith) will need to grow.

READ Acts 3:19.

What does the word "repent" mean?

When we repent (this is a matter of our heart and our will that will later be seen in our actions), what is it we are to turn away from?

Can you think of another word for *"turn to God"*?

What is the result of repenting and turning to God?

READ II Corinthians 5:17.

Faith and repentance can be viewed as two sides of the same coin. According to this passage, what happens to someone who repents and believes (and is therefore "in Christ")?

Describe this new change, or transformation? What does it look like?

READ John 3:3.

Paul used the term *"new creature"* to describe the Christian's transformation. What term does Jesus use here?

READ Matthew 12:33.

And what term does Jesus use here?

What does it produce?

List some *"good fruit"* the believer in Jesus will produce (use Galatians 5:22-23 to help you).

Let's stop at this point and reflect on a truth that is often overlooked today. True, genuine faith and repentance are necessary for salvation, granted. God's grace is poured out into the new believer's heart and a transformation process begins. This always happens, and there are no exceptions. The dead sinner becomes alive in Christ. His sins are forgiven, and he is changed.

So, here's the question: What then is the assurance of our salvation? Is it a stake driven into the ground that reminds us of our decision to follow Christ? Is it the fact that we walked a church aisle or prayed a prayer at the altar? Though these may be helpful in our coming to Christ, Scripture never refers to them as assurances of our salvation. Apart from the Holy Spirit's confirmation in our heart (Romans 8:15; Galatians 4:6), which can be subjective and difficult to discern (though important), then what is? The entire book of I John details the answer. It is this and only this: a changed life. If there has been no change, no good fruit produced, it is because the wrong seed was planted, and the tree is bad.

Again, the result of genuine faith and repentance is always some measure of transformation. If I told my children that while I was jogging today, trying to cross Rt. 46A, a semi-truck going in excess of 50 mph hit me square on, they would laugh at me (then probably mock me!). Why? Because anyone hit by a semi-truck going over 50 mph would never live to tell of it. On impact they are drastically changed—for the worse! As believers in Jesus, we are changed— for the better, in no less of a dramatic way. This is the incredible transforming power of the gospel. We are taken from death to life, from enemies of the Father to being reconciled with Him, and are thereby empowered to live a radically different life. Our assurance, then, is found in the change that Christ produces in us. Please don't miss this truth. It is important as we move on.

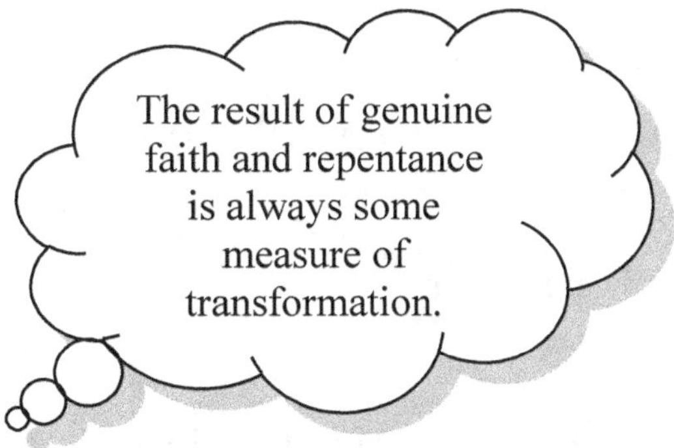

This concludes *Study Section 1*. You may stop here for now and finish at another time if you choose, or you can continue on. Either way, a summary may be of help here. We have learned that our sin has spiritually killed every one of us and that God's gift of life and forgiveness can only be received through faith in His

Son Jesus. This requires a surrendering to His Lordship. But genuine faith is always accompanied by repentance. You cannot have one without the other, because in our repenting we are choosing to turn away from sin *to* God. This is the essence of faith. And this initiates a transformation process that continues throughout our life with Christ.

Study Section 2

READ Matthew 6:33.

What should be our top priority?

Can you define these?

READ Matthew 22:34-40.

In your own words, what is the greatest commandment?

In your own words, what is the second greatest commandment?

How are they alike?

The focus of the kingdom of God then is love, first for God, then for others. Everything else falls a distant third. What else could be in this last, third category? List several.

If we love anything(-one) in the last two categories more than God, what would we call this? (see Ephesians 5:5)

READ Revelation 2:1-3.

This is one of seven letters Jesus dictated to John to be given to seven different churches. This one was addressed to the church in Ephesus where Paul had spent nearly three years proclaiming the gospel and establishing the church there, his longest stay by far of any city he evangelized. His companion, Timothy, also had spent considerable time there training and setting in leaders. In addition, tradition says that the apostle John had ministered there for several years. As you can see, it had a vast legacy of strong Bible teaching. What does Jesus commend the church for? List them.

In your own words describe or assess the church in Ephesus?

Now **READ** Revelation 2:4-5.

What does Jesus rebuke them for? What does He mean?

What things do you suppose they *"did at first"*?

These hard working, persevering, theologically correct Ephesians had grown cold in their love for Jesus. Do you see this happening in the church today? If so, what are you seeing?

Is Jesus *your* first love? How can you tell?

The truth of the matter is that our love for Jesus needs to be the foundation for what we do for Him. It apparently was not for the Ephesians, even though Paul, Timothy, and John had ministered extensively there.

Describe the difference between knowing about Jesus and knowing Jesus (see Matthew 7:22-23, especially verse 23, for a clue).

READ Psalm 27:4-8; Psalm 42:1-2; and Psalm 84:1-2, 10.

What is meant by the *"beauty of the LORD"*?

Does David, who is not a Levite or even a priest, really want to live in the temple?

If this is not his point, what is?

In 27:8 the Hebrew for "face" is many times translated "presence." Give some examples then of how David might seek God's presence?

What does David long to do in Psalm 42 and 84?

Have you ever been so overheated and thirsty you thought you might faint? How might satisfying that kind of thirst be similar to a longing for our First Love, Jesus? (And this is very masculine by the way)

Do you have a friend you really look forward to spending time with? God invites us to want to be with Him even more.

Let's close out our Bible study with one more passage.

READ II Chronicles 16:9.

How does God strengthen us? (Note that a more literal translation suggests that God shows Himself strong on our behalf. The concepts of blessing, working on our behalf, God's favor or grace, and even miraculous intervention are included in the meaning.)

Can you use some personal examples (for King Asa in the context it was winning a battle against the evil northern kingdom of Israel without relying on wicked Ben-hadad king of Aram)?

What is needed on our part for God to act on our behalf like this?

What does half-hearted commitment look like? Give a few examples if you can.

Can you name some people in the Bible who were wholeheartedly committed to the Lord?

Can you name some people you know in your life today who are fully devoted to God?

This concludes our study. We have seen that loving God and living in His kingdom are to be our highest priorities. We are called to have a passion for Him that is wholehearted. Everything in the disciple's life flows from this. As you read through the "**THINK ABOUT IT!**" section you will see how all of this forms a solid foundation for our life.

THINK ABOUT IT!

The alarm was bleeping so loudly I quickly, though reluctantly, shut it off so as to not awaken my wife. "5:00 A.M.," it glared at me. "What? Who set my alarm so early?" I wondered, trying to sort through the cloudiness of my mind. As the haze lifted, I remembered that my city pastors' prayer meeting was that morning and *I* was the culprit who had set the alarm so early. I pulled myself from bed, walked into my closet and got dressed in the dark, again so as not to awaken my wife. Upon entering the bathroom and turning the light on, I realized a problem as I stared into the mirror. My button-down shirt was completely cock-eyed! Because I got the first button wrong, the rest were misaligned. I'm not a very particular dresser, so my wife says, but this was a little much. I could imagine Jeff, a pastor friend of mine, say, "Hey Mike, I see you got *yourself* dressed this morning!" So, I promptly re-buttoned the shirt and headed out.

The First Button
Our relationship with God is like that first button. If we get it wrong, everything else gets misaligned: family, job, relationships, ministry, studies, finances, dreams, and goals. Everything is affected. The real question then becomes: do we love Jesus more than anything or anyone else? But this is a tough question to answer for several reasons.

God's Love Must Be Experienced
First, it *is* hard to love someone you cannot see, because relationships are by nature experienced. How then do we grow to deeply love the invisible God? By

experiencing Him. But to experience Him, we must first understand what this love of the invisible God is.

Scripture is very clear that every one of us has sinned (Romans 3:23). Sin broke that image of God we were created in. The curse of Genesis 3 is that brokenness in all of creation caused by sin. In essence then, we are all broken people. It is seen in how we relate with God and people. It pushes us away from our Creator and leads us to do things we deeply regret.

Scripture also says that we were God's enemies as a result (Romans 5:10), trapped in Satan's snare and in bondage to sin (II Timothy 2:25-26; Romans 6:6-7; Galatians 3:22). We must be rescued from our sin in order to have this relationship with God. The only way for this to happen is for an exchange to take place. Since *the wages of sin is death"* (Romans 6:23), someone must suffer the punishment of death for our sin that we clearly deserve. Isaiah 53:5 tells us that Jesus did this: "But he was pierced for our transgressions, he was crushed for our iniquities; the punishment that brought us peace was

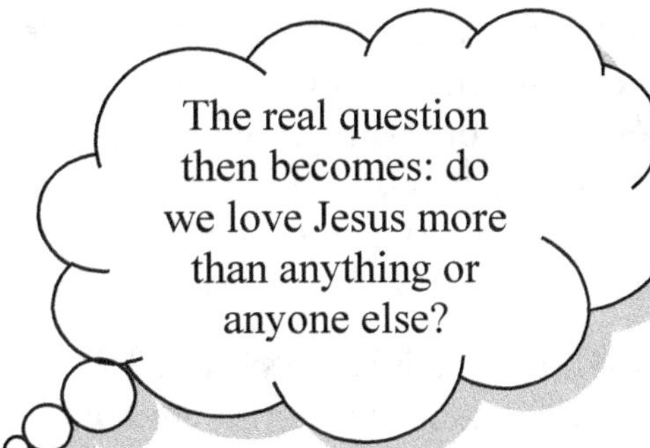

on him, and by his wounds we are healed" (NIV, 1978). And justice demands "life for life" (Exodus 21:23). For this reason, Jesus laid down His life for us in a Great Exchange, whereby my sins are placed upon Him and forgiven when I put my trust in Him. It was His life for my life. This is the amazing significance and utter necessity of the cross.

Consequently, when we are forgiven by Him, we experience His love. But before we are forgiven, it is merely a concept, a truth we have read about. The greater the forgiveness, the more we experience and understand God's love for us and, consequently, the more we usually desire to love Him in return.

This is the point of the story of the woman who anointed Jesus' feet in Luke 7. Because she was forgiven much, she loved much. So, should we sin more that we might be forgiven more and thus love more? Is this Jesus' point? Of course not! The Pharisee who was chiding Jesus was simply not very aware of his own sinfulness, whereas the woman at Jesus' feet felt quite convicted of hers. The more we are able to see the utter offensiveness of our sin to an infinitely holy

God who patiently extends His forgiveness to us over and over, day after day, the more we discover the depth of His love for us (Ephesians 3:18-19), a love that is so vast we will never be able to fully know it (read "fully understand and experience it"). We can experience God through answered prayer, promises that He fulfills, and more. These experiences are personal. Jesus becomes someone who is more than words on a page but our intimately loving Savior.

Love Is Masculine Too

Second, when we speak of loving Jesus, it can somehow seem a little feminine. This is unfortunate but true. Loving God, however, can be very masculine. It is not gender specific. As men we can tend to downplay our emotions, thinking this mushy stuff is for girls. But love is not just emotional. It can be passionate. This word "passionate" may be a little easier to connect with, because it speaks of zeal and intense devotion, and as men we usually better understand these. They deal more with our will though still have an emotional thrust. Young men, let us never be afraid to speak of our deep love and devotion to Jesus. Let us always be full of zeal (Romans 12:11), or passion, as we follow Him second to none!

David was certainly passionate for God. In II Samuel 6, while bringing the Ark of the Covenant into Jerusalem, David danced enthusiastically before the Lord. The Ark was God's very presence on earth, and David longed for this. You may need to revamp your views of this particular article from the tabernacle's Holy of Holies if it's solely based on the movie Raiders of the Lost Ark. There was certainly an austerity about the Ark, but God is not just holy, He is also loving. David knew this. It was exhilarating for him to have God's presence in Israel's capital city where he lived and ruled. So, David *"celebrated before the LORD"* (verse 21) and expressed his love for God in such an unkingly (though not irreverent) way, it was viewed as "undignified" by some (verse 23—NIV, 1978). David's love for God was far greater than his concern about the opinion of others. There was but one opinion that mattered, and only that captured David's attention here. Again, being passionate for God is very masculine and is weighed in the devotion of our heart to Him and Him alone.

Delighting In God

Third, it can be hard to know if we love Jesus more than anyone or anything else, because it is rather subjective. It will require that we weigh the desires and motives of our heart—not an easy thing. It can be seen in our hunger for God's Word, prayer, worship, evangelism, serving, and so on. But it's possible for a person to do all of these things and still not be passionate for God. Been there, done that, as they say. Psalm 37:4 challenges us: *"Delight yourself in the LORD."* As we shall see, delight is the key here.

When I was a teenager, I ran track and cross country. This required quite a bit of devotion as I had to run between six and fifteen miles each day. After watching Wide World of Sports, I was motivated! This carried me for a few days, but my "desire" soon faded to "duty". I was shallow here and quite a bit of discipline was required. Needless to say, I failed in my consistency quite often. Many athlete wannabes camp out here, lots of sporadic "desire" (or motivation) with little sense of "duty" (or self-discipline). Even-

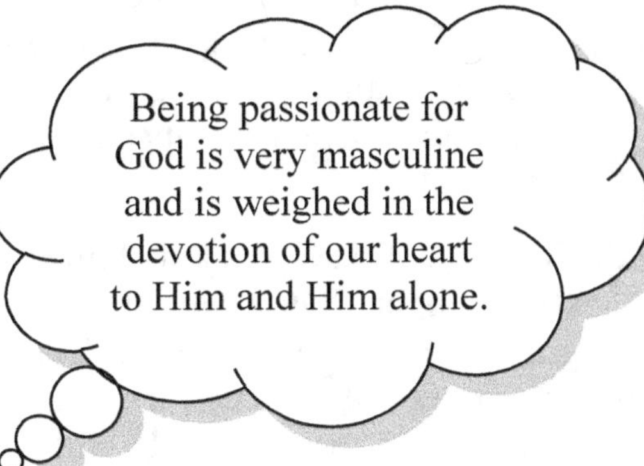

tually, perhaps, one matures and becomes more dutiful. They get better but only to a point. They experience some burn out and the consistency begins to lag again. They need to "find another gear."

Many Christians live their lives just like this: initial desire, mix in some duty with eventual burn out, and a lackluster walk with Christ results. They need to "find another gear!" But what is that "gear"? Psalm 37:4 says that gear is *"delight."* We need to move from initial desire, to duty, then to delight. Athletes that don't thoroughly enjoy the sport they compete in rarely succeed. It's the same with Christians. Please don't misunderstand. Duty is important. Faithfulness, doing what we should do even when we don't want to, is necessary, just not enough. If we do not find ourselves regularly delighting ourselves in the Lord and our default "gear" in following Christ is "duty," we will not be able to discover what it means to be a truly godly man.

Godly Men are excited about their walk with Christ. They look forward to a daily time in God's Word and prayer. They don't just skim the surface in the study of the Scriptures, they try to dig deep, asking lots of questions. They discover it is a goldmine of truth that is relevant for them in their daily lives. They regularly experience the power of its promises.

In addition, they delight in praying for the lost that they are seeking to reach with the gospel and for others who desperately need God to intervene in their lives in some way. I've heard it said: "Pray when you want to, pray when you don't want to, and pray until you want to." My long distance runs were similar. As a runner I found that other "gear," but my runs didn't always start out enthusiastically. I knew to get in shape I needed to run that day, so I threw my clothes and shoes on and started out. I did this out of duty. Eventually, within a short while, I was enjoying my run and cruising at a good speed. I ran until I wanted to. I became delight-driven. Similarly, though I did not always start my morning out eager for the Word and prayer as I wiped the sleep from my eyes, the time soon enough shifted to delight.

Godly Men seek first God's kingdom and His righteousness. They delight in the things that delight God. Their heart hurts for the things that hurt God's heart. They grieve for what grieves God. They rejoice in what God rejoices in. Their values are God's values. Their desires are what God desires. You see, when you delight yourself in the Lord, "He will give you the desires of your heart." You want what He does.

Godly Men sacrifice anything for God, because they delight in Him. He makes daily hard decisions to safeguard this, allowing nothing to compete for his affections. He has died to self and is willing to lay down even his life for Christ and His kingdom. This is the meaning of *"carry his own cross"* (Luke 14:27). As Jesus' disciples once put it, *"We have left everything and followed you"* (Matthew 19:27).

A Word About God's Grace
"We love, because He first loved us" (I John 4:19).

Though Scripture declares that you were God's enemy, He initiated in rescuing you. He fought for you to win you. Whether you recognized it or not, His grace worked in innumerable occasions to draw you to Him. His rescue plan for you was accomplished as you responded to this grace in heart-surrendered faith and He forgave you, brought you to life, made you His child, justified you, initially sanctified you, and by His indwelling Spirit gave you a vast inheritance in His kingdom. All by His grace. All because He loved you. But His grace didn't stop there.

Throughout your friendship with Him, He desires to pour out His grace to you daily. This grace is more than forgiveness of sin for salvation, it is ***everything***

He has that you do not but desperately need. It is a vast reservoir of His abundance—of anything you need. You will discover numerous obstacles along your pathway to fulfilling God's will for your life, difficulties that seem impossible or immoveable. God delights in these opportunities to display His love and strength, His kindness and power. He will permit circumstances in your life that will press you hard against the wall. They will make you feel helpless and weak. But this is ok, since it's not really about you but about Him. When you desperately cry out to Him in these hard, seemingly dark moments, He will shine His light, flex His muscles, and show Himself mighty—but according to His great plan not yours.

In these moments of weakness in your life, His grace will be displayed. It will be more than enough. In your weakness, His strength will be shown to be perfect (II Corinthians 12:10). These moments are meant to humble you *("He gives grace to the humble"*—James 4:6) and stir up faith in you to completely rely upon Him as He works these things together to maximize His glory and your good. All of this will be used to endear your heart to Him, forging an even greater devotion to and love for Him. This is the path of the impassioned disciple of Jesus. It is from this increasing depth of love for Him that you will serve Him, sacrifice for Him, deny yourself for Him, and stay true to Him. And it is all part of His amazing plan for your life.

This will become the source of your devotion to him and delight in Him. In my own life, these deep, agonizing struggles have become the most treasured moments of God's greatest miracles for me. So, I encourage you to step into the yoke and live in submission to Him always. He is completely trustworthy. And in your reliance upon Him, He will pour out His more-than-enough grace for you to walk in every character quality this book will call you to. Then you will find yourself delighting in your Rescuer and finding every measure of grace you will ever need—every day!

Living At 210?

Perhaps, moving from duty to delight has been difficult for you. You want to but just can't seem to do it. You're frustrated, even weary. What can be done? Let me share an illustration, then several points of application that may help.

Water can be found in three states, the most common, of course, is its liquid form. When water moves from a liquid state to a solid state, it first must reach a critical temperature point. Then it goes through some interesting changes. At

32°F water turns to ice and actually becomes lighter than its liquid form and floats. Can you imagine if this were not the case? The ice of frozen rivers would sink to the bottom where fish find their food supply, making it impossible for them to feed. The result? They would die! Pretty amazing stuff how God created this world.

Water's other critical temperature point is when it turns from a liquid to a gas. This happens when it boils at 212°F. This transition produces an incredible abundance of energy. Older engines were powered by steam. Some people use steam for cooking. Recently, we used it to clean our carpets. Many things steep or dissolve much better in boiling water. Let's note something of interest: water does not reach this critical point at 150°F or 200°F. Neither does it reach it at 210°F.

Do you remember II Chronicles 16:9? It is relevant here. God desires wholehearted commitment on our part. Half-hearted devotion is less than adequate. Many truly believe in the "Just Enough" mentality, nothing radical about their relationship with Christ. They don't live full out, over-the-top with total abandonment, or passionately for God. They do "Just Enough," that is, "just enough" in their mind. Like the hourly employee who punches in at 8 A.M. and punches out at 5 P.M., gets his hour for lunch with other smaller breaks, and who is unwilling to work after 5 P.M. or come in early, or who refuses to learn his job more efficiently to excel in the company, he does "Just Enough" to get by and his wage reflects this. Is this how you live? Serving God "Just Enough?" Do you expect His blessing in return? Many Christians do—and they expect water to boil at 210°F.

Life at 210 goes nowhere and accomplishes little! God's promise is to show Himself mighty on behalf of those whose hearts are fully committed to Him. They live life at 212. Full surrender, no holds barred, to the limit. Or perhaps as our cartoon hero Buzz Lightyear says, "To infinity and beyond!" For us, that means that Christ has captured our heart's devotion fully. He has won us completely. In the midst of great accomplishment, David chose to live at 210 for a season. The results were disastrous. When other kings went out to war to secure their borders and protect their land and their people, David relaxed. He felt he had done enough. He had succeeded. Nations bowed in service to him. Their tribute was his. He felt pretty good about himself. Consequently, at an unguarded moment, he fell into adultery and murder. He hurt others. His sin devastated his family and his kingdom. In his moment of pride and self-satisfaction, David's heart was unyielded to God. You see, living life at 212 isn't really about **doing** more for God but **surrendering** more to God. It's an attitude of the heart that will **eventually** be seen in what we say and do. Water at 212°F goes through profound change. Expect God to do nothing less for you!

Beware the Passion Killers

Let's admit, though, that for the most part David did live life at 212. For this reason, in spite of some lapses, he was seen as the moral measuring stick for all subsequent kings. Their devotion to God was measured by this "man after God's own heart." But as we've seen, even such men can allow certain things to douse the flames and cool their passion for God. Let's look at a few of these "passion killers" that may cause us to live at 210.

First, sin, or compromise, can neutralize us. It is merciless, even the small ones. We may think it's no big deal, just this one time, this one look, this one lie, this one angry remark. But it still seems to sap us of our zeal for the Lord. Romans 12:9 tells us to *"abhor what is evil; cling to what is good."* We must learn to hate as God hates. No, not people but our sin. Sin appeals to us because we like it. Ask God to help you hate it. Sometimes God must show us the horrible consequences of our compromise in order for us to detest it and turn away from it. When people tell me of their struggles with being passionate for God, inevitably we find a sin issue that has been allowed to fester, grow, and take control in the person's life. One teen had allowed a secret relationship to develop through texting, even though his parents had forbidden it. This one compromise began to seriously steal his heart. He soon had little desire for the Word or the things of God. He had been neutralized. Once confessed, he began on a healthy track to ignite a passion for God again.

Second, as we saw with David, success is not always a good thing if we handle it wrongly. As you read II Samuel 10, you find David gaining victory after victory. He had "arrived". He was the man! His fame spread. Other nations feared him. His people were delighted with him. God was delighted with him and all he did—until chapter 11. There David began to feel his success. It went to his head. He was proud. He was the best, the mightiest, above others, even above the law, so he felt. That's when he figured he was entitled to another man's wife and had to cover it up by any means possible. Psalm 51 is the result of David's repentant heart. In verse 12 he says, *"Restore to me the joy of Your salvation."* His joy was gone. His passion doused. His zeal snuffed out. Post-Psalm 51, however, David recognized his complete dependence upon the Lord and tried hard to avoid stumbling into that neutralizing deception again.

Third, possessions and pleasure can turn the flames way down. There is nothing inherently wrong with either of these, but should they steal our heart, we can become a casualty. Jesus put it this way: *"For where your treasure is, there your heart will be also"* (Matthew 6:21). He concludes in verse 24 that *"no one can serve two masters."* Why? Because *"he will hate the one and love the other."* Eventually, our treasures displace God from the seat of His throne in our hearts. Sometimes it's a video game we love too much or a TV show or girlfriend, or the newspaper or social media that steal us from our appointment with God. We can put God on hold. Do this enough and don't be surprised if you get a busy signal! (Psalm 66:18)

Fourth, an improper view of our problems can suffocate us. The truth is that an incredibly loving God has allowed suffering in our fallen world for a reason.

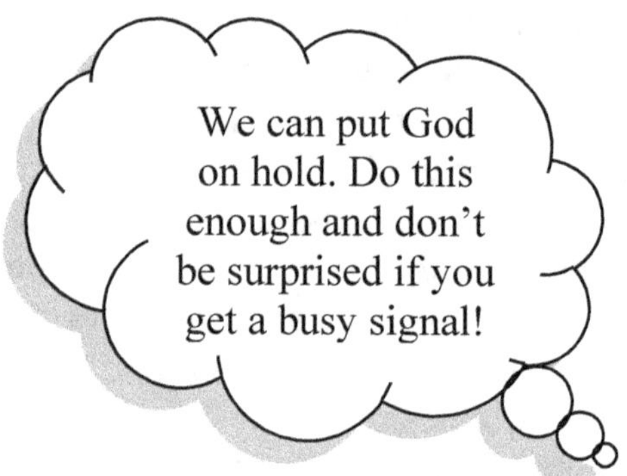

When we can face these trials with His divine perspective, then we can truly *"consider it all joy"* (James 1:2). God uses our struggles to refine our character (do I hear a "Whoo-hoo"?), discipline us, redirect us down a different path, and strengthen our faith. For many this does not seem very attractive. Perhaps, because we value comfort over character. Without a proper perspective, however, we can become disillusioned. We expect blessing and seem to get only hardship. We feel we have served and sacrificed enough to warrant God's rewards but get stuck with another dose of unpleasant spiritual medicine. We swallow hard but it tends to leave a bad taste in our mouth that seems to last forever. We have bargained with God at the table. 50-50. We give, He gives. That's the way this Christian deal is supposed to work, we figure. He has become our Jesus Genie. We've rubbed the lamp and are expecting our three self-serving wishes—I mean, answers to prayer. Many truly believe God has failed them. They are hurt, even embittered. Serving God is withheld like a ransom. When God's ready to make good on His end, then and only then, are we ready to serve Him.

Let's back the Truth Trolley up a moment! Who's driving this runaway contraption anyway? Last I remember, Romans 8:28 said that God works all things together for our good and His glory. That means the year I gave my heart completely and irretrievably to my Savior and boldly prayed, "No matter what it takes, make me more like Jesus," He purposed to use my injury that sidelined my sports dreams for my good and His ultimate purposes. Well, He didn't fail me! My heavenly Surgeon cut me wide open and began to remove some seriously cancerous character. It was admittedly painful. I kicked and cried the whole time as my dreams faded. And Romans 8:28 became my life verse in the process. Let it become yours, too. Let Him who knows best do His best to shape you, mold you, and transform you into that person who looks like Jesus, a man passionate for Christ, a Godly Man.

Love Is a Reflex

Over the years, as both a father/husband and pastor, I have been amazed that when someone truly understands how much someone else loves them, they love in return. It's like a reflex reaction. Know this then: Christ's love for you is vast, beyond measure. The more you can grasp this biblical truth, the greater the desire will be in you to return that love. We will discuss this more in the next chapter, but for now let God's love fully capture your heart. Let his compassion displayed on the cross stir you up. Let it ignite a raging fire in your chest that compels you to live for Him at 212. Don't hold back! Be aggressive. Be intentional. Let God point out and remove any barriers, anything that would douse those flames. Repent of compromise. Cry out to Him to change you. This certainly is His heart. Let it be yours!

BRING IT HOME!

Have you truly repented and chosen to follow Jesus as your Lord and Savior? If not, take some time right now and cry out to Him to rescue you from your sin and your brokenness. Have your mentor pray for you.

Do you have an assurance of your salvation? Why?

Do you have any questions about being a Christian (write those down and share them with your mentor)?

(This is a very subjective question) What temperature are you at today? 150°F? 200°F? 210°F? 212°F?

Are you "delighting in the Lord"?

Can you identify any "Passion Killers" in your life? If so, list them along with any others not mentioned in this chapter (for example, dwelling on negative emotions like self-pity, hanging around and being influenced by ungodly people, watching too much TV or listening to music or engaging in social media that doesn't honor Christ).

Do you have any idols in your life (refer to the **"DIG IN!"** section of this chapter)? If so, list them here.

Do you have a regular time each day for Bible study, prayer, and worship (personally, my worship is scattered throughout the day, whereas a good chunk of my early morning hours are for study and prayer)? On average, how many times per week do you meet personally with God? (Please, be aware that how many times a week you spend with God in the Word, prayer, and worship is never a measuring stick for maturity in Christ. It is only a means to become mature in Him.)

How do you express your passion for God?

In your own words, how has this chapter's study helped you?

What will you do differently now with God's help?

NOTE: It is easy for us to regularly feel as if we do not measure up, that we can be doing more for God. This chapter is NOT an invitation to step onto the proverbial hamster's treadmill of performance. This only produces guilt and burnout. Instead, it contains some basic biblical principles that call us to deeper surrender and delight in Jesus. Properly balance these truths with the vastness of Christ's love for you explained more fully in the next chapter.

Godly Men
Find Their Significance in
Christ

What makes you valuable? Awards you have earned? People's positive opinions of you? A girlfriend who thinks you're attractive? Cool clothes? That expensive iPhone? The one principle laid out in this chapter of where you find your sense of significance has far reaching implications for your life. It revolutionized my entire character as a young man. Let me tell you how it began.

As the horn sounded the end of the second period, I got up from the mat. Suddenly, pain pierced my concentration. I almost fell back to the mat as my right knee buckled underneath me. In a second, thoughts raced through my mind. What had happened to me? Should I forfeit and concede defeat? I had missed half the wrestling season due to a simple twisted knee injury. My doctor had given me clearance to wrestle but expressed significant doubts. I weighed the odds and being in the tournament was more important, in fact necessary—for me. Had I made a serious mistake?

I quickly limped to the center of the mat, hoping my opponent hadn't seen my strained efforts. I dropped down into "referee's position." Since I was on the bottom, I figured I would just wrestle out the period defensively, seeing that I had the point advantage. My strategy worked. The buzzer sounded and the match was over. I jumped to my feet to shake hands and head to the tournament's platform. Again, my knee immediately crumpled underneath my weight. After the quick ceremony, my coach helped me to my seat with the rest of the team. My dad, who was a high school track coach and had some knowledge of leg injuries, was waiting there for me: "Michael, let me see how bad it is."

As he put one hand under my heel and the other on top of my knee for leverage, my dad attempted to straighten my leg out. Severe pain let me know this was not going to happen. The excitement of the victory allowed me to downplay the tragedy of the moment, but the months that followed soon revealed a devastating reality: I would never wrestle again. In fact, this injury affected all my sports competition. It doesn't take much to fill a young man with inflated dreams of the Olympics. These dreams had occupied a large part of my life. I lived for sports—until then.

After four months of crutches, uncertainty on my doctors' part, and arthroscopic surgery, my rehabilitation was painstakingly slow. The severe atrophy that had set in with my leg muscles was overshadowed by the devastating discouragement that imprisoned my dreams. I struggled to know why the God that I had recently given my heart to was "destroying my life." Over the months that followed, God chose not to reveal answers to my "why" questions. Instead, He began to redirect my focus more completely to Him. Could I trust Him to lead me and do what was best? Only as I daily chose to rest in his sovereignty and the truth of His love, did God begin to show me the need for this life-changing turn of events. What He actually did was start me on a years-long journey that revealed much about myself and God. He opened my eyes to tremendous insecurities I had and that He desperately needed to remove in order for me to become the man He had called me to become.

Before we begin this Bible study, I need to warn you. Most men do not believe they wrestle with insecurity. The frank reason for this denial is that the admission of having such a problem feels so very un-masculine. We imagine Linus with his "security blanket" or a person riveted with phobias or a little boy with "daddy issues" (whatever exactly *they* are). We just know that's not us. Nothing, however, is probably further from the truth. As a pastor very involved in discipling men (young and old), I believe this is the number one problem in becoming Godly Men. Yes, the number one problem! As you will see, its symptoms are vast. The world sees the issue but offers only skewed and upside down solutions. The Bible provides us with God's solution. It appears so simple when in fact it is so hard to implement. The truth is that it is a life-long quest. So, as you begin this study, open your heart to the illuminating work of God's Spirit. Be honest. Be humble. And allow Him to peel back the layered issues one at a time. This will probably be the biggest wrestling match of your life.

DIG IN!

Study Section 1

Before we define what "insecurities" are, what causes them, and how we can deal with them, let's see them in action. Scripture gives us an excellent picture of this problem in the life of King Saul. It also gives us a contrasting picture of a "secure" leader in King David. So, let's begin and fill out the chart below. All Scriptures are from I Samuel, unless otherwise noted. After reading the passage, describe each person. The first is filled out for you.

Saul	David
1) <u>9:2</u> - Impressive, young man; without equal; head taller than others.	<u>13:14</u>; <u>16:7</u> - Man after God's own heart; qualified by his heart not his appearance.
2) <u>10:20-22</u> -	<u>17:32-37</u> -
3) <u>13:9</u>; <u>14:24,27,29,44</u> -	<u>II Samuel 6:20-22</u> -

4) <u>14:19,35; 28:5-7</u> -	<u>22:15; 23:4,9-11; 30:6-8</u> -
5) <u>15:3,9,11,22</u> -	<u>Psalm 51:16-17</u> -
6) <u>15:12,30</u> -	<u>22:1-2</u>
7) 15:24; 17:11 -	17:45-49 -
8) 18:8 -	25:32-33 -
9) 18:9,12,15,16,28-29 -	II Samuel 23:8-9 (especially "honor" in 19, 23—who probably initiated this?) -
10) 22:8; 18:8 -	24:5-7; 25:39; 26:18,24; II Samuel 12:13 -

Before we go any further, let me give you a definition of "insecurity" that will help tie things together: ***It is finding our value in things or people's opinions*** *so that when those things are taken from us or people's opinions of us change for the worse, we feel devalued, inadequate, and less significant.* Our sense of value then is not secure. Below is a list of some symptoms of insecurity which can be easily recognized in King Saul's life and in anyone struggling with insecurities:

- Pride

- Self-centeredness

- Boastfulness

- Feelings of rejection

- False humility

- Sense of inadequacy

- Argumentativeness

- Feeling like a failure

- Defensiveness

- Over competitiveness

- Anger

- Constant use of excuses

- Jealousy

- Hard to praise others

- Outwardly religious

- Not open about sin or weakness

- Love of money

- People-pleaser

- Love of possessions

- Compares with others

Check the one's that you wrestle with more frequently. Then, if it would be helpful, have your discipler check the ones he sees in you. This last step will probably be very difficult. Discipler, please be sensitive and judicious here and not overly critical.

I have chosen to include here some personal observations and insights concerning the Scriptures studied earlier that contrasted the insecurities of Saul and the security of David as a man of God (check your answers with these):

1) Already done. Understand that the people, and most likely including Saul, placed greater value on external qualities than on the internal ones that David possessed.

2) Saul hid among the baggage, because it seems he was fearful of leadership responsibility. His focus was on his inabilities. David was bold to confront Goliath, the enemy of both Israel and God, and quickly accepted responsibility to fight him. His focus was on God's abilities. Now, read the rest of this paragraph very carefully. ***Saul compared Goliath to himself and feared. David compared Goliath to God and was confident. This contrast highlights the difference between where each found his strength.***

3) Saul readily engaged in burnt offerings and fasting, hoping to gain God's favor by religious observances. David, however, cared little for outward religious displays but had great concern for the heart, especially expressed in ardent worship of God. Saul was focused on man's opinion of him, whereas David sought God's favor alone.

4) Again, Saul had no "devotional life." Prayer was more an outward display, a formality, rather than a foundational principle of leadership. David, however, inquired of God regularly. It was central to his effective leadership. Here too we see David's dependency upon God.

5) Saul was a compromiser. He rationalized his sin away to make it seem acceptable. He gave excuses. David realized that God sees through our

rationalizing and truly repented, refusing to dress up his sin.

6) Saul sought personal glory and honor from people not God. David cultivated humility and a brokenness of spirit before God.

7) Saul feared the people, even Goliath. He lacked trust in God's wisdom and strength. David, however, did not fear men, especially Goliath, but fully trusted in God's deliverance.

8) Saul was easily angered, experienced rejection that created misinterpretations of others' actions, and became paranoid. He regularly feared losing people's praise. David understood that his reputation lay with God and that God's ultimate plans were more important than the temporary satisfaction of vengeance. He was teachable.

9) Saul was filled with jealousy, fearing the honor the Lord and the people were giving David. He longed for such success and honor for himself. David's heart was quite different. He wanted his men to succeed and be honored. In fact, he led the way in honoring these men.

10) Saul loved his "pity parties." He could not see his own faults but falsely accused David. David was a man who left vengeance to God and extended mercy. He did not hide behind false accusations by blaming others for his own sin.

Is there anything you do or anything you own that makes you feel valuable or important (example: wearing expensive sneakers that make you feel cool, popular, or significant)?

We have found that Saul was an unfit king. He possessed many of the symptoms of insecurity. David on the other hand was a Godly Man, a man after God's own heart. He showed few, if any, signs of being an insecure leader.

Study Section 2

READ Galatians 1:10.

Why is people-pleasing so bad?

Be aware that people-pleasing is placing someone's desires above God's. You will want to please your parents when they ask you to do something within God's will. This is not the people-pleasing the Bible warns against. When you are more concerned about others' opinions of you than what God thinks of you, this is people-pleasing.

Whose opinions matter a lot to you? More than God's opinion of you? Is there anyone you really want to impress?

READ I Peter 2:23 and Luke 23:32-43.

How was Jesus insulted?

Have you ever been insulted or made fun of? If so, give an example.

How did it make you feel? What did you do?

If you responded in a negative way, why?

Jesus did not retaliate, because He did not trust in or personally value others' opinions of Himself.

READ Luke 3:22.

Whose opinion *did* Jesus value? The Father expressed three truths about how He felt about Jesus. What are they?

-
-
-

Look at Luke closely. What miracles had Jesus done or sermons had He preached to prompt this response from the Father?

What was the Father's love based on?

READ Genesis 1:27, 31 and Psalm 8:4-5.

What kind of stamp of approval did God give over his creation of man?

Why did God choose to love (or value) man so much?

READ Ephesians 3:17-19.

What is Paul's concern here? What goal should the Ephesians have?

What does it mean that Christ's love *"surpasses knowledge"*?

Is this a life-long goal or do we achieve it at conversion?

Grasp this very important principle: *we value the things we love*. Growing up, my family spent every Christmas Eve at my grandmother's. We always lit the fireplace with matches that seemed well over a foot long and gathered around while my grandmother told of her adventures as a missionary in China at a time when pirates raided both land and sea. Of course, we had our traditional meal of Chinese cabbage, rutabaga, mashed potatoes with gravy, and beef tongue. You heard me right—beef tongue! I have come to love beef tongue so much, I consider it one of my favorite meats. Consequently, I place very high value on it. I would be willing to pay almost any price to taste that succulent meat that practically melts in your mouth. You see, *when we love something, we place high value on it*. When God loves us infinitely, He has assigned immeasurable worth to us. He highly values us!

READ John 3:16.

How did God show us how much He valued us?

God's love for us is boundless. It has no limits. It is infinite in measure. It is beyond our complete understanding (which is limited). In view of this, how much has God chosen to value you?

Does God's view of you change? Does His love for you or value of you change?

When people speak hurtfully about us (as Jesus' accusers spoke of Him), do their words value or devalue us?

When this happens to you, how do you respond? Why?

READ Luke 12:15, 21.

Why do people place so much value on their possessions?

So, we can see that our value does not depend on what we accomplish, what others think of us, or what we possess. Again, what does our value depend upon?

Why should we only draw our sense of value from Christ's love for us and nothing else?

The Father's love for His Son was not based upon His Son's performance, any miracles He had done or sermons He had preached. It was solely rooted in His eternal and unchanged relationship with Him.

We can see that when we fully recognize God's amazing love for us, we find in it our true sense of value. We weigh our worth not by the opinions of others but by the inestimable opinion of the God that laid down His life for us.

THINK ABOUT IT!

As a young man of fourteen, I placed my sense of significance in my sports accomplishments. I relied on them for my sense of personal value. But take them away and who was I? Not someone who would be praised or respected, I felt. I had propped up a false sense of value with my accomplishments. But when my future in sports turned to false hopes, my inadequacies surfaced.

Striving For Praise

We all tend to use our accomplishments, our possessions, our looks, our intelligence, our personality, our job status, or our abilities to win people's favor at times. We want them to like us. We want them to think we're special, important, and successful. We can live for this. Our decisions can be based on how others will respond. We will crave admiration. We will sacrifice principle for praise. We may build big businesses so others will want to be like us. We may own nice cars and large homes so others will think we are important. Even some pastors will try hard to grow large churches, perhaps sacrificing family along the way, so others will recognize their obvious skills and "anointing." They crave speaking opportunities with large venues. They love people needing them, the nice reviews and the momentary applause. All, of course, for the kingdom! Or, at least, so they have convinced themselves.

Not too many national level speakers include in their bios: "He is his sons' greatest hero, his daughters' first love, and his wife's sole sweetheart. His first priority is his family." Why? Perhaps because people praise accomplishments. Big accomplishments (as if the above in quotes is not). Some pastors of large churches have become like this, because this is what *we* value. *We* have sung the Sirens' song, and our pastors have been seduced. I have felt its call and deception myself. I am so grateful that *many* have refused to bend the knee to this idol. America still has many godly pastors who have not sold out.

Wrongly Defending Our Perceived Value

Shortly after surrendering to Christ, I noticed some encouraging changes in my life, but one thing seemed untouched. At first, I wrote it off as my brother's problem, not mine. I grew up in a family of six children. We always fought. Always! It was our way of life. Wasn't it Jesus who said, "Those who live by the fist, will die by the fist", or something like that? If so, I "died" weekly, if not daily. My problem was that this issue remained in my life even after my conversion. Granted, the fights were more with words than with fists, but hostile, nevertheless. My brother just older than me would say something attacking, and I would return with an snide reply. My mother realized what was happening, so when I complained to her one day about this, she turned the tables on me. She put the ball in my court. I was not the innocent victim I thought I was. Much of the fault for these fights *did* lie with me.

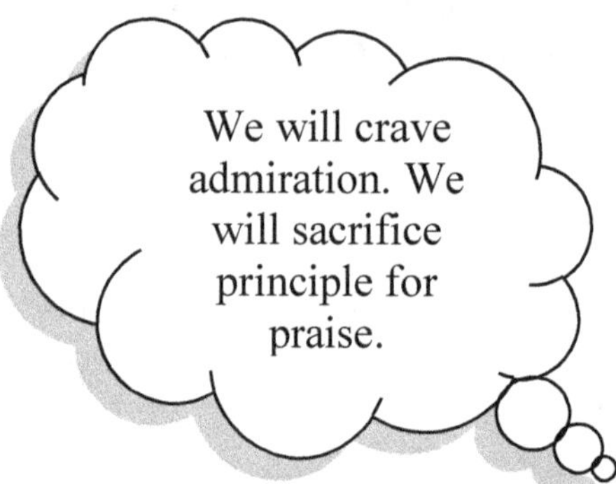

When Jesus was verbally assaulted, He did not retaliate. Why? In truth, my understanding of the answer to this question took years to solidify. I just knew that He didn't get angry and respond defensively. Years into my marriage I still found myself seriously struggling with being defensive while "discussing" what my wife saw as my shortcomings. Again, I felt attacked. How did these discussions always turn into arguments? The Lord needed to put the ball in my court and for me to examine my own heart.

If my wife was right, why did I resist it so? James 4:1-2 asks, *"What is the source of quarrels and conflicts among you? Is not the source your pleasures that wage war in your members? You lust and do not have."* What was it I was really wanting? I wanted my wife to always be agreeable with me, even when I was boneheaded. Her highlighting my weaknesses made me feel…well, weak. It made me feel attacked, so I defended myself. I defended my sense of value. I defended my need to be admired and respected. I was consistently confusing my abilities (or inabilities) with my sense of significance.

Our Source of True Value

Jesus did not do this. His value did not come from what He did or even what He said. It came from who He was, the Son of God, loved by the Father from all eternity which could *never* change. It was a rock-solid truth that Jesus, while being mocked on the cross, grounded Himself in. Man's words could not shake Him from that. The world's opinions could not nullify His knowledge of the Father's love, so there was no need to defend and bolster what was immoveable. Jesus cared little about men's opinions. Therefore, if I could be grounded in Christ's love for me, my wife could speak truthfully into my life, and I would not feel the need to defend my value. Being wrong did not lessen God's love for me nor my value. I could listen to any rebuke and be teachable, not argumentative.

"Could." That's the key! But we forget. We humans are so susceptible to the lies of the enemy that we need to defend our value found in things instead of Christ's unchanging love. We forget simple truths so easily. Our flesh still craves men's praise and cowers in the face of correction. May God set us free from this, so we might fully *"comprehend with all the saints what is the breadth and length and height and depth, and to know the love of Christ which surpasses knowledge"* (Ephesians 3:18-19).

Let's take a moment and see these simple truths played out in the lives of King Saul and David. Saul was an insecure King. This especially came to light when the Spirit of God left him, no longer anointing him for his kingly duties, and an evil spirit tormented him. Just as Jesus explained in Matthew 18:34 that the unforgiving servant was turned over to the *"torturers"* (jailors who tortured the guilty criminals), so Saul in his bitterness was turned over to this torturer. And

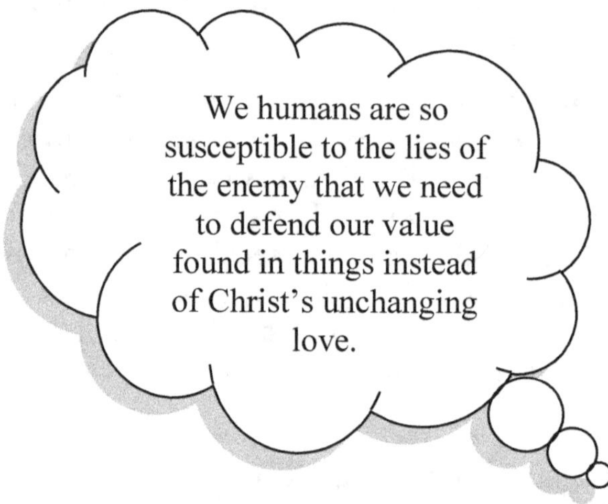

he was merciless. Even before I Samuel 16:14, Saul was characterized as an outwardly religious king who cared more for man's praise (even building a monument to himself) than for God's honor. But *"to obey is better than sacrifice"* (I Samuel 15:22) Samuel challenged him as he invoked God's rejection of Saul as king over Israel and his replacement by one "better" than him (verse 28). The fact that Samuel needed a guise to go and anoint David in chapter 16 speaks plainly that Saul was hurt and angry, even wanting to kill him if necessary (16:2).

In 17:11 Saul feared for his life before Goliath and shrank from the courageous faith that bolstered David's challenge in 17:45-47 to the Philistine champion. Incidentally, as like begets like, Saul and his men slew no giants in their day, whereas David and four of his mighty men slew a total of five. In 18:8-16, we see Saul's anger, jealousy, and fear that David's popularity might potentially open the door to his stealing the throne of Israel. Saul felt abandoned by the Lord as he saw David empowered by Him to victory in every battle. Saul even slew 85 priests whom he thought aided David in his flight as a fugitive in 22:18.

Saul wallowed in feelings of rejection and in excuses to defend his wrong decisions. He found his value in the wrong things. David, however, did none of these. Though Saul was a slave to people's opinions, David was a man after God's own heart. He desired the things God desired. When reading the Psalms, we are struck by this resounding chorus over and over: *"Give thanks to the LORD, for he is good, for His lovingkindness is everlasting"* (Psalm 136) and *"But I have trusted in Your lovingkindness"* (Psalm 13:5). David was secure in the love of his Redeemer. Saul was not. David fully trusted in his Deliverer. Saul could not. David was well-known as a herder of sheep, an animal compliant with his master. But Saul was known as a herder of donkeys, animals stubborn in their willful ways. Get the picture?

A Transformation of Insecurities

In spite of our insecurities, God can still transform us though. Mike is a very good friend of mine. He's a leader in our church with a true servant's heart. He's teachable, humble, and not necessarily given to anger. Eight years ago was quite a different story, however. Mike had just joined our church and started working for my business. He was a hard worker, but, let me say, zealous for the approval of men. He felt rejection rather sharply and easily. Somewhat awkward in a social setting, he even scared off a girl he had interest in.

He was taking several college classes while working full time for me. After one particularly grueling semester, he heaved a sigh of relief that it was over and he had passed. I asked him his grades, and he sheepishly, though excitedly, told me he had gotten straight A's. I stopped him in his work, looked him in the eye, and said, "Mike, I want you to know, I'm really proud of you!" He had been the only one in his family to graduate from high school, much less go to college. Several minutes later with tears in his eyes he approached me and said, "Thank you for saying what you did to me. No one's ever told me that before."

God began peeling back the layers of insecurity in Mike. It was an arduous process. Many jealousies and much rejection surfaced. Like stubborn weeds, they resurfaced again and again with different testings from the Lord. I could tell the conflict inside him was intense. Both my wife and I extended some serious challenges to him. Not to be defeated, Mike soon came to me and requested, "If you ever see any hint of insecurities in me, please speak to me. I'm done with this. It's ruining my life. I'm moving past this thing." I saw Mike at the altar during worship and after the Word week after week. He meant business. Within a month everyone noticed the difference in him. Two months later, the change was so noticeable, the girl he had run off before approached me, inquiring about his growth. I'm no matchmaker, but even I could see the sparkle in her eyes.

I'm so grateful we serve a God who believes in happy endings. Or maybe I should say happy beginnings. Two years later I had the privilege of marrying Mike and Sarah. A year and a half later, after several heartbreaking miscarriages, they gave birth to an absolutely adorable little boy, Micah. At the present writing of this workbook, he is four months old and stealing everyone's heart. That's just like our God. When we fully yield to Him, choose to be fully grounded in His infinite, unfailing love for us, and delight ourselves in Him, He gives us the desires of our heart. Is that good or what?

The Power of a Dad's Blessing

I would like to close their story with a word of challenge to you dads. Please look for regular opportunities to praise your son and tell him how very proud of him you are and why. Although each of us must find our sense of worth in Christ and Him alone, this does not preclude us giving words of affirmation to one another. On the receiving end we must say Christ and His love is truly enough, but on the other end, God asks us to lavish those around us with words that bring life: "Death and life are in the power of the tongue, and those who love it will eat its fruit" (Proverbs 18:21). Your son must know, however, that your love for him is not contingent on how obedient he is. I have told my son (and daughters) at times I was disappointed in the wrong course of action or wrong words he chose and disciplined him, but this was always followed by a reaffirmation of my love for him.

Every child needs the blessing of his father. When my dad was in his early 20's, he performed a vocal concert at a church. Some fifteen years later, his father, a music teacher of a Philadelphia Christian college, said to him, "Dave, I don't know if I ever told you this, but you did a fine job in that concert several years ago." The buried hurt resurfaced as my dad replied, "I wish you would have told me that fifteen years ago!" My dad had grown up with a father who was short on praise. In fact, my dad related to me that that incident in his mid-thirties was the first time he remembered his father ever praising him. My dad has a rich baritone voice and has done numerous such concerts in his life. But my grandfather had failed to wield the power of life with words of affirmation to his son. This had serious consequences that my dad has had to work through in order to be healed of the wounds.

Dads, be that wellspring of life to your son. Be quick to praise, slow to be critical, and always speak the truth in love (Ephesians 4:15). It is common understanding that a father who neglects to speak this way to his son will foster great issues of pride in him as he yearns for others to recognize what his father failed to. Additionally, a dad who neglected to lavishly praise his daughter, including her beauty, will tend to foster in her a desire for another man's attention, typically found in promiscuity. Dads, this is what's at stake here. The situation is serious. The consequences are far reaching. Set the pace for your son. Be a man of lavish praise and encouragement. Be a man who takes the time to say, "I'm so proud of you!" Be a man you want your son to be like.

The Real Solution

The world has its own answers to many of life's problems. They are almost always insufficient, upside down, and very man-centered. Their solution to the problems discussed in this chapter is "self-respect." Slogans like "Be a better you," or child-raising advice like "Never say 'no' to your child or they won't have self-respect," or self-help tips like "Learn to love yourself" represent the backwards philosophy of our day. It is empty, powerless, and self-defeating. In short, it is a lie.

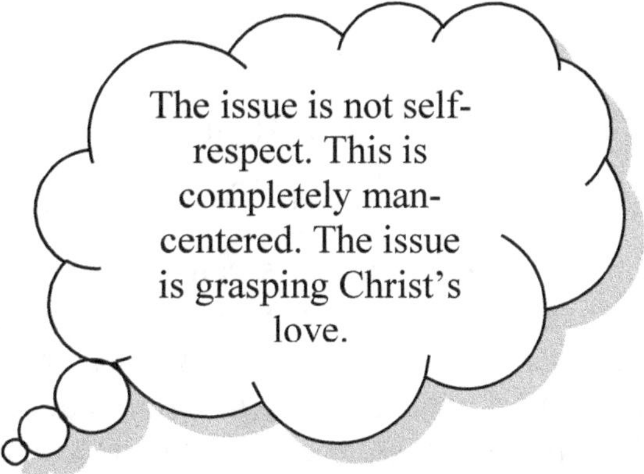

The issue is not self-respect. This is completely man-centered. The issue is grasping Christ's love. The whole of it, not just the hem of it. Not just "God loves me," but stepping back and seeing the entire picture. This picture starts in Genesis 1 and speaks of man's special place in God's creation, then moves to Genesis 3 where man willfully becomes God's enemy by rebelling against Him. Genesis 6 speaks of God's judgment for mankind's total apostasy yet offers a glimmer of hope in Noah and later, even more so, in Abraham. By the time we turn the page to Jesus' life, death, and resurrection, we are struck by a love revealed from heaven that willingly lays down everything for the sake of God's enemies, those who hate Him—that was you and me. The grace of God, that He rescued us from the stranglehold of sin and translated us from death to life, is truly amazing. This persistent love of God that pursues us to overtake us and restore us is the message of this chapter and the true solution man needs, not the paltry proposal of "self-respect." Loving ourselves is not the answer, it's the problem!

Unlocking the Floodgates of God's Love

Deep seated hurts can act as a barrier to receiving this rich, lavish love God has for us. Harsh, attacking words spoken to us over and over can wound our heart and create an embittered spirit. Such wounds need healing. The crucial step must be our willingness to extend forgiveness, otherwise we will not be able to grasp the depth of Christ's love for us. Should we refuse to forgive, we will not be healed, and we will not be forgiven. We will remain untouched by God's outrageous display of love for us. Our harboring of hurts will serve to keep God's affection at bay. This is the nature of bitterness.

"You're so stupid!"

"You'll never amount to anything!"

"You're a lost cause!"

"Can't you do anything right?"

"Why can't you be more like your brother?"

All of these accusations can hurt very deeply, and the accusers need to be forgiven—for your sake! You are not declaring them innocent, that's God's responsibility. You are merely releasing them from any debt you believe they owe you. Cancel any obligation you believe they owe you and any desire to see them punished. Let it go! As you free them, God will free you to experience His love and forgiveness in far greater depth. He will enable you to truly know His love that is beyond knowledge, and you will unlock the floodgates of His lavish love for you. Let it wash over you, cleansing, restoring, and empowering you.

How Much Are You Worth?

Because we wrestle with sin issues, we are constantly in need of Christ's forgiveness, an aspect of His Love. We can even wonder if Christ will continue to forgive our stubborn, reoccurring sins. We may begin to believe God is weary with us, tired and frustrated with our failings. Consequently, we can fall into the trap of a performance-based relationship that believes God loves us less when we sin so much.

Does God withhold love when we sin? Does He love us more when we are more obedient? No, His love that He has lavished upon us has no limits (though He is grieved when we sin—Ephesians 4:30). It does not fluctuate. Neither God nor His love change. They are infinite. Therefore, if God's love is infinite, so is our value. It too never changes.

Let me illustrate. If I displayed a $1,000 bill to you and asked its worth, you would respond, "$1,000. And my pocket would be a really safe place for that right now!" O.K., simple enough. However, if I crumpled it up and threw it into the mud, stomped on it and ground it in, then picked it up, straightened it out, and asked, "*Now* how much is it worth?" you would probably say that it is still worth $1,000 regardless of its condition (though you may not want to put it in your pocket just yet). Why? Because its value is fixed and does not change (in an ideal world with no inflation anyway). And so it is with your worth in the eyes of God. Why? Because God's love for

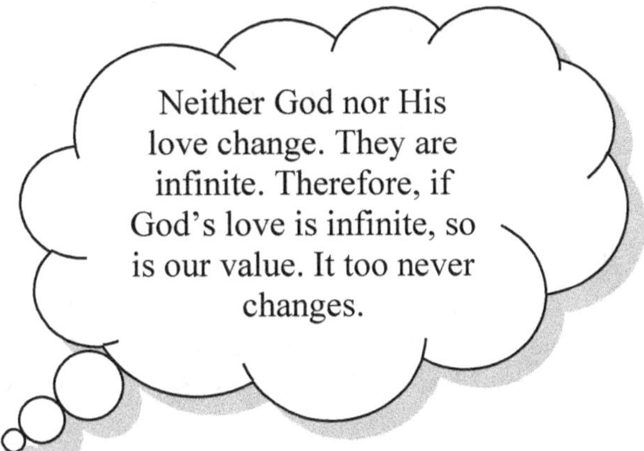

you is fixed and cannot change! Be comforted in this truth then: nothing you do can cause Him to love you more, and nothing you do can cause Him to love you any less. It is constant. Infinite. Lavish. Enduring.

Far Reaching Implications

As you go through these ten Bible studies, you may notice that a large number of biblical, masculine traits are tied to this one truth of God's love. Every time anger flares up in you, or jealousy clouds your reasoning, or feelings of rejection cause you to nose-dive into self-pity, or any of the number of symptoms of insecurity surface, allow that emotion gone awry to serve as a red flag to you. Pause in your downward spiraling thoughts or knee-jerk reaction to reflect on the cause and ask yourself this one very important question: "What aspect of Christ's love am I failing to grasp at this moment?" Reflect again upon this truth of God's resolute, lavish love. Drink it in like the sun-scorched land receives rain. Thank Him for it and choose a different course of action. Refuse to go down that old, rocky road again.

The enemy wants to take you down. Wrestle with him to the buzzer. As you humble yourself in this process and avail yourself to God's empowering grace (James 4:6), don't hesitate to slam your enemy's shoulders to the mat. I promise you, a rich reward awaits you at the awards platform.

BRING IT HOME!

Now having read the chapter, go back to the list of some symptoms of insecurity (pp. 35-36) and with a different colored pen, check any more that apply to you.

Write down a recent incident in which you struggled with impressing someone.

If your desire to be liked or accepted had been completely fulfilled at the time (such as, by Christ's love), how might you have responded differently?

Think of a recent argument you were in. What caused it and why was it so important for you to be right? What was really at stake?

Reflect on some of your daydreams. Do any of them highlight a need to feel important, be better than someone else, or protect your personal sense of worth? If so, write them down.

Is it hard for you when others are praised or honored? If so, list a recent incident.

Can you think of any ability or possession you have, a personal trait such as intelligence, looks, or personality, or any job status or accomplishment that, if taken away, would make you feel less valuable? If so, list them. [Hint: if someone insulted you about one of these and it made you angry or feel very hurt, you might want to list it. Nearly every honest person will need to write something here. So, if you do, you are certainly not alone.]

Lastly, list any hurts you need to forgive. Many times, a parent is completely unaware of any hurts they may have caused. Dads, if you have been the cause of some of these wounds to your son, take some time right now and ask for forgiveness. Be humble and teachable. Allow God's Spirit to minister healing to your son and to your relationship as you meet together to discuss the lesson.

Use this time right now to ask God to help you fully grasp His love for you and get it down to the core of your being that that rock-solid truth would become the platform from which you act and react to every life situation. Cry out to Him that His love transform you into that mighty, secure man of God you desire to be.

Godly Men
Are Full of Integrity

Integrity is a difficult word to grasp. Its meaning can be very broad or very specific. How it can be undermined in a man's life is equally difficult to grasp, because it usually goes undetected at the start. Perhaps this rather sarcastic, personal story will help illustrate this.

So, there I was in my doctor's office for a routine physical exam as he was doing his doctor's thing, you know, probing and prodding and acting very "doctorly," like testing my ability to answer questions with a tongue depressor wedged so far into my throat that I think he found yesterday's lunch. Of course, he had me inhale and exhale over and over (minus the tongue depressor), I guess to make sure that at the very old age of 48 (and apparently with one foot in the grave) I had remembered how to breathe correctly. I was mildly satisfied as I passed the tests, that is, except the last one. With latex gloves donned to check me for prostate cancer, he plunged his hands into what appeared to be a 55-gallon drum of Vaseline. I was sure it would humiliate me, that he'd probably find that Lego I swallowed as a boy.

When he was done, he sat down with an expression of disappointment. I, however, was quite relieved. He proceeded to hold up his gloved hand and say,

"This is not good!" I don't think anyone would have disagreed with that. Personally, I would have ripped the glove off and burned it, then sanitized my arm, the bench, the whole room, and probably pulled the fire alarm to clear the waiting room, just to be on the safe side. Instead, he held his finger up and boldly declared, "I found red blood!" Stupid me, I didn't realize there was any other kind. But after a full, technically sophisticated, medical explanation that involved something about the difference between blood from the upper colon and blood from hemorrhoids, I came to the most logical conclusion — he really *did* find that Lego!

Actually, he went on to explain that I might have a malignant polyp, so I would need to schedule what all men dread who are nearing fifty—the endless viewing of "Get Smart" reruns. If that were only the case (and, truth be told, I love "Get Smart" reruns)! Seriously, he told me I would need that notorious procedure called a Colonoscopodectomy, or something like that. This is where they remove your entire colon and clean it out completely (I've heard they dump the contents somewhere in New Jersey in the vicinity of one of those white "No Dumping" signs off major roads that everyone pays so close attention to—pretty good cover if you ask me). Then they put it back in with lots of duct tape and Liquid Nails. I know what you're thinking, "Is this stuff even sanitized?" Apparently so, says that endless fountain of knowledge where I get all my trustworthy information— Wikipedia.

Well, the day for the operation came and I was informed, much to my delight, I would only need to have a "colonoscopy." To the uninformed, this is a very simple investigative procedure where they take approximately 12,000 feet of flexible drill and feed it through your colon Roto-Rooter style. I was told not to worry. After all, it was made of "fiber optics." I would like to say I was relieved, but that word fits all too well in this context. After putting on the surgical gown and laying down on the gurney, I began wondering what I had gotten myself into. My thoughts were very confused, wandering from fiber optics to Get Smart reruns to, of all things, counting backwards from 100, my favorite thing to do whenever I'm preparing myself for terrifying experiences.

As is typical, I never remember anything after "96" and awaken to some nurse asking me, "So, how do you feel?" What does one say after sitting on the toilet for 24 hours and then having Mr. Roto-Rooter clean you out? "Flushed"? "Wiped"? "Drained"? Or respond with your own question: "So, how much duct tape *did* they use?" forgetting this was only a colonoscopy and not that "colonoscofiberopticectomy," or whatever.

Eventually, the doctor came in apparently very impressed with his color photo shots of what looked like slides from the movie *Alien*. He drew my attention to one frame in particular where it looked like Sharknado got swallowed by one of those alien creatures. It took some convincing, but I realized that what I was looking at was really a two-inch polyp that showed every sign of being benign, and I was told not to worry. Sharknado had been removed, and I was going to be fine. On my way out the door, he shook my hand (and I really let him do this?) and said rather convincingly he'd look forward to seeing me in five years. Really? Five years? I could hardly wait!

As I relate this story, I have become franticly aware that I am due for my next colonoscopy in a few short months, and I cannot find my Get Smart DVDs. I'm just trying to get mentally prepared for it.

"100...99...98...97...."

So, what does a colonoscopy story have to do with "integrity" you might ask? Fair enough question, seeing that is what this chapter is *supposed* to be about. The other half of the story was unfolding some 3,000 miles away in California where one of my older brothers was not quite as fortunate as I was. Not long after my colon was declared cancer-free, my brother received some very different news. After being rushed to the hospital from passing out, his doctor told him that cancer stemming from his colon was engulfing and destroying his liver. The cancer had advanced too far for radiation, so their only recourse was chemotherapy. For about a year or so his cancer count went down drastically, only to reverse and quickly increase. Within about six months, shortly after Christmas, my brother at age 53 found himself taking his last earthly breath before being ushered into the very presence of his Savior he had known for over 35 years. This is that same brother who had introduced this squirrelly fourteen-year-old to this same loving Savior. To this day, my heart still aches and misses him.

Consider this: just a very small, malignant polyp in an otherwise very healthy colon can wreak havoc and breed utter destruction, devouring everything around it. It is truly and unfortunately amazing how something so small can do so much damage. Our integrity is no different. Small character flaws, or weaknesses, can potentially destroy a man, devastating his life and those around him.

Let me again illustrate. One day as I was sitting in a chair that had metal cross-supports, one of these supports gave way and bent under my weight. Naively, I simply bent the cross support back so it was straight. The next time I sat on this chair, however, it crumpled, sending me to the floor. Why? The bend in the metal had weakened it, compromising the integrity of the bar's strength. Webster defines "integrity" as "an unimpaired condition, soundness; the state of being undivided, completeness; firm adherence to a moral code; honesty" (***Merriam-Webster Collegiate Dictionary***, Tenth Edition, 1993). In other words, the bent support bar was no longer "sound." When my brother developed a cancerous tumor, albeit undetected, it affected the sound health of his colon and eventually his entire body. Yes, even as a minor defect in a piece of metal can compromise its strength, so a minor character issue in a person's life can weaken his walk with Christ. Consequently, we call this "compromise." Many believe that little compromises are no big deal. God, however, has a different view.

Godly Men are full of integrity, not compromise. So, as you go through this study, reflect on any weaknesses (that is, sins) in your own life that God will want to clean out completely. Thankfully, He does not use a Roto-Rooter. But trust me, those little malignancies can be very destructive. They typically start small but, unchecked, eventually affect one's entire life. Our goal will be to identify and remove those cancerous character flaws before this happens. Are you ready?

DIG IN!

Study Section 1

READ Psalm 78:70-72 and I Kings 9:4.

How did David rule?

READ I Kings 15:3.

How did Abijah rule? What comparison is made?

READ I Kings 15:11.

How did Asa rule? What comparison is made?

The Hebrew words for "integrity" is literally "completeness." It communicates character that is unflawed and a heart that is undivided. King David became the measuring stick for subsequent kings of Judah concerning character, as we saw in Abijah and Asa above. This does not mean David didn't sin. We observed this in chapter one. He repented of his pride and lust, preventing them from becoming patterns of evil behavior in his life.

READ I Timothy 3:2 and Titus 1:6-7.

What is the first character requirement for an elder/overseer?

"Above reproach" means to be "blameless" or "beyond accusation." Why would this character quality be important in a leader?

Describe the similarities between "above reproach" and "integrity."

READ Colossians 3:9.

What is being warned against?

In our day, the word "integrity" is many times used to mean "honesty" or "not lying." Why is this? (Hint: you will want to refer to Webster's definition mentioned earlier and use the words "truth" and "complete" or "completeness" in your answer)

Can you think of a time in which you lied? Briefly describe it.

Why did you lie?

READ II Timothy 3:5.

How does someone have a form (or appearance) of godliness but deny its power? (Hint: the word *"denied"* here implies "closed off access to" or "refused the presence of.")

What word might describe someone who looks godly on the outside but on the inside is not?

READ Matthew 7:15.

What example of this lack of integrity does Jesus give here?

Describe how these types of people lack integrity?

Can you give five examples of these types of people? (The first two are done for you.)

- A boss who tells you to be honest with the customer but lies to his employees.
- A leader who encourages people to be responsible but is always late to work.
-
-
-

We have seen the value of integrity and our need to live it out and model it like King David. To do this we should seek to live beyond the accusations of others and to always be a man of our word.

Study Section 2

The opposite of integrity is compromise. And it is sin. Let's look at an Old Testament example of an otherwise godly man who allowed a series of compromises into his life and what the outcome was.

READ Genesis 13:8-13.

Why did Abram (or Abraham) and Lot part company (Abram was Lot's uncle)?

Where did Lot choose to live? Why? What was so appealing about this region?

What city in this region had a bad reputation? Why?

Lot *"moved his tents as far as Sodom"* (13:12). Considering he could have chosen to live nowhere near this wicked city or to live in the city, what does this phrase tell us about Lot's heart?

READ II Peter 2:7-8.

How does Peter describe Lot?

Describe Lot's initial compromise by filling in the blanks: Although Lot was a ___________________, he chose to ___________________________.

READ Genesis 13:18.

Do you see a contrast between Lot and Abram? Describe their difference.

READ all of Genesis 19.

What was Sodom's deep rooted sin issue for which God judged them?

    A. They had a serious loitering problem.

B. They really loved children's games and got ticked that Lot refused to come out and play.
C. They were horrendously bad at Blind Man's Bluff.
D. The sin of homosexuality was rampant.

Now refer to Genesis 19:1-3 again. This story in Genesis 19 occurs approximately 15-25 years after the incident in Genesis 13.

Where is Lot living now?

What significance does the phrase *"Lot was sitting in the gate of Sodom"* have? (If you aren't sure, research this to find the answer)

READ Proverbs 31:23.

How does this help to answer the previous question?

Refer to Genesis 19:9 (and perhaps reread II Peter 2:7-8).

It says, *"**Now** he wants to play the judge!"* (NIV, 1978). What does this imply?

If Lot was so unhappy about the sin in Sodom, why didn't he speak out against it before "now"?

Can you think of a time you saw or heard something very wrong and chose to say nothing? Why?

Refer to Genesis 19:14.

By compromising and living in Sodom, how did this affect his two daughters' choice of future husbands?

Refer to Genesis 19:15-16.

By living in Sodom, how did this affect Lot's response to the Lord's command?

Why do you suppose he hesitated?

Refer to Genesis 19:26.

By living in Sodom, how did this apparently affect Lot's wife (you will need to understand *why* she probably looked back)?

Refer to Genesis 19:33.

By living in Sodom, how do you suppose this affected Lot's personal ability to draw the line with respect to alcohol?

Refer to Genesis 19:36.

By living in Sodom, how did this affect the morality of his two daughters?

In summary, list six ways that Lot's choice to live near Sodom and then eventually live in Sodom as an involved leader affected himself and his family:

-
-
-
-
-
-

Can you remember what Lot's initial heart issue was in Genesis 13 that led to his compromise or lack of integrity? Write it here.

So, we can see that Lot is an example of someone who at one time had a heart for the Lord but allowed it to be filled with compromise. We could say then that he lacked integrity. Some small, unchecked heart issues turned into life devastating problems that cost him his wife and two daughters. None served the Lord.

THINK ABOUT IT!

Many years ago as a young pastor, I was tested in a phone conversation with a very wealthy businessman. This particular man had been extremely generous to numerous churches and non-profit organizations. At one point, he expressed his anger toward a particular pastor, whom I had never met, and had hurt him. He went on to say how much he had helped this pastor's church out financially. What he had given over the years was an enormous amount. His feelings of betrayal were quite evident in his words. I quickly realized I needed to help this gentleman work through his rejection, so in response to a single question, he began to unfold his story of hurt.

Several years prior, he had gotten a divorce. Shortly afterward, he began dating another woman, whom he eventually asked to move in with him. The pastor confronted him on the issue. My well-to-do acquaintance described the pastor as "overzealous," "uncaring," "slanderous," and "ungrateful" for the financial gifts and counsel this man had helped his church with. He left the church very hurt, convinced he had done little wrong, and, since he owned the building the church was using at no charge, he pulled the lease and kicked them out. The pastor had been "demonized" by this man's embellished story, I was sure. But how could I help him see this? Or even *should* I help him see this? There was a risk involved here for me.

I began by coming along his side, letting him know I was not against him. To do this, I affirmed some of the obvious wrongs my friend claimed the pastor had committed. Maybe if I could avoid offending this man unnecessarily and show him I was an understanding person, I might be able to casually show him he shouldn't have been living with his girlfriend. For a moment, I felt my heart in the balance. I knew I might potentially be closing the door on a financial gift from this man. I also knew I was wanting to tread too delicately, because at the moment my heart was in the crucible of compromise. But there was so much we could do with a generous donation. The slime and filth of wealth's deception was enclosing around me. It was suffocating! The Spirit of God in me was repulsed and rose up from within. "No! This is wrong. I will not compromise. I refuse to march to the tune of this pied piper," I thought. I quickly changed my course and showed him how very right the pastor had been and how very wrong he had been. I was embarrassed that I'd struggled at that moment, that I'd considered speaking softly for fear of offending with the truth. I'd played the coward, and the Devil had almost bought me.

The Price Tag On Compromise

Here's my question to you: how much can you be bought for? An amount of money? Sexual pleasures? Popularity? A sale? A good grade? Success? At what price are you willing to compromise and cater, to abandon your principles for people's praise or some personal profit? What's your price tag? After fasting for forty days and enduring numerous temptations, Jesus told the Devil He would not sell out to the highest bidder (Luke 4). Temptation can feel like our soul is being bartered for. We must stand firm. There is no other option for Godly Men!

When I had almost been bought in my phone conversation with the wealthy businessman, my words began to reveal a desire for financial blessing at the risk of righteousness. So, when our actions do not match our beliefs or our words, it reveals a lack of integrity. We play the hypocrite. I use the word "play" purposefully here, because the word "hypocrite" originally was used for a play actor; one who wore a mask. He was a pretender. In Matthew 6 and 7 Jesus referred to these types of people as ones who did good deeds but whose hearts were filled with evil. What they were outwardly was quite different than what they were inwardly. As we can see, our outward actions must match our inner beliefs, attitudes, and values.

Similarly, understand that who we are publicly should match who we are privately. When I was in my first youth pastor position, I remember trying to disciple a young man. Tom claimed to be a Christian but lacked any desire for spiritual things. He was a strong influence in this small teen group, so I chose to work with him. But I met with constant frustration and disappointment. I prayed for him regularly, but no breakthrough was in sight. He said all the "right things" but something seemed wrong under the surface.

One day, I got a call from his mother (who was not a Christian). She began to unfold for me the events of the past weekend that led to Tom's arrest. He and his cousin (also in the group) had gotten drunk and drove through a neighborhood smashing mailboxes with a baseball bat. Well, I guess they smashed one too many and got caught. This ended up being the best thing for him. Later, he personally confided in me that this type of reckless behavior characterized this dark side of his life. Outwardly, Tom was funny, outgoing, and a relatively good guy. This made him quite popular with the other teens. But underneath revealed a different story. What Tom said and believed did not line up with his actions. Who he was publicly clashed with who he was privately. That truth-telling day marked the beginning of a drastic change in Tom's life. His repentance became evident as he began to pursue Christ and be a bold witness to the transforming power of the gospel.

Who Are You Really?

Ralph Lauren, a clothes designer, once said: "The crux of a person's identity…resides in the trappings, not in the person himself…One needn't be well read so long as he surrounds himself with books. One needn't play the piano, so long as one has a piano. In short, one can be whoever he wants to be. Or—more accurately—one can seem to be whoever one wants to be" (Stan Moneyham, *Dancing on the Strait and Narrow*, San Francisco: Harper and Row, 1989, pp.1-2, 68). This is the hypocrite's problem. Life to him is a one act play with no curtain at the end and no removing of the mask, only continual bows to the audience. What he fails to realize is the mask *always* slips. What's really underneath is *always* revealed. And the critic's reviews will *always* follow. Who we really are will eventually surface. The private self becomes public. Our lack of integrity will inevitably become evident.

So, what are you like in private? Who are you there? Is it any different than when you are in public? Are you an angry person behind closed doors but jovial and compassionate in public? If so, the next question comes as no surprise: Why? If the presence of people helps you exercise self-control and curtail anger, then you probably value man's opinion above God's, who sees you in private when others do not.

Correcting Compromised Integrity

First, come to grips with this skewed value system. Learn to fear God and accept His love. Yes, you read that right. God's holiness and His love are not polar opposites or contradictory. The fear of God helps us avoid sin, whereas the love of God draws us closer to follow Him. They are the two guardrails that keep us on the straight and narrow. They stir us and motivate us. They challenge us and encourage us. They protect us and comfort us.

Next, simply dispense with the show. Remove the mask. Image is what people see. Integrity, or its lack, is who we really are. So, let God's holiness and love so thoroughly pierce you and cut to your heart that you hate the pretense. Long to be genuine. Be the man God wants you to be everywhere and at all times. Be a Godly Man!

An Example

When my son was twelve years old, he appeared to be doing well with his course work. He was homeschooled, but we made the mistake of relying too much on his self-accountability. He graded and recorded his own test results. Math was where his problem became highlighted. We noticed numerous pencil erasures on his tests and "accidental" misplacements of homework he said he had done. The mask slipped on his mid-semester test. We corrected it and discovered that his grade did not match his weekly test results nor his promise that he was on top of the work. His past test results, his work assignments, and his self-accountability were not what they appeared. He would now need to redo three months' worth of work. As a result, his summer was very busy!

My heart broke for my son. I knew what needed to be done, but it would be hard. Needless to say, he and I had a sit-down talk. I explained at length the need for complete honesty, in tests as well as in life. Integrity was at stake. Little lies become huge lies. A small problem now (in his eyes) would become a life-controlling problem later. For one month, day and night, including the weekends, he could only do schoolwork and chores around the house. No TV. No computer. No video games. No football or play. No fun movies with family. The one exception was our Sunday Family Nights, where we watched a movie or played games together.

On several occasions during that month, I sat down with him to see how he was doing. I wanted to make sure he gave no place to hurt or bitterness. He didn't, and the punishment produced the change of heart needed. Our house, cars, and garage never looked better, but more important, he never lied like that again. Actually, he has become a very honest, transparent young man (and excellent in math) as he rounds the corner to sixteen. During that month, several nights he chose to go to bed early, quiet and almost unnoticed. I crept into his room and laid down next to him as he rolled over to reveal his tears. Again, my heart broke. Truthfully, however, this was a small price to pay compared to the devastation that awaited a life of compromise.

What Lies Beneath the Surface

Young men, realize that a lack of integrity will eventually be revealed. It will always catch up with us. It can go under the radar for only so long before it shows up. And when it does, I have learned it is usually only the tip of the iceberg. The greater concern lies beneath the surface. Minor character flaws usually hide bigger ones.

Did you know that what we see of an iceberg is only about 15% of what is actually there? Before the Titanic sunk in 1912 it was touted as amazingly well engineered and unsinkable. Such was its reputation. However, the night it went down it received six iceberg warnings. After the last, the operator responded, "Shut up! I'm busy." Thirty minutes later it began to make its way to the bottom of an abysmally dark Arctic Ocean, surprising everyone (John Maxwell, *Talent Is Never Enough*, Thomas Nelson: Nashville, Tennessee, 2007, p.195). Icebergs are nothing to trifle with. What one doesn't see is what will eventually destroy. The truth is, men, we must be men of truth. We must be men of the Word and men of our word. Little compromises now will yield devastation tomorrow.

How Character Is Built

Our character is the sum total of our decisions. Think about that. What is character? How do you recognize a loving person? By their words alone or by their choices, as well? How about a humble person? By the fact they say they're humble or by a series of decisions in which their words backed by their actions reveal a humble heart? Regardless of what we say we believe and value, our actions (determined by our choices) demonstrate what we really believe and

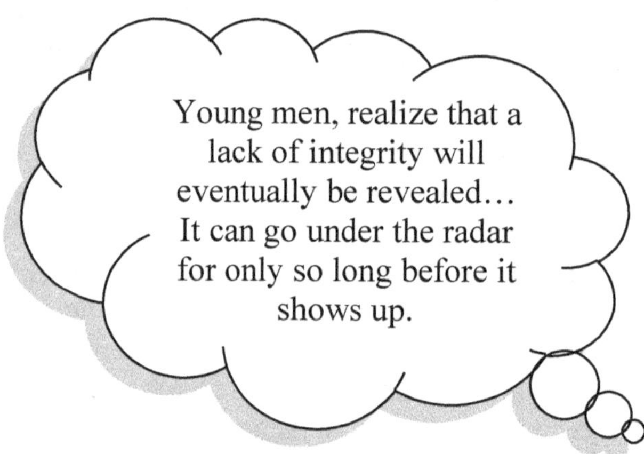

value. This can become very evident, for example, in the arena of politics. The candidate makes numerous promises, but if elected, his voting record (his decisions) shows where he really stands. For this reason, many politicians seek to hide how they voted, so the public does not receive a contradictory message. I've heard it said the word "politics" can be broken down as follows: "poly" meaning "many" and "tics" meaning "blood sucking parasites." For many, this is all too true.

If our integrity is built one decision at a time, then what lies before every one of us are two roads, each paved by right or wrong decisions that lead to good or bad character. First, the heart must change, then a series of godly decisions must follow, if we are to become men full of integrity. Neither step can be overemphasized. A changed heart will always reveal itself by a series of right decisions. Let's take a brief look at our friend Lot to see how this principle worked—or in his case, didn't work.

A Lot of Temptation

Lot was Abraham's nephew and as such owed him everything he had become. After Lot's father (Abraham's brother, Haran) died, Abraham took Lot in much like a son. He even allowed Lot to travel with him to Canaan, the land God had promised to him. There with God's favor and Abraham's leadership, the two became quite wealthy. As their flocks and herds outgrew their land, the tensions rose and they knew their families needed to part. But who would go where? There was the land to the east that was well-watered but had a bad reputation of wickedness or the land to the west where the Promised Land lay that was well-occupied by the Canaanites and as such could offer only meager opportunity to grow livestock. Abraham yielded the decision to Lot. What would he choose? Sin-soaked Sodom or the land of promise? Lot's decision revealed his heart. Though God-fearing, Lot was torn by compromise. The seed of greed had taken root, and this nasty weed would eventually spread and overrun Lot's heart.

He settled in the green grasslands outside of Sodom. Nothing permanent, only a temporary stay to regroup before moving on. The allurements of Sodom preyed on Lot's mind, however. Greater opportunity for business and political advancement lay within the confines of the city where sin abounded and compromise awaited. As God usually does, He sent Lot a wake-up call before his fatal step toward embracing Sodom's empty promises. Four mighty kings came down from the north and raided the surrounding cities, taking Lot and many others captive. But Lot was too lost in his downward spiral of greed to recognize God's disciplining hand. So, when Abraham came to his rescue and delivered him, he went back to his comforts of compromise.

Some fifteen to twenty years later, we find Lot settled *in* Sodom, owning a house and apparently holding some form of leadership in the city council which sat by the gates making their decisions. There are no signs of his once nomadic lifestyle that typified the patriarchs' desire to avoid the settled, sinful culture of the Canaanites. Instead, he has grown accustomed to Sodom's upgraded lifestyle, his daughters have found soul mates that have left them morally soulless, and his wife has become fond of the simple security of finally settling down, albeit in a sinful city. When fleeing Sodom, her seduced heart is betrayed by a longing glance back, and she is turned into a pillar of salt. This is rather ironic, seeing that in Jesus' words they all had lost their saltiness and weren't even fit for the dung heap! But such is the outcome of all who allow compromise to steal their hearts and lead them astray. It starts small, only to control them in the end. Their bad decisions reveal a heart lacking in integrity. So, we must let God change our heart. Then choose the right road that leads to good character, remembering that integrity is built one godly decision at a time.

Integrity Galvanized In Trials

Perhaps the best way to discover what lies beneath our surface is times of testing. It's easy to make godly decisions during times of success and things are going great. But when trials come our way, as they say, our cup is shaken and what's inside spills out, good or bad. If we have issues of anger or worry or love for the world, then these trials will tend to reveal them. But God can use trials to **build** character not just reveal it. We are told: *"...we also exult in our tribulations, knowing that tribulation brings about perseverance; and perseverance, proven character; and proven character, hope"* (Romans 5:3-4). How does this happen? Because of the intensity of the trials, or suffering, we become much more dependent upon God and the decisions made during these times tend to become galvanized into character.

Let me explain with some examples. The Israelites needed to learn to rely completely upon God and obey Him no matter what. After leaving Egypt and wandering in the wilderness, they lacked water and food at times. How did they respond? What decisions did they make during these times? They usually grumbled against God and His leaders, demonstrating a faithless heart. It took an entire generation to learn the godly character of faith and total reliance upon God and His promises.

Moses told them: *"He brought water for you out of the rock of flint. In the wilderness He fed you manna which your fathers did not know, that He might **humble** you and that He might **test** you, to do good for you in the end"* (Deuteronomy 8:15-16). The bad decisions to grumble only brought God's judgment. The consequences of sin were severe. For us, we may put our hand on a hot stove only so many times before this painful experience teaches us to make the wise decision to **not** touch the hot stove. Those painful consequences help galvanize good decisions to obey the parental command, "Don't touch the hot stove!"

Eventually, after forty years of numerous character failures, the Israelites began to make good decisions to obey God, and He richly blessed them. He humbled them constantly until these difficult circumstances began to reveal godly character. In this way God uses trials to build integrity in His people one decision at a time.

I have mentioned my personal struggle with anger, particularly when I was a young Christian. I blamed it on my brother. If only he would stop irritating me, I thought, then I would not get so angry and start fights with him. But the truth is that no one and nothing can *make* me angry. Anger is always a choice. Don't let anyone, including present day misguided, secular psychologists, tell you otherwise. We consciously choose to be angry. It may not feel this way because it has become so ingrained in us that it has developed into a knee-jerk reaction.

The only person I could ever blame for my anger issues was me. As I learned this truth, I found that when I made the tough choices to respond with kindness in the face of irritation, I was able to get rid of anger (Ephesians 4:31). Over time my good choices replaced my old, bad habits of anger. They soon became my default response. This happened one decision at a time, building proper, godly character. Trials, therefore, either reveal the ugly that is already there or become the stepping stone to galvanizing integrity in our lives. The choice is literally ours.

Decision Time

Men, we must realize what is at stake in our day. People are selling their souls to the system of this world one small compromise at a time. Dealing with the Devil in this way is always a lose-lose proposition. What lies behind his veneer of promise is always destruction—shipwrecked lives. And why wouldn't it be? The Devil is the Father of lies! He deals in deception. This is his trade. He is unfair and callous. He cares nothing for you and will only be delighted when you take the bait and discover a hook in your jaw. So, take a step back and assess where you are at. Is there anything you have been covering up with a lie? Do you tend to act differently around different groups of people? Do you act one way at church and another way at home? Are there promises you have made to others that you have not made good on? Until a problem is brought to the surface and admitted, it cannot be dealt with. This is the simple purpose of this chapter. Our next lesson will show you how to uproot stubborn sin issues once we have recognized and confessed them.

Right now, allow God's Spirit to gently bring His correction and to steer you back on course. Allow Him to remove the cancerous character and heal you. Do not put this off! And do not cut short the process. Small spiritual malignancies today become life-threatening problems tomorrow. As Godly Men, let us take our stand now and become men full of integrity.

BRING IT HOME!

Write a short paragraph describing King David's character.

Now write a short paragraph describing your character.

Remember, Godly Men seek to live "above reproach" and "blamelessly," free from accusation. Does anyone have a legitimate accusation against you? What is it? Are you taking proper action to resolve it?

If not, why not? What's holding you back?

I do not like asking the following rapid-fire questions, but I have come to learn that we tend to cover up or "sugar coat" these areas in our lives where we lack integrity. Challenging, soul-provoking questions are about the only way to uncover them.

If you are a student, have you cheated on any tests or homework? If so, which ones?

Do you read books you've been asked to? If not, which ones have you not read or just skimmed?

Do you check off work you haven't really done?

Do you plagiarize your reports, essays, or other writing assignments?

If you are employed, do you nap when you're supposed to be working?

Do you lie to get out of potential trouble?

Are you frequently late? If so, why? (Personally, I hate wasting time, but I can't use this as an excuse for being late. And that's what it is, an excuse. When we're late, we generally make people wait for us. This then is selfishness. Let's get rid of our excuses, young men, and thereby honor others by being early.)

When running an errand for your boss, do you take "smoke breaks" or make other pit stops to relax on company time?

Do you talk negatively about your boss behind his or her back?

Do your work habits change whether your boss is present or not?

If you are married, are you keeping secrets from your spouse? If so, what are they? Share these with your mentor and plan out how you will "come clean." If it is of a significant nature, get with a pastor and plan out a rehabilitation process (the next chapter "Godly Men Walk in Freedom" can help with this).

Does your private self match your public self? If not, list where they are different.

Do you flirt with girls? This is communicating in a way that says, "I am interested in you" without obligating yourself. You are hoping for a response that says the same thing. This is playful deception and can be hurtful.

Have you noticed any compromises (even small ones) in your life lately? If so, what are they?

What steps of action (decisions) do you need to make at this point?

Godly Men
Walk In Freedom

Sin rarely presents itself initially in all its horrid destructiveness. It is far too subtle. Camouflaged with appeal, it allures and seduces. Once entangled in its web of guilt and shame, we often wonder how we had been so naïve and how we can be freed from its merciless grip. Though God's answer is certain, we must be prepared for the fight of our life.

I grew up in the suburbs of Wilmington, Delaware. Just two to three miles from my house lay the green, rolling hills of the country. It was the perfectly innocent and unsuspecting scene for Sin's set up. Winding roads curve their way through these hills and reveal numerous large estates with high stone walls to keep the curious out. Large state parks dot the map of northern Delaware, making it inviting for those who want to take in its picturesque scenery by car, bicycle, or foot. It became a favorite place for my long-distance runs. At fourteen, I regularly ventured along the twisting roads to get in shape for cross-country.

I still remember one run in particular. It was daylight during the Fall, so it was not too hot, not too cool. I was headed home but still in the country with several miles left to go when nature began to call. It wasn't long before the call turned to a shout, and I knew I needed to pit stop behind a tree somewhere. I frantically dashed into the woods and ran nearly 100 yards from the road (being a very private person), ensuring I would be unseen from any passing motorists. As I began to relieve myself behind a huge oak tree, I noticed something at its foot. It appeared to be some folded up papers. Some interesting bathroom material? I preferred the comics myself, sometimes the sports section. It was neither. Instead, I apparently had come across someone's disposed pornographic magazine. Curiosity and desire won the moment as I tucked it inconspicuously into my shirt and shorts and finished out my run.

Like it was for Gollum in **The Lord of the Rings**, it became my Precious. I was soon addicted to pornography and regularly felt the darkness of a different lord around me. Later, it became apparent to me that Satan had set me up like breadcrumbs on a path. I felt controlled and defeated, even helpless. He is a ruthless task master, merciless in his rule. It was about the same time I had truly given my heart to Christ, so a serious tug of war ensued. I wasn't about to quit fighting, but I felt so powerless. What could I do?

Many men of all ages walk in similar defeat, wondering if the God who saved them is truly powerful enough to rescue them from such self-absorbed sin. Lust is a powerful temptation, but never stronger than our conquering Christ, the "Anointed One," who is able to break every stronghold and empty any prison cell. This chapter is about walking in freedom. Not just freedom from lust. Freedom from anger. Freedom from greed. Freedom from the control of sin. It is one of the toughest battles in a man's life. Though the answer lies in self-control, it is more than that.

If you are running the race of faith and have found yourself tripped up by Satan's snares, I assure you victory is still within your grasp as you train yourself in godliness and learn to run (and yes, very long distances) in God's enabling grace. This He did for me two years after that fateful pit stop, and this He can do for you as you *"run with endurance the race that is set before [you]"* (Hebrews 12:1).

DIG IN!

Study Section 1

READ Galatians 5:22-23.

What is "self-control" called in this passage?

Who produces this character quality?

Is it right to say then that it is a product of will power?

READ Romans 8:9.

What is another result of the Spirit of God living in us?

READ Ephesians 1:13-14.

What does the Holy Spirit do when we believe in Christ and are included in Him?

So, do all believers have the Holy Spirit living inside them? [NOTE: The sealing and indwelling of the Holy Spirit for all believers are different from the empowering work of the Spirit described in Acts.]

According to God's Word, does the Spirit of God live in you? Does He control you? (Do your best to answer that last question)

READ Ephesians 4:26-27.

What can happen with unresolved anger?

KJV -

NIV -

NASB -

I will later discuss the word used here for what Satan can do. Suffice it say for now, it is a weakness in us that our enemy wants to exploit to gain control in our life.

READ II Corinthians 10:3-5.

Paul is talking about a spiritual battle here in which we fight with weapons unlike our military's. What are our weapons able to demolish? (one word)

Verse 5 explains what is being demolished. They are typical of strongholds. List them.

These strongholds are in what form?

    A. Stone.
    B. Knowledge.
    C. Pretend.

In what part of us then would Satan want to erect his stronghold?

    A. Our foot.
    B. Our chest.
    C. Our mind.

Though the immediate context here is a false gospel that Paul's enemies are preaching and leading many Corinthians astray (see II Corinthians 11:3-4), it is falsehood, or lies, that we must battle concerning any stronghold. According to 10:5 but in your own words, how are we to solve this problem?

READ Romans 12:1-2.

In order to not become like the world and fit into its mold of evil behavior, what must we do?

So, in order to change our wrong behavior, what must first change?

If we want to control our temper, what needs to be controlled first?

How about if we want to control our greed?

How about if we want to control a drug or alcohol addiction?

Consequently, both our behavior and our emotions are the product of the way we think. List some things that require self-control.

As we have seen, the fruit of the Spirit called self-control is really Spirit-control. Satan our enemy seeks to gain footholds in our minds to control the way we think and therefore the way we act. God's Spirit must change our thinking if we are to be Spirit-controlled and transformed.

Study Section 2

READ Psalm 119:11.

What is the most powerful way to transform the way we think?

READ I Peter 5:8.

Why is Satan compared to a lion?

What is his goal in our lives?

How does he do this?

READ John 10:10.

What is Satan's goal?

How might he do this?

READ I Corinthians 10:13.

Are you the only one wrestling with the sins that entangle you?

What promise does God give us here?

What then does this promise imply about potential victory?

Do you know what *"the way of escape"* looks like? Describe one (perhaps use a personal example).

READ James 4:6-10.

According to verse 9, what should our attitude be toward sin? Have you ever done this? If so, share a brief example.

What two things does God do for the humble according to verses 6 and 10?

The word used here for "resist" literally means "to stand firmly against" and is very aggressive, not passive. It is also translated "oppose." I find helpful the image of Gandalf in *The Lord of the Rings* slamming his staff down before the evil balrog, shouting, "You shall not pass!" When we oppose the Devil like this, what must he do?

What very important thing must we do before we oppose the Devil?

How do you do this? Can you list some practical ways?

So, we have seen that Satan our enemy tries to control us as followers of Christ. This usually starts small, such as a "foothold," and grows more dominating as 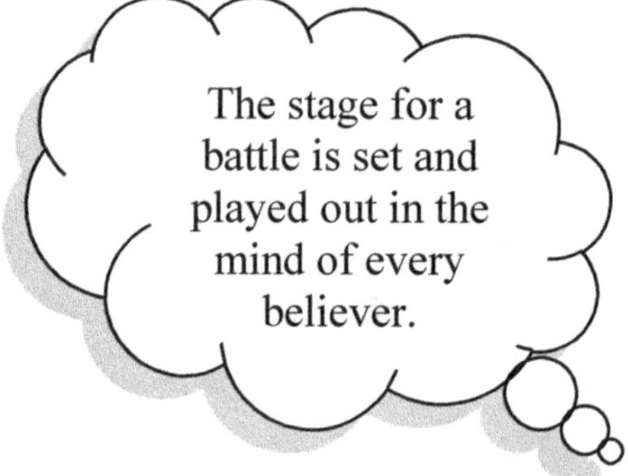

we allow him. But we also saw that the Holy Spirit is to control us. We do not have to be controlled by the Devil. The stage for a battle is set and played out in the mind of every believer. Thoughts that we permit in either feed our spirit to yield to God's Spirit more or feed our flesh (see Galatians 5:17). In the next section I will guide you through some very specific steps of action you can take to regularly walk in freedom. Remember though that victory is not measured by the moment but by a continued, consistent life of self-control, yielded to God's Spirit.

Much of what is contained in this chapter can feel like a list of things to do, and if done in the "arm of the flesh" can feel burdensome. This is certainly not the intention. Perhaps much of Jesus' Sermon on the Mount can feel this way as well. For this reason, Jesus began with eight beatitudes, the first four of which focus on the gospel and our need to *rely upon God* for our transformation. In view of this, please make sure you have a good grasp on the principles of the gospel and reliance upon Christ laid out in the first few chapters before proceeding. These highlight the beauty of God's grace, the only true means by which we can ever walk in genuine freedom.

THINK ABOUT IT!

Growing up, I heard this story about Little Tater that will help us understand the control sin can have on us should we allow it. He was a good old country boy who grew up in a small, backwards town. One Christmas he got a moped and was so excited about it, he drove it around town nearly all day showing his friends. At one point as he came to a stop at a red light, the finest Mercedes Benz he'd ever seen (which admittedly were few) pulled up right next to him. Tater leaned over, pressing his face against the driver's window and exclaimed, "Golly, the dashboard looks like an astronaut's panel!" To impress the little fellow, the driver lowered his window. "Them's nice leather seats!" Tater commented in his slow southern drawl.

About this time the light turned green and off our Mercedes driver went, accelerating furiously to demonstrate its power. As he looked in his rearview mirror, Tater was a speck of dust, he was so far back. However, not but five seconds later, there went Tater on his moped speeding past the surprised driver. "Holy smokes!" he muttered with obvious embarrassment as he pressed down on the gas pedal, passing our little friend. He soon looked in his rearview mirror and Tater was, yes, a speck of dust, way back there! About five seconds later, as the Mercedes owner was chuckling to himself, there went Tater again on his moped. "Why, this here's impossible!" the driver exclaimed. So, he put the pedal to the metal and streaked past our bewildered mopedist. You guessed it, as he checked his rearview mirror, there was Tater, only a speck of dust, he was so far back.

Now, as our confident motorist began to settle comfortably into his leather seat to enjoy his drive, not but *five* seconds later, Tater came smashing into the back of this beautiful, sleek Mercedes-Benz. The driver came to a screeching halt, jumped out, and frantically ran to the back of his car, yelling, "Tater! Tater! Is there anythin' I can do for ya?"

Shocked and dazed, Tater looked up at him and replied, "Sure. Can ya unstrap my suspenders from yer side view mirror?"

Every time I hear this story, I imagine poor Tater rocketing back and forth on his moped like a yo-yo. The truth of the matter is that this is a vivid picture of many of us caught in the stranglehold of a sin. At one moment, it appears we have victory, but the next moment, we are at its mercy, caught in its trap. Eventually, we lie there in a smashed heap of defeat, wondering if there's any possibility of truly conquering this problem. But resignation is not the answer. Jesus is. Luke 4:21 tells us that Jesus is the Anointed One who has come to set the captives free.

Jesus Our Bondage Breaker

Let's take stock here a moment. When you became a Christian, the Bible clearly states that your sins were forgiven. Fact. As Savior, Jesus cancelled out every sin and, therefore, every accusation the Evil One could throw at you. Fact. But for most of us, that's the sum total we believe our Savior accomplished for us on the Cross, that He saved us from our sins. Now read that last phrase one more time, slowly: "He saved us from our sins." This great salvation we have received is not just forgiveness *for* our sins but salvation, deliverance, rescue *from* our sins. As Isaiah put it: *"to proclaim liberty to captives and freedom to prisoners"* (61:2). Jesus is the Freer of captives. He is the Rescuer of sinners. He is the Bondage Breaker!

Jesus' mission as the Christ, the "Anointed One," is both to forgive and set free every sinner who surrenders to Him. Now I hope I didn't surprise you with that word "surrender." Perhaps you were expecting it to read "every sinner who *believes* in Him." The truth is that we have redefined this word "believe" in much of Americanized Christianity. We have turned it into a rather wimpy word with no grit and no challenge. Consequently, we have stripped it of much of its power. The Greek word can mean to acknowledge certain facts, but when Jesus repeatedly said, "Believe *in* me," He certainly meant far more than this. The word also means "to commit oneself to." This is the essence of surrender, and understanding this is key to grasping the principles and steps of freedom I believe Jesus our Bondage Breaker longs for every one of His children to walk in.

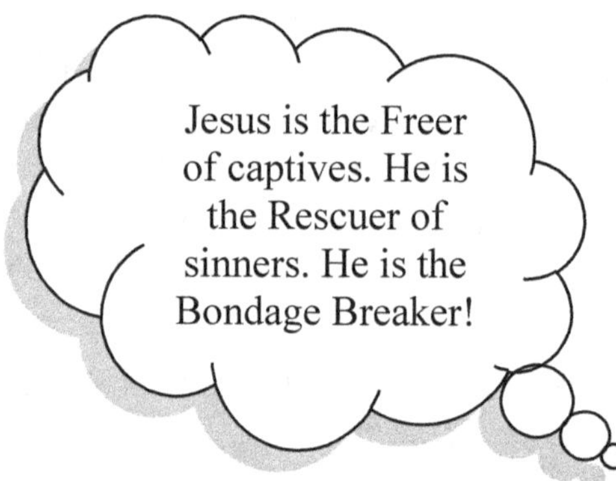

Before I share these truths with you, allow me to illustrate the seriousness of what God is requiring of us in our surrender to Him. Four years ago, my children and I got my wife an orange tree for her birthday. They grow well here in the sandy central Florida soil as long as they are properly cared for. We planted, watered, and fertilized it accordingly and didn't expect much the first year or two. However, though those first two years produced one or two oranges per season, the third year we anticipated a good number, seeing the tree was nearly six feet tall. Sadly, it managed a meager handful. Peering out into my backyard one Saturday morning during my prayer time, I noticed something very unusual. Nearly half the leaves were dying. These withering leaves weren't randomly scattered over the tree's foliage, they were all on one side.

I decided to check this unusual sight out, putting my prayer time on momentary hold, and slipped through my sliding glass door. As I investigated the tree, I noticed that all the dying leaves stemmed from two main branches. Following the branches to the trunk I discovered the problem. Apparently, the orange tree came with tags dangling from ribbons. Only portions of the two ribbons could be seen as the branches on which they were tied had grown around them, completely engulfing them. These ribbons were severely restricting the proper flow of nutrients to the leaves and subsequently to any potential fruit.

If I didn't do anything, I knew the branches would either die or perhaps retain some foliage but stop producing fruit altogether. Taking drastic measures, I took a sharp utility knife from my tool box and proceeded to cut very deeply into both tree branches. With each successively deeper slice, I attempted to feel for the ribbon. Eventually, the knife caught the ribbon and severed each restriction. Days passed as I waited to see how the branches would recover. Had I dug too deeply? Had I permanently damaged their ability to produce fruit? The cooler months soon settled in (there are no "cold" months here), and the Spring and Summer would soon reveal the success or failure of the surgery.

As I sit here recounting this story on paper, we are closing out our thunderstorm-filled summer. The tree has produced nearly ten times the number of oranges as the past three years combined. I'm sure you get the principle in play here. The restrictions that hinder the grace of God from flowing through our lives and producing an abundance of fruit are the strongholds we've allowed. Perhaps for better illustration purposes, I should say "strangleholds." The point then is that the Chief Surgeon must cut deeply into our lives so these sins can no longer strangle the fruit bearing limbs of character growth and ministry. May I say from personal experience that the process is painful. There's no way around it. As we submit to His knife, He cuts out what He needs to. He breaks the stranglehold. He sets the prisoner free! This will require some serious self-sacrifice, choosing God's way above our own and His desires above ours. As Jesus said, *"Not as I will, but as You will"* (Matthew 26:39). This promise of freedom then is to everyone who truly surrenders to ("believes in") Him.

The Battlefield

So, how do we apply this and walk in freedom? First, let me lay out for you what we'll call the battlefield. Here, we will confront our enemy many times with the goal of complete conquest. Then I will walk you through a behind-the-scenes training regimen that will enable you to sustain victory in the face of further temptations.

Our Authority as Soldiers of Christ

"When He had disarmed the rulers and authorities, He made a public display of them, having triumphed over them through Him" (Colossians 2:15).

This pictures for us the typical scene of a Roman general leading his conquered captives through the streets of Rome in a triumphal procession in which they are scorned and humiliated. This is what Christ, the Freer of Captives and our General, has done to Satan and his demonic entourage for us by the cross. As John put it, *"Greater is He who is in you than he who is in the world"* (I John 4:4). And again, John tells us, *"Who is the one who overcomes the world, but he who believes that Jesus is the Son of God?"* (I John 5:5). Sometime later, John wrote in the book of Revelation: *"The accuser...has been hurled down....And they overcame him because of the blood of the Lamb and because of the word of their testimony"* (12:10-11).

The authority every believer has is "in Jesus' name." For this reason, when we rebuke the Devil, he must flee, we studied. But any authority can be yielded. Should we do this, Satan gains a "foothold" as Ephesians 4:27 (NIV, 1978) states. The Greek word used there is *tupos* and literally means "place." It is more than just an "opportunity" (NASB). It is ***not*** an abstract noun. It has a locale. The word can carry a military usage like our phrase "beach head." When the Allies of WWII took Normandy Beach from the Germans, it was a turning point for them. They had gained the high ground and a military advantage to retake France and eventually secure access to Germany. They had obtained a "beach head" or "foothold," a "place." Remember, Satan starts small but his influence increases. The authority, or right, to gain control back is within us as representatives of Christ. When Jesus dealt with His adversary, He did so with a command. We do the same "in Jesus' name," a phrase expressing power of attorney, that is, we function in the authority of Christ, in His stead, as His representative.

The truth then is that by Christ's authority we can walk in constant victory. But when we stumble repeatedly into sin, we can *feel* enslaved by it. This enslavement, however, is a lie, a deception. Let me explain. During his imprisonment by the Japanese, General Wainwright was tortured and succumbed to the power and authority of his captors. However, when WWII was finally over, word spread slowly. Though his captors knew of their defeat, they refused to tell him and treated him no differently. Eventually, he discovered the truth and, emaciated and weak, marched into the Japanese commander's office, demanding full and complete surrender to him and his men. The commander complied and Wainwright was in control.

Many believers live without the full realization the battle has been won, so act as if it is not, thus unwittingly yielding authority to the enemy. As the truth set General Wainwright free to walk in his authority, even so it should with us. We have been set free from our prison and our chains have been broken by the cross. However, when we yield authority to the enemy and he obtains a "foothold," it's as if we walk back into the prison cell and sit down in "defeat." The door remains unlocked, and the chains are not secured. So, let me repeat, this enslavement is a lie, not real. It is smoke in mirrors. But where we allow the enemy to dominate, he gladly will. So, what do we do?

Engaging the Enemy

Now, let me introduce you to two very important words: repentance and renunciation. Both are integral in our battles with our adversary.

Repentance means a forsaking of past actions that have seriously grieved God and now grieve us. Yes, it is emotional. It is also an act of the will that we shall purposefully carry out in action. This is not a sorrow for being caught. It is a grief and sickness over our sin. With a repentant heart, we cry out to God in desperation to forgive us and set us free.

Renunciation would be like the captured general saying to the Japanese commander, "I refuse to live in these squalid conditions any longer. I am walking out of this compound and absolutely refusing to obey any further directions from you. You are the defeated enemy, and by the authority of my Commander-in-Chief I am free to go home and have nothing to do with you!" Renunciation is a resolute, willful turning away from sin and a clear, determined declaration of one's new intentions. It requires bold authority—a firm faith in who Christ is and what He has accomplished for us.

Let me illustrate this. A veteran cop will boldly step into oncoming traffic, forcefully blow his whistle, and confidently extend his open hand to bring traffic to a halt. A rookie traffic cop, however, usually is somewhat timid when trying to stop traffic for the first time. Will the oncoming cars stop in time as he hesitantly extends his hand, lightly tweets his whistle, and cautiously stands directly in their pathway? Is there any guarantee that they will see him and obey him? He wrestles with the uncertainty. In the same way, it is hard for the timid believer to completely walk in the authority of Christ and wriggle free from our adversary's clutches. Like the veteran cop, confidently put your foot down. Demand the enemy to cease and desist. This is faith—courageous, authoritative faith. Run to God! Leave the chains behind. Don't look back. Be free. If a porn addiction is the chains, then leave it. Be resolute in your decision. Understand the devastating consequences of your sin and long for it no more. God responds to this kind of faith with ample grace.

A simple example of this principle is found in the disciples' attempt to cast a demon out of a young man but were not able to. Why? When His followers asked why their attempts failed, Jesus said, *"Because you have so little faith"* (Matthew 17:20—NIV, 1978). Lean into this challenge, then, young men and be resolute in your faith here.

At this point, you will want to have your mentor (or another man of God) pray over you, commanding the enemy to leave, to release his foothold that has become a stranglehold in your life. He should do so, exercising the faith and authority he has been given in Christ. Then both of you cry out to God for sustained strength for you to daily walk in freedom.

Ongoing Confrontations

The temptations may continue, but a new freedom will be present. Choose to walk in this freedom with each subsequent temptation. James 4:7 tells us how: submit to God whenever the allurements seek to entrap us again and then rebuke the Devil. He *must* flee! Submitting to God comes in many forms, but they are all expressed in actions and words: worship, prayer, quoting Scripture, thanksgiving, declarations of faith or God's promises, etc. As you engage in one of these, boldly command the Devil to stop his tauntings and leave you. Jesus had the Word memorized and frequently quoted it against the enemy, wielding it like a sword.

Let me offer a suggestion here. When it comes to lust in particular, don't keep praying about it over and over somewhat mechanically when tempted. This can inadvertently cause you to think about it more. Rather, submit to God, rebuke the Devil, and move on. Don't become preoccupied by the very thing you are trying to escape. Instead, think about pure things and occupy your mind with what is true, noble, right, excellent, or praiseworthy (Philippians 4:8).

In this way, you can take back the authority Christ has given you and successfully submit to Him, walking in daily freedom. *Repent* of your habitual sin, crying out to God to forgive you and set you free, then *renounce* the sin, declaring you will have nothing to do with it any longer. Be aggressive. Be adamant in this decision!

A Rigorous Training Regimen

What I have described is the actual battle, yielding to God and confronting the enemy to gain victory. But every warrior submits to rigorous training so he can win each conflict. No shortcuts should be permitted. Remember that the story of Luke Skywalker breaking his training with Yoda short and confronting Darth Vader is fantasy. That means it is based on imagination and does not happen in real life. Though Luke was ultimately victorious, such is not the case outside of Hollywood.

Recently, a local pastor that had fallen into an adulterous affair had stepped down from his responsibilities and submitted himself to the care and direction of an older pastor in our area who had dealt with this issue in other pastoral leaders. Within three months this fallen man removed himself from this corrective covering and found another. Why? The prescribed process of restoration would be a minimum of two years, far too long for the impatience of this man. Within eight months, another pastor set him back in as a spiritual leader. A four-to-five yearlong affair corrected in eight months? The causes of such a secretive addiction (this is what it was) run very deep. Very deep! But like Luke, many refuse the necessary steps of correction and training needed to rebuild.

What follows is a training regimen, a step-by-step plan of what you can do to be strong, implement correction, and sustain freedom. It is hard work and will require considerable discipline on your part, but such is the life of a warrior. But let me repeat, reliance upon and submission to Christ will be key.

STEP 1: A Mindset

Romans 12:9 says, *"Abhor what is evil; cling to what is good."* Though referred to earlier in chapter one, it is relevant here. The warrior needs a certain mindset. The battlefield is not a playground. Wooden swords are discarded for sharp, tempered steel that can sever limbs with one swing. Seriousness of the situation is required. This is where boys become men. For Godly Men in pursuit of freedom in Christ, sin is nothing to be trifled with. As I say, "If you pet the piranhas, you'll get bitten!" Hatred for evil is mandatory. One cannot be casual, or he will become a casualty. All too often, however, we attempt to see how close to sin we can get without really sinning. This is both dangerous and deceptive.

What would you say to a friend in the following situation? While walking up a winding, abandoned, mountain road with the mountain to one side and a one-thousand-foot drop to the other, your friend attempts to see how close to the edge of the cliff he can get. Although a guardrail is present, he climbs on top of it and begins to walk it like a balance beam. One misstep to the side, however, and he plummets to his death. The truth is it's a beautiful scene and the risk of the "adventure" is very alluring. Your friend even tosses clods of clay over the side to see what happens to

them as they fall for what seems like forever before hitting the rocks below and shattering into thousands of pieces. Do you join in the "adventure" yourself? Or do you quickly grab his arm and pull him to safety? Are you content to encourage him to walk beside the guardrail as long as he doesn't climb on top of it or lean over it? Or do you firmly challenge him to avoid the guardrail altogether and walk in the center of the road, where it is much safer. We must have the mindset that truly hates evil and avoids it at every turn.

Consider also a wrestler. He has a fixed mindset. He must if he wants to win. He rises early to run his prescribed miles before school. He eats only what is healthy and avoids overindulging, because he realizes he must make weight. If he's too heavy for his weight class, he doesn't wrestle. He's disqualified. He trains both on the mat and in the weightlifting room. He thinks like a wrestler, acts like a wrestler, and trains like a wrestler. He eats, breathes, and dreams wrestling. It becomes his life. Equally so, Godly Men who follow Christ think like a Christian (read, "spiritual warrior"), act like a Christian, and train like a Christian. Christ consumes them in thought and action. As a wrestler wouldn't even think of eating a double whopper with a side order of fries, so a Godly Man ***should refuse*** to entertain the possibility of delving into porn or lusts or explosive anger or harsh, demeaning words. These are poison to his soul. They are contrary to his new nature in Christ. His mindset says, "No!" He's serious about sin and demonstrates it by his actions. "Should refuse" is key here. His fleshly desires may lead him astray. If this happens, he repents, fully embraces Christ's forgiveness, and resets his mindset.

STEP 2: God's Word

The other half of Roman's 12:9 commands us to *"cling to what is good."* To do this, we must first fill our mind with what is good. Psalm 119:9 says, *"How can a young man keep his way pure? By keeping it according to Your word."* And how does he live this way? Verse 11 declares: *"Your word have I treasured in my heart, that I might not sin against You."* Psalm 1:2-3 says about the blessed man: *"But his delight is in the law of the LORD, and in His law he meditates day and night. He will be like a tree firmly planted by streams of water, which yields its fruit in its season and its leaf does not wither; and in whatever he does, he prospers."* Such a blessed man meditates on God's word "day and night," that is, regularly. He will be like the tree planted by streams of water, constantly being nourished. God blesses him in all his undertakings.

While we lived in Phoenix, Arizona for three years, I was introduced to "desert landscaping." Due to the lack of rain, many filled their yards with rock—white or, if they were creative, red lava rocks. Lawn mowers were discarded for a bottle of Round Up. Some, however, bore the expense of watering their lawns on a regular basis. Here in Orlando, sprinkler systems water lawns a couple times per week. One particular friend of mine, who lived in Phoenix on an acre lot with a horse in his backyard, used a different system of irrigation. Once a week, he flooded his backyard with about four to six inches of water. At first sight, I thought this was a waste and would surely result in a dry, sun-scorched lawn by the end of the week. But he explained that the water percolates down into the ground some twelve inches. As deep as the water goes, the roots will grow. This results, of course, in grass roots twelve inches deep. By the end of the week only the top several inches of soil are dry. But since the grass roots go much deeper, they continue to draw moisture from much further down, well below the surface. My friend's backyard was actually very green and very healthy in spite of the frequent 115° temperatures.

As you dig into God's Word on a daily basis, don't just read it, meditate on it. Think about it. Ask questions and search for answers. Seriously consider its implications for your life and your world around you. What is it asking you to do? How will you accomplish that? Ask God what portions you should memorize. As an athlete increases his training over time, running two miles, then four, then six, so increase your time in God's Word. Let it saturate you. Allow it to percolate through your mind down into your spirit. Let it challenge you and encourage you. Let it sift your thoughts, attitudes, and motivations (Hebrews 4:12). Allow it to examine your actions and change you. Don't be satisfied with only information. Seek transformation! Pray back to God what you believe He is challenging you to do in response to your time in His Word.

Study Scripture with one eye on yourself and another on others in your life. Reservoirs with no outlet become stagnant pools empty of life. How might God want you to reach out and encourage someone else? Your focus here is to bless or minister to them. Be careful of pride. Paul said, *"Knowledge makes arrogant, but love edifies."* (I Corinthians 8:1). Let your heart be filled with love as you build them up, instead of pride, demonstrating

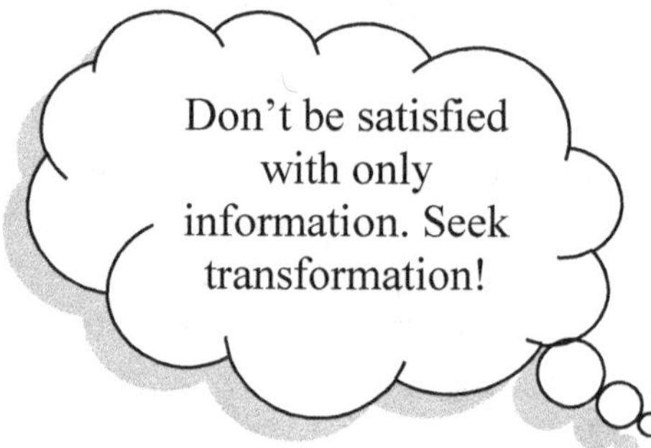

how much you know. God's Word in you and spoken through you will potentially accomplish great things for Christ's kingdom (Isaiah 55:11). So, daily sit alone with God's Word and let it saturate your mind and percolate down into your spirit, renewing, restoring, and refreshing. And then go do it!

STEP 3: Into the Light

Some years ago, while my family and I lived in Phoenix, I became convinced the roaches in the Southwest were the result of radioactive testing gone awry. My wife, Meredith, complained our first summer in this desert city that she saw a roach ("palmetto bug") three to four inches long. I admittedly did not believe her. A college friend who was visiting us at the time encountered this beast one night and left a note on the bathroom door: "The battle was fierce. Life threatening. The enemy was so big you could saddle and ride it. But I triumphed, me and my can of Raid. Signed, the Palmetto Kid." He affirmed my wife's fears: these creatures were huge, arrogant, and bold. "Su casa es mi casa!" I think they even had the accent down.

Anyways, southwestern roaches were nothing to trifle with. Since I worked with my friend's pest control company, leading crews door-to-door, selling the service, I was made aware that if you saw a few, you had to act fast before they took over. So, when potential customers complained to me about their problem, I asked them, "When you turn the kitchen light on at night, how many do you see?" As I say, a few are bad news. When they would respond, "A dozen or two," I knew right away the house needed to be bombed—some of them with C4! The bombing of course was with chemicals, so our technician would look throughout the house for signs of the nests. One particular tech told of a time he was searching the air conditioning vents. These were located in the ceilings and were not small. As he unfastened the latches of one and let it swing down, what happened next was nothing short of revolting and nightmare-inducing. Hundreds (yes, **hundreds**!) of roaches poured over him! Nest discovered. Roaches uncovered. Tech **not** recovered! I think I still feel a twinge of fear every time I open an air conditioning vent of any kind.

My point is that one must turn the light on to assess the roach problem. If some are discovered, one must act fast before the problem gets out of control. But the truth is, roaches typically run from the light. They hate it. It's as if they know that they will be discovered and killed. So it is with our sin. Truthfully, we don't want it to come into the light and be exposed and dealt with. Jesus said in John 3:20, "For everyone who does evil hates the Light, and does not come to the

Light for fear that his deeds will be exposed." Here's the principle: sin thrives in secrecy. Unexposed, it grows. The more it grows, the more it controls. It takes over. It infests.

Several years ago in 2004, we central Floridians experienced three hurricanes in the space of about four weeks. A first for us. My family room and kitchen flooded each time. We pulled about seventy gallons of water from the floor during each hurricane. Needless to say, afterwards, some repairs were in order. However, after three months, we continued to smell a strong mildew odor in our kitchen. In my endeavor to discover its source, I pulled the four-inch kickplate out from under our cabinets along the wall. Underneath was dark with mildew. It was everywhere! I donned a charcoal filter mask and latex gloves. Well equipped, I scrubbed every square inch under these cabinets with a strong bleach solution. As long as the mildew had remained in the dark, it grew and took over wherever it spread. I had to expose it and take thorough measures to get rid of it.

Can we do any less with our sin habits? Left alone in the dark, unconfessed, they will only grow. We need someone we can confide in to help us bear this burden. Then and only then can we be healed. *"Therefore, confess your sins to one another, and pray for one another so that you may be healed."* (James 5:16). Scripture also says, *"Bear one another's burdens, and thereby fulfill the law of Christ"* (Galatians 6:2). The context is dealing with sin. Remember then that with healing comes the freedom. With freedom comes the restoration. Confession, repentance, and prayer are essential. This will require humility and willingness on our part. Confidentiality will be necessary. Dealing with the sin issue in the past by yourself hasn't worked, so don't think one more try will be any different. Do it God's way. It's hard, yes, but the only effective way. Pull this confidant in as an accountability partner. Don't be fooled into thinking you're the only one wrestling with this issue. I assure you, you are not. Paul says that it *"is common to man"* (I Corinthians 10:13).

Some men I have ministered to have needed multiple accountability partners.

One young man with an alcohol problem had a habit of going out with his co-workers after clocking out to a local bar for a few drinks. This never ended well for him. After surrendering his heart to Christ, he needed an accountability call after his work hours. The problem was he got off at 1 A.M. After he surrendered his heart to Christ, another brother volunteered to call him every morning at 1:15 A.M. He did so faithfully. Others regularly called him or met with him. God truly set this young man free, in part because he unveiled his secret sin, bringing it into the light, and was held accountable. These brothers loved him and supported him. They were faithful and required complete truthfulness. They constantly sought to encourage him, breathing life into his daily situations. The beautiful thing is he does this for others now and is becoming a key part in helping grow strong men in our church.

STEP 4: Radical Amputation

When I was a boy, I looked for odd jobs to do around our house. My mother would pay us a small wage, and by saving up our dimes, nickels, and pennies (these are the small coins in our monetary system that most kids today are unfamiliar with except as tiny pieces of metal they try to see how far they can throw), we could buy a pack of baseball cards, gum, or penny candy (I'm not even going to explain what this is). One of these odd jobs was pulling up dandelions in our backyard. I wasn't sure why my mom wanted our yard rid of these. I kind of liked the small yellow flowers. The apparent problem was that they were everywhere. So, we plucked the flowers, putting them into small brown lunch bags while pulling the ones that had the cool looking spores and blowing them into the wind (and no, I'm not sure our mom ever saw us do this—she would have had our hide!) Apart from blowing the spore seeds into the wind, the problem was we were only plucking the flowers. The dandelion population did not decrease in our yard as a result. We needed to dig down several inches and pull the stubborn weeds up by the roots. But doing this would have taken considerably more time and *definitely not* cost effective—for us, that is.

One day, my mom introduced us to a new tool. I came to hate this tool. It was long and thin, with a "Y" at the end for pulling up the roots of the weeds. It really cut into our productivity. We filled fewer bags in more time, so we made less. Over time, however, I did notice something very different. Our backyard stopped looking like the front cover of a Country Gardens magazine—less yellow, more green. It was actually working. The weeds were being eradicated and allowing the grass to thrive. Even though I had fewer baseball cards to trade,

I did find great contentment in the hard work that produced a beautiful yard.

Even as Christians, we can be creatures of comfort. We choose the quick and easy route, hoping for the desired results. And we're surprised when we don't get them! The truth is we need to eradicate these stubborn sins in our life. Dealing with surface issues is not enough. We must go deep, and we must be ruthless in the process. Just the head is insufficient. We must get root and all. Jesus said in the context of dealing with lust, *"If your right hand makes you stumble, cut it off and throw it from you"* Matthew 5:30). This calls for radical amputation! Now just for the record, Jesus was using hyperbole here (that means exaggeration) to get His point across. Put another way, He was saying, "Drastic problems require drastic measures."

If lust is an issue, get rid of anything contributing to it (more on this later). If greed is a serious problem, put a tight rein on your finances and stop the "Windows shopping" (window shopping online). If a drug or alcohol addiction has gripped you, then avoid people and places where access to these are available, and by no means allow it into your home. If bad language or coarse joking have become part of your lifestyle, cut off the influences, such as bad friends or media. All of these will only serve to feed the problem. It will cost you, but in the long run you will be far better off. Even if someone as close as a girlfriend is a source of temptation, pull back on the relationship or cut it off completely—at least for a season. Then consider reading **Real Men Talk about Freedom, Girls, & Marriage**. List the negative influences for each issue and decide how they best need to be handled.

Be smart in your fight. If lust or pornography has been an issue, protect yourself. Guard against the seductions on the internet. I recommend Blue Coat K-9 Web Protection be downloaded onto your computer, cell phone, and any other device you have that can access the web. K-9 is free (as of the writing of this book). So are many other software programs. You will need someone to be an administrator to help with this. Get it today if you don't have it. Never assume you are strong enough. Never!

If anything acts as a trigger that sets you up to stumble, be aware of it. Avoid it if possible. Some triggers cannot be avoided, and self-control will be necessary. For example, an inappropriate billboard may be unavoidable. You can't help driving by it, but you can help what happens next. Though it may not create thought problems at the moment, during some mental down time later it might.

Be aware of this and refuse to allow the enemy to set you up. Rein in the stray thoughts immediately. Choose not to think about the inappropriate billboard. Denying yourself the down time by mentally engaging in something different, like reading a good book or putting on worship music, may be in order. To put it bluntly, don't let the "fire" get started! Whatever the "weed" problem is you are seeking freedom from, be merciless in pulling it up, roots and all.

STEP 5: Self-Control

Recently, my family and I were able to grab some much-needed vacation time in the mountains of northern Georgia. We all loved it. I grew up vacationing in the mountains, so there was a certain nostalgia I enjoyed. One part of vacationing, however, is *not* enjoyable to me: the late-night driving. Weariness begins to set in, and the eyelids get heavy. As tiredness steals my focus and the lines on the road begin to blur, the car may start to drift to one side. On more than one occasion, I have been grateful for the fluorescent road bumps and rumble strips on the side (or center) of the highway. I usually find a close rest stop, pull over, and walk around to clear my head.

"Clear-headedness" is the idea behind the Greek word translated "self-control" in I Peter 5:8, concerning our dealings with our adversary, the Devil. It means "sober, sensible, disciplined, sound minded." Personal desires can cloud our thinking. Strong ones can intoxicate us, dull our sense of right and wrong, and lead us astray. Staying focused is key here. So, how do we keep wrong desires from taking the steering wheel and veering us off course? Our English word "self-control" means to control self. Though we may be the helmsman, Jesus captains the ship and we must learn to rely on the Holy Spirit for our navigation. "Self-control" is a fruit of the Spirit not the fruit of self. Submitting constantly to the Spirit and crucifying self of fleshly desires is absolutely important here. This becomes easier the more we do it.

Though self-control is actually at heart Spirit-control for the Christian, we must play a part in it, too. To do this, we can view self-control like a muscle. The more you exercise it, the stronger it grows. In my teen years I ran long distances to train for races. Some of these runs were 15 miles long. Somewhere around the 10- or 12-mile mark I would want to stop, making the last few miles painstaking. I just had to "grind it out." And it was hard. This helped teach me, however, to say "no" to what my body wanted. When I began to sincerely follow Christ, I was already learning to exercise my self-control muscles. Now I needed to learn to yield my desires completely to Him. His desires began to sober me and control me.

Take stock of the disciplines in your life. How self-controlled are you in keeping your room or your car clean? Are you staying on top of your studies, if you're a student? How about your chores around the house? Your finances? Your desk? Your garage? Okay, okay, that was some serious toe-stepping! We could mention physical exercise, diet, and even personal hygiene. Then there are the spiritual disciplines in a regular Quiet Time. The point is that self-control is not an isolated issue. It affects many areas. Even so, a lack of it in a few areas can easily affect it in other areas. The physical and spiritual are very much connected. When counseling men in sexual addictions, I eventually challenge them to find other areas where they lack self-control. As they exercise the "self-control" muscles in those areas, it invariably affects other areas, including the sexual.

STEP 6: Perseverance

"Let us run with endurance the race that is set before us, fixing our eyes on Jesus, the Author and Perfecter of faith, who for the joy set before Him endured the cross, despising the shame, and has sat down at the right hand of the throne of God. For consider Him who has endured such hostility by sinners against Himself, so that you will not grow weary and lose heart" (Hebrews 12:1-3).

Be careful not to confuse endurance and perseverance with patience. Though similar, they are very different. The marathon runner exercises perseverance. He must endure the grueling 26-plus miles. His coach, the one who holds the stopwatch, however, must have patience! The one must have perseverance, the other patience. II Peter 1:6 says specifically to add to your self-control, perseverance as opposed to patience. So, let's do that.

In order for us to truly be victorious over any sin, we must learn to say "no" to what is wrong and "yes" to what is right and good and to keep doing this without lapsing into old ways. This requires perseverance. Jesus did this by setting His focus on His Father's goal, the joy set before Him. That joy was you and me, for us to once and for all be cleansed and set free from sin and to be with Him forever. This enabled Him to endure the opposition of His enemies and the suffering of the cross.

What joy is set before you? What noble goal do you seek to obtain? Perhaps it's the example of purity for your children or the restoration of a relationship gone bad due to a serious lying habit or the passing of a class potentially forfeited by the lack of diligence in studies or the much longed-for words of our Savior to you, "Well done, good and faithful servant!" The last of these goals should cast a shadow over all others. It is our ultimate and most significant joy. To persevere we must have a God-centered goal, something we are striving for. The light at the end of the tunnel, so to speak. It drives us forward during the most difficult of times. It motivates. It sustains. It cannot be temporary. It must be eternal. It calls to us daily: *"Forgetting what lies behind and reaching forward to what lies ahead, I press on toward the goal for the prize of the upward call of God in Christ Jesus"* (Philippians 3:13-14).

A few years ago, my family encountered a very stubborn problem. In our wonderful state of Florida many were not sleeping well. An epidemic of bedbugs had hit. These little blood-sucking creatures had no discretion. They preyed on anyone regardless of cleaning habits. They leave small itching welts and are otherwise invisible, hiding during the day while feeding at night.

When they invaded our home, they initially went undetected. They quickly multiplied and spread to several bedrooms in our house. By the time I discovered what the real problem was, they had hunkered down. They were more than ready for a fight. What ensued was more like a war, however, something along the lines of Armageddon. Treating all the rooms was a time-consuming process. It took most of the day. After two treatments of my own, we chose to hire the big guns, a pest control company who brought in heavy artillery.

Now a bedbug's ability to live for a year without feeding make them particularly scrappy in battle, fiercely determined to survive. It took nearly eight months and over half a dozen assaults strategically planned before these nightmare-inducing, persistent pests flew the white flag. When the war was over and the smoke had cleared, I for one was exhausted, battered from the battles, and ready to be Baker Acted (but the white jacket was terribly uncomfortable!). Though at times the discouragement was overwhelming and I felt like surrendering, perseverance eventually won the day. What a lesson learned. Still to this day, I believe I have a twitch every time the word "bedbug" is mentioned.

Strongholds of sin can be just as resistant in battle. You must be determined to win. Mark out your goal and set your sights. Be resolute. Persevere no matter what. Quickly work through the discouragements of lost skirmishes with the enemy. Get back up on your feet and keep fighting. ***Never*** give up!

STEP 7: Be Battle-Ready

The great city of Babylon, though nearly 200 square miles, well-fortified, and weapon-ready, was overthrown in one night, because its people were partying while the enemy lay just outside its thick, strong walls. Having diverted the Euphrates River that ran through the city, the Persians then marched under these walls on a waterless riverbed and defeated an unsuspecting, drunken people who were definitely not pre-pared.

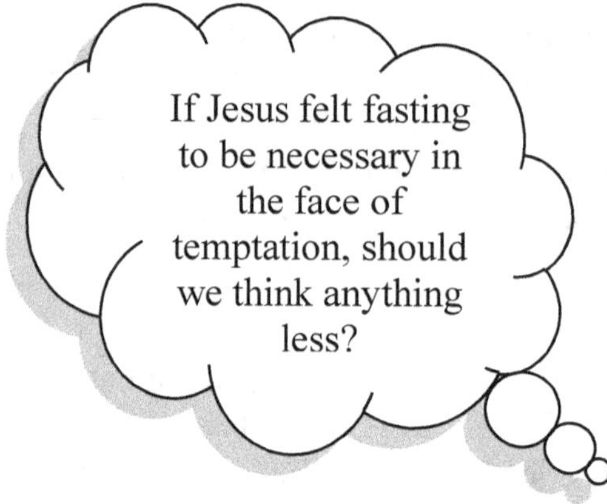

To defeat our adversary, we must constantly be battle-ready. *"Therefore, prepare your minds for action, keep sober in spirit, fix your hope completely on the grace to be brought to you at the revelation of Jesus Christ"* (I Peter 1:13). The first phrase literally says, "Gird up the loins of your mind." In the days of long robes, before pants became fashionable, when a man wanted to run, he would reach down about his knees, grab the back portion of the bottom of his garment, and pull it up, tucking it into the front of his belt. This would allow greater freedom to move his legs. Elijah, for example, did this after his victorious duel with the prophets of Baal on Mt. Carmel in preparation of running ahead of Ahab's chariot all the way to Jezreel—some twenty-five miles (I Kings 18:46).

It's like rolling up one's sleeves before a fight. It's preparation for a battle. It's being mentally set for the enemy's strike at any moment, never letting your guard down. It's lifting up the shield of faith to *"extinguish all the flaming arrows of the evil one"* (Ephesians 6:16). It's praying in the Spirit on all occasions (verse 18). It's fasting for extended periods of time to remind you how physically weak you are and yet how very strong He is. If Jesus felt fasting to be necessary in the face of temptation, should we think anything less (Luke 4:1-2)? It's daily surrendering to His kingdom purposes, pursuing His agenda above our own, His desires above ours, His passions in place of ours.

In many ways this takes us back to "Step 1: A Mindset." That mindset is fixed on battle, to not yield one inch of ground to the enemy or a single foothold in our lives. When Christ establishes a Beachhead in our lives, we must maintain it and not slip back into old ways of thinking or old practices. We refuse to allow wrong desires like lust, greed, or men's approval to lead us or to follow negative emotions like sinful anger, worry, or fear that cause us to sin. When these come knocking at our door, we cry out to God, surrendering to the Holy Spirit's control. Don't play into the Devil's tactics. This is no playground. He fights for blood—your destruction. There is nothing innocent in his ways. Stand your ground. Be strong. Fight him till the temptation is gone. Jesus did this in Luke 4, and the enemy left Him for a season.

The Devil is a roaring lion, seeking to devour (I Peter 5:8). He comes to steal, kill, and destroy (John 10:10). His goal is to take you down. But always remember: *"greater is He who is in you than he who is in the world"* (I John 4:4). So, let the Spirit arise in your heart, men of God. Be steadfast in your convictions. Firm. Unwavering. Be the first to draw the sword. Don't wait. Slam down your staff as you solemnly declare to your adversary, "You shall not pass!"

BRING IT HOME!

Discuss with your father or mentor any strongholds you are dealing with. Repent and renounce these sinful habits. Have your father or mentor pray over you with authority. Circle any of the following that are strongholds:

- Lust
- Pornography
- Sexual immorality
- Greed
- Anger
- Rejection
- Bitterness
- Pride
- Controlling fears
- Criticalness
- Procrastination
- Self-condemnation

- Inappropriate joking
- Showing off
- Flirting with girls
- Other

Do you have someone who will hold you accountable? You may need both a mentor and a friend involved in this. Remember: leave no sins in secret.

Are there any sins you have been flirting with? Have you been walking the guardrail?

Are you feeding on God's Word regularly? How often? Where in the Bible are you meditating? List one thing God recently showed you in this time with Him that you need to act on.

The following has been used for some young men I disciple in our church. Use it if you feel it will be helpful:

Young Men's Discipleship Accountability

Quiet Times (QTs) are never a measure of one's spiritual maturity. They are a means to an end: to draw us closer in relationship with Jesus our Savior.

1. How many QTs did you have this past week?

2. Did you fall into porn this past week?

Viewed immodestly dressed women?

If applicable, how many times?

3. Is there anything(-one) seducing your heart, drawing you away from Christ?

4. On a scale of 1-10, 1 being very poor and 10 being very good, how are you doing controlling your thought life (sexually)?

---

5. What other strongholds are you presently dealing with?

Are you seeking help?

Is it going well?

6. Did you lie on this accountability questionnaire?

I have used this written questionnaire in a group setting. With one-on-one discipleship, verbal accountability is always best. List any and all drastic measures you need to take in order to gain freedom from the stranglehold of any sins in your life.

The following story may be helpful here. I read it some time ago and have paraphrased it below. It is entitled *An Autobiography in Five Short Chapters* (Portia Nelson, *There's A Hole in My Sidewalk*, Beyond Words Publishing: Hillsboro, Oregon, 1993).

DAY 1: I traveled down a certain road one day and fell into a deep hole. I tried for hours to get out. I met with much frustration. It wasn't my fault. I wondered why God would allow this in my life. Finally, after much sulking and digging, I managed to climb out of the hole. Dirty and exhausted, I headed home.

DAY 2: I traveled down the same road and fell into the same hole. Angry with myself, I chose not to blame God. I struggled for a long time but managed to climb out of the hole quicker than I did the day before. Once out, I headed home.

DAY 3: I traveled down the same road, being very careful not to fall into the same hole again. As "luck" would have it, I fell in but wasted little time in climbing out. I headed home.

DAY 4: I traveled down the same road, taking every precaution imaginable to avoid the hole. I did so successfully and joyfully walked home.

DAY 5: I traveled down a different road!

Go back to the last question. If you need to travel down a "different road," then list what you need to do differently to avoid the sin: different friends, different music, different TV shows (or none at all), etc.

Looking over this list, are there any triggers that you need to avoid (stores, "primping" or flexing in the mirror, the beach, certain magazines, sports games that incline you to yell at the umpire or referee)?

Check your personal disciplines. How clean is your room? Your car? Your workplace? Are you on top of your schoolwork? Physical exercise? Bedtime and morning rising time? List where you need work and begin to get on top of these. Have your mentor hold you accountable.

If you struggle with lust, do you have internet protection on all your web access devices? If not, do not let another day go by without installing it on each one.

Write down some Scriptures on 3x5 cards and place them strategically in your room, bathroom, kitchen, study room, workplace, etc. The following are helpful:

- Ephesians 4:26-27

- Psalm 119:11

- Galatians 5:22-23

- Psalm 1:1-3

- I Corinthians 10:13

- John 10:10

- Philippians 4:13

- I Peter 5:8

- Romans 12:1-2

- Ephesians 6:10-11

Consider setting one day this week aside for fasting and prayer. Liquid fasts are preferable, but consult your parents, a pastor, and/or a physician about what type of fast will be best for you. Fasting the day of your next meeting is advisable. ***Have your mentor fast with you.*** Cry out to God for freedom. Walk through repentance and renunciation. Have him pray over you and command the enemy's release from any and all strongholds that you circled earlier. Believe God for freedom and victory.

Godly Men
Never Give Up in Battle

ave you ever faced failure so many times you thought, "What's the point? I'll *never* succeed!" Our valiant efforts don't seem to be quite enough, and we want to give up. Whether trying to score well in a class, start a business, or gain victory over sin, failure *seems* final. But God has an important lesson for us to learn that, if we pay close enough attention and grasp it, will eventually yield tremendous dividends in success.

Nearly twenty years ago, I moved my family down to central Florida to start a church. Much prayer, planning, and godly counsel from church leaders went into this venture. I chose to support my family with a paint touch up business that catered to car dealerships. I had done this business before graduating from seminary, so I had the skill and know-how. Several months of preparation, including some test marketing in the Orlando area, preceded my start date. As the launch of the business neared, my family and I spent considerable amounts of time in prayer and fasting. We knew that if the business failed, my plans to plant the church would be halted. I was confident God would open wide the doors of opportunity.

The initial phase of the business began. As I traveled from dealership to dealership, reality refused to line up with my projections. Day after day I got turned away. Not one manager even let me touch a vehicle to demonstrate my services. After two weeks, I thought I had seriously missed God at tremendous expense to my family and great disappointment to myself. There was no ray of hope and no light at the end of the tunnel, except the proverbial train bearing down on my dreams. Depression hung over me like a dark cloud—with no silver lining.

At the height of my frustrations, I remember pulling over to a lake beside the highway to eat my lunch, not that I had an appetite. My small meal turned into a party—a pity party, that is. As I nibbled at my sandwich, watching some construction workers refurbish an historic house, I complained and argued with God. I accused Him of leading us a thousand miles from home only to abandon us. I had completely failed and had no Plan B to fall back on. I had graduated seminary at the top of my class, only to find myself at the bottom of the barrel. I was discouraged and humiliated. What was I to do now?

God decided to crash my pity party. Up to this point, He had just listened, but now He spoke. Though His words were compassionate, they were not gentle. As I observed the renovation of the house across from me, God began to show me I had rotten wood in my life that He desperately needed to remove, plank by plank. He would need to strip me down to my basic framework and rebuild. Much painful testing lay ahead for me as He would need to build the necessary character for what He had called me to. At this point, I wasn't sure I wanted any part in this plan, but I also knew that was the wrong answer. He then told me to stop playing the blues, get up, and get back to work. Ouch! That was direct. Party over!

I walked, or rather, crawled back to my vehicle and continued down the road to the next dealership several miles away. With tremendous reluctance I walked the used cars until I found one I could repair to demonstrate my services. My attitude was still in the trash can as I approached the manager. I might as well have said, "You don't want me to repair this car, do you, even if I do it for free?" Apparently, he had just gotten rid of his painter, so he gave me a shot: "Sure, go ahead. You can do your work over there."

I stood there for about a minute as he walked inside, and I began completely repenting for my attitude. That car dealership was the beginning of a landslide of accounts that soon filled my schedule. God had taught me a lesson in perseverance and faith that had broad implications in my walk with Christ. Especially in view of the last chapter's lesson on walking in freedom as soldiers of Christ, we can become battle weary. The fight can be intense and the failures frequent. How does a young man keep fighting a battle in which he has gotten knocked down repeatedly? How does he get back up more bent on victory? Truthfully, many never learn to press in with such determination and choose instead to live for Christ half-heartedly, nothing radical to stir up the enemy's ire. But we've learned that life at 210 is both powerless and unfulfilling. As warriors for the cross, we are destined for victory. So, how do we press on to gain this? The truths we will discuss are liberating, but the process of building them into our lives, for God to renovate and reconstruct, will require the stripping of rotted planks and the unexpected crashing of any pity party.

DIG IN!

Study Section 1

READ II Samuel 23:8-10.
What status or position did Eleazar have among King David's warriors?

Was he a beginner or a veteran? Did he have little or much experience?

I Chronicles 11:12-14 makes it clear that though the Israelite army fled, both David and Eleazar remained in the middle of the field to fight the Philistine army. What does this tell us about Eleazar?

Why do you suppose Eleazar's hand froze to the sword? (circle the best answer)

A. It was a very, very cold day!
B. Before the battle, Eleazar was trying to repair some equipment and spilled Super Glue all over his hand.
C. The sword was magical.
D. The battle lasted so long and Eleazar killed so many Philistines, his hand muscles would not release the sword.

What does this tell us about Eleazar's character? What type of warrior was he?

The word that comes to my mind as I read about Eleazar is "determination." This is absolutely necessary when entering any battle.

READ Proverbs 24:16.
Why might a righteous man "fall"?

Should he fall, what does he do? Why?

Tell of a time you failed at something and wanted to quit. Why did you want to quit?

READ Philippians 4:13.
What should our mindset be about failure?

READ I John 1:9.
Should we fail by stumbling into sin, like lust or anger, what should we do and what does God promise *He* will do?

READ Psalm 103:11-12.
Describe what God does with our sin.

Why?

READ Zephaniah 3:17.
What does this say about God?

From this verse, do you get the picture that God gets so frustrated with us (e.g. our sinning) that He abandons us? If not, what "picture" do you get?

Have you ever felt that He has abandoned you?

Why did you feel this way?

READ Romans 8:1.
What does God promise will **not** happen to those who truly believe in Jesus Christ?

What is "condemnation"? Use a dictionary.

CONDEMNATION:

Sometimes when we repent, we still feel condemned, accused, or guilt-ridden so we feel like a complete failure, written off as worthless. But God promises He won't condemn us. Where are those feelings coming from, do you think?

READ Revelation 12:10.
What is Satan called in this verse?

What does the name "Satan" mean? Use a good English dictionary or Bible dictionary that will tell you what the Hebrew name means.

SATAN:

How is this significant in answering the question about where our feelings of condemnation come from?

READ Romans 8:33-39.
Can anything or anyone separate you from God's love?

So, what do these verses tell us when we *"feel"* condemned, or abandoned by God, or separated from His love?

So, let's put this together. If we are to be victorious in battle, like Eleazar, we must be determined to fight to the end and not give up. This will mean _______________________ (fill in the blank) when we fall into sin. We do this by asking God to forgive us. If afterwards, we feel guilty and condemned, this is not from God but from _______________. We know this, because God promises that nothing will separate us from His _______________.

Study Section 2

Let's conclude our study with a look at a familiar story from the Old Testament.
READ I Samuel 17:8-11.
Was Goliath polite or rude and "in your face" as he challenged the Israelites?

How did this make both King Saul and the Israelite army feel?

READ I Samuel 17:20-24.
How were the two armies positioned?

When Goliath stepped out from battle line formation, what did the Israelites do (circle the best answer)?

    A. Ran up to greet him, saying, "May the best man win."
    B. Yelled back: "Sticks and stones may break our bones, but words can never hurt us!"
    C. Tattled to a Philistine King about how incredibly rude Goliath was being to them, and that such behavior was clearly out of line with the Geneva Convention.
    D. Broke battle line formation and ran away from him.

READ I Samuel 17:48.
Contrast what Israel's army did with David's response?

What does this say about David?

READ I Samuel 17:41-44.
Describe Goliath's attitude toward David?

Was Goliath confident of David's defeat?

READ I Samuel 17:33.
Was King Saul confident in David defeating Goliath?

READ I Samuel 17:45-47.
Was David confident of victory?

Why? (circle the best answer)

    A. He was really Superman in disguise, and there was a convenient phone booth on the front lines.

    B. David was wearing his lucky underwear that day.

    C. There was a Jaeger from Pacific Rim standing behind Goliath ready to pound him.

    D. David's special training in Saul's elite forces made him into a "skilled ninja dude you never want to meet in a dark alley."

    E. David completely recognized that the Lord would defeat Goliath, and so he trusted in God's strength not his own.

Was this one-on-one battle really about who was the strongest and most skilled warrior?

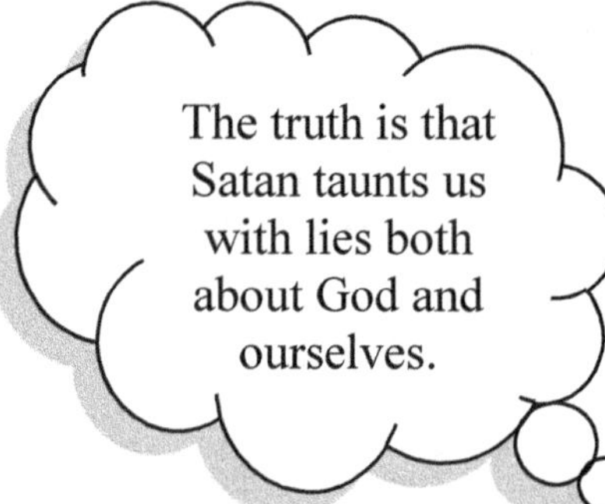

What was it really about?

Let's relate this to us today. Fill in the chart, writing in the second column what the first column represents today in view of our lesson. Think carefully. This may not be easy. The first one has been done for you.

I Samuel 17	Represents Today
Goliath	Satan. Big problems. Temptations.
David	
Saul and his army	
Goliath's taunts	
Vs. 46: "I'll strike you down and cut off your head."	
David running to the front line	

The truth is that Satan taunts us with lies both about God and ourselves, just as Goliath taunted David and the Israelite army. We must meet these accusations head on with truth and in full faith, because God is bigger and stronger and will help us gain the victory.

THINK ABOUT IT!

Though failure is not final, it can certainly seem that way at times. As a young man having just graduated from high school, I had my share of failures, sins that seemed to snag me regularly. While attending many young adult Bible studies, I was plagued by this growing sense of failure. My inadequacies compounded the issue. Though a leader in the group, I many times felt discouraged, that others were much further along in their spiritual maturity than me and that perhaps I would never become the man of God I needed to be. I wrestled with condemning thoughts regularly. I wanted so much to succeed and for God to be truly pleased with me. But how could He be if I consistently failed Him? These were **not** the imprisoning thoughts of an unregenerated young man. God had truly rescued me, filled me with His Spirit, and called me to full time ministry. But I felt like the little hamster on the treadmill of performance, condemned to run as hard as possible but get nowhere.

Proverbs 24:16 tells us that *"a righteous man falls seven times and rises again."* Do we just need to learn to become numb to the feelings of failure? Do we lower our goals or standards to make them easier to attain? Many men have chosen to do this, to coast through life, never attaining to the call of God on their lives. Understand that this call is not given exclusively to full time pastors but to **everyone** in Christ's kingdom! Why should we run so hard only to fall repeatedly, we wonder? How do we fall, even seven times, and get right back up?

Dealing with the Pain of Failure

Listen to this truth: what we are really trying to avoid is *pain*. When we fail, it hurts. When we disappoint God, it hurts. When we are guilt-ridden, it hurts. How do we deal with the pain? Consider this. During WWII, the Japanese proved to be such a devoted people, their armies were extremely difficult to defeat. The Japanese Kamikaze thought nothing of sacrificing his life if that meant greater loss to the enemy. I have even heard that many of Japan's soldiers wore a tie on each arm. If they got shot in the arm, they would tie it off just above the wound and keep fighting. This both restricted blood loss and helped numb the pain. They were almost an invincible foe.

So, how do **we** "numb the pain" of failure to stay in the battle? To answer this question, we must realize that there are two main reasons why our pain of failure persists so that we want to give up in the battle: either we fail to truly repent so the guilt remains, or we lack a deep understanding of God's grace expressed in His forgiveness of our sins. Let's discover our answer here.

Do We Have Godly Sorrow?

First, we must understand that true repentance springs from godly sorrow. Paul tells us, *"Godly sorrow brings repentance that leads to salvation and leaves no regret, but worldly sorrow brings death"* (II Corinthians 7:10—NIV, 1978). Worldly sorrow is self-centered. It focuses on personal failure. We are disappointed in ourselves. "How could I have done this? I'm such an idiot!" we tell ourselves again and again. Shame settles over us. We feel humiliated that we would do something like this. It causes us to feel like failures. We've messed up again! We just can't seem to "get it." The focus is all on us.

Godly sorrow, however, focuses outward and understands the offense is first and foremost against God. David confessed: *"Against You, You only, I have sinned and done what is evil in your sight"* (Psalm 51:4). We understand that David's offense was against Bathsheba, Uriah her husband, his family who bore some of the fallout from his sins, and the people of Israel, whose leader had fallen and set a very bad example for them. But it was God's holiness that was truly offended here and no one else's. It was God's righteous standards that were violated.

Godly sorrow recognizes this and, though desires to make amends with his fellow man, cries out to a holy God for forgiveness. It does not wallow in personal failure as a result. It quickly moves past this, because the focus is God and His holiness, not ourselves, our failure, or our shame.

Romans 12:9 states: *"Abhor what is evil; cling to what is good."* It is this hatred for evil that prompts us to have godly sorrow and true resulting repentance. This type of God-focused sorrow and repentance brings about divine forgiveness. Regrets can quickly fade in light of this. Self-pity and feelings of failure and condemnation can be halted, because these have to do with us and our view of ourselves. But I emphasize "can" here. The next step is crucial.

Understanding the Extent of God's Forgiveness: The Heavenly Battle
Second, obtaining complete freedom from these feelings of failure can only come when we also ***fully*** embrace God's forgiveness. So, how do we do this and walk in such freedom? The answer is found in warfare. Let me explain.

I must confess, I love intense battle scenes in both books and movies when good triumphs over evil. There is a sense of justice served, of victory and vindication gained. Such a battle scene is found in Revelation 12. Michael the archangel with the support of fellow angels is battling Satan and his evil hordes in heaven. Satan loses and is cast down forever to earth, never to be able to approach God's throne again as he did, for example, in Job 1. When was this battle fought? Before creation? During the "end times"? The context tells us. Just prior to this battle we are told in symbolic form that the woman Satan ("the dragon") was chasing gave birth to a son who will rule the nations. The woman managed to flee to safety for a season. Who is this woman and who is her child? They are the nation of Israel (or perhaps more specifically, the Old Testament community of believers) and Jesus the Messiah.

"And there was war in heaven" (12:7) indicates this battle took place during this time (Jesus earthly ministry and ascension). In addition, it should be noted that immediately following this great battle we are told, *"**Now** the salvation, and the power, and the kingdom of our God and the authority of his Christ have come"* (emphasis added—12:10). When was "now"? When did this salvation, power, kingdom, and authority come? These clearly came at the cross and no other time. It was during the cross and resurrection (and ascension—12:5) that Michael's army fought the Devil, definitively defeated him, and cast him down to the earth.

Now keep following me. What was the effect of this on **us**? Let's keep reading: *"For the accuser of our brethren has been thrown down, he who accuses them before our God day and night. And they overcame him because of the blood of the Lamb and because of the word of their testimony, and they did not love their life even when faced with death"* (12:10-11). The name Satan means "Accuser." He and his horde were hurled down and overcome. How were they overcome? How was Satan defeated and thereby lose his place of accusation before the throne of God? The simple answer is he lost the battle with Michael and his angels, but this is only the spiritual backdrop of the real cause. Satan was forever displaced for two reasons.

Understanding the Extent of God's Forgiveness: The Accuser's Defeat
First, the blood of the lamb, Jesus Christ, defeated him. Paul describes the scene this way: *"When He had disarmed the rulers and authorities, He made a public display of them, having triumphed over them through Him"* (Colossians 2:15). In both Ephesians and Colossians, the phrase "rulers and authorities" as used here depicts spiritual forces of evil—Satan and his minions. As mentioned earlier, Paul paints here for us the typical scene of a Roman general riding on his horse, parading his chained, defeated captives through the streets of his beloved city, heralding his victory before the people to the utter embarrassment of his captured enemy. This is the victory Christ won for us upon the cross. The apostle John worded it this way: *"The Son of God appeared for this purpose, to destroy the works of the devil"* (I John 3:8). So, there we have it, by Christ's sacrifice on the cross, Satan has been thrown down forever. But one more thing

needs to happen.

Second, this great salvation secured by the cross must be personally applied. By faith we apprehend it. *"The word of their testimony"* is the applied blood of the Lamb to each sinner as he repents, believes, and is freed from his sins (Revelation 1:5). This is no weak belief in the mere facts of Jesus' sacrifice, but a faith that chooses to disregard personal pursuits for that one great pursuit of Christ. Such a faith is willing to lay down one's life, even to death, for the cause of Christ, the Victor (vs. 11). It denies self, takes up its cross, and follows the One who chose death for us.

In view of this, picture the bar in a courtroom. It separates the gallery, where the general public sits, from the court proceedings. For a lawyer to pass this barrier and have legal authority to prosecute or defend, he must pass the "bar exam." Satan, the Accuser of the brothers, has lost his legal standing to prosecute believers. His authority to do so was grounded in our sin. In other words, our sin gave him the legal right to accuse us. We were guilty and worthy of his charges and the punishment incurred by our sin. But Jesus' blood washed that sin away for good along with Satan's authority to prosecute us. He has been cast down, no longer permitted in God's heavenly court (as he was allowed in Job 1). He has been disbarred!

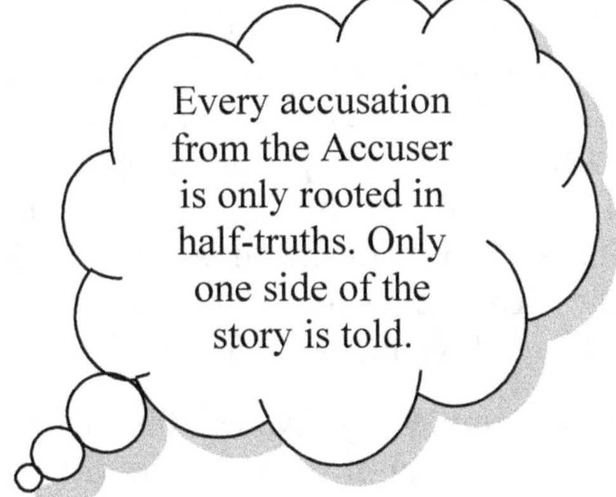

So, let's come full circle. What does this mean exactly for us when we are facing regrets, self-pity, failure, and condemnation? What's its significance when we hear that old recording played over and over: "You've failed again! How many times do you think God will forgive these acts of rebellion? You've gone too far this time. You're worthless, second-rate. God will never bless you now. You're condemned to bear this guilt, and you deserve it. Scum! Failure! Useless sinner!" Not too far off? Unfortunately, this is where many Christians live, crippled with guilt and accusations. It seems unbearable at times. But the truth is, we must cling to this truth: Satan, the Accuser of the brothers, has been hurled down forever. Never again can he bring such accusations before the throne of God. Our Advocate, Jesus Christ, makes sure of this.

But not every one of the aforementioned accusations falls on deaf ears. Though heaven's ears are shut, ours are not. We listen. We indulge. We press "play" over and over. But this is our choice. It certainly is not God's. In fact, Romans 8:1 states very clearly, *"Therefore there is now no condemnation for those who are in Christ Jesus."* Every accusation from the Accuser is only rooted in half-truths. Only one side of the story is told. We have sinned—truth. But remember, Christ has completely paid the price of our sin, and His love for us remains unchanged—***truth***! There is nothing we can do that will cause Him to love us more, and there is nothing we can do that will cause Him to love us any less. His love remains constant—infinitely vast.

Silencing Satan's Accusations—Our Personal Battle

How then should we respond to Satan's half-truths, which are really lies dressed up like truth? Paul reveals the answer in his prayer for the Ephesians: *"that you, being rooted and grounded in love, may be able to comprehend with all the saints what is the breadth and length and height and depth, and to know the love of Christ which surpasses knowledge"* (3:17-19). This then is the answer: know Christ's love. Though this knowledge is rooted in truth and should be intellectually grasped, it is more. God invites us to ***experience*** this love. That is the clear implication of this word "know." Constantly walk in the truth of Christ's love for you. Understand it. Experience it.

Your complete forgiveness found in Christ's love covers and washes away every sin. Your debt of sin has been fully cancelled. God holds ***nothing*** against you. Reject then Satan's lies that say otherwise. Turn a deaf ear to accusations that put God's love and forgiveness in question. Don't press "play" to listen any longer to the Accuser's words of condemnation that make you out to be a failure. God's truth says you are a "super-conqueror" (the literal Greek translation—Romans 8:37). He always leads you in triumphal procession in Christ (II Corinthians 2:14). You are His treasured possession (Deuteronomy 7:6), the apple of His eye (Zechariah 2:8). You are ***not*** a failure!

When the accusations come and you feel condemned, rebuke Satan and tell him you will not believe a single one of his lies (Zechariah 3:1-2). Remind him of the truths of God's grace, love, and forgiveness. Memorize some of these Scriptures and quote them back to him. Say to him, "The Lord rebuke you, Satan!" Then stand firm. Don't give an inch. Choose truth. Choose victory. This is your heritage in Christ! If the courts of heaven are closed to the devil's demands for justice, then ***you*** give him no audience. Do so in the authority of

Christ, in Jesus' name. He must submit. He has no other option. As it's been said, "When the Devil reminds you of your past, you remind him of his future."

Let's review. At the time of the cross, Satan lost a significant battle in the heavenlies which resulted in him being shut out from God's throne room. He can no longer bring any accusations before God. This truth is directly applied to you when you surrender to Christ and become His child. Satan's accusations against you go unheard. Should they assault **you**, discard them promptly from your mind and choose to embrace Christ's love found in His forgiveness toward you. Then rebuke the Devil every time he whispers his lies in your ears.

The Song of Our Savior

If you have truly repented out of godly sorrow and regularly cast down the empty lies of the Accuser, then there is no room for regrets, because God's grace covers every sin, releases us from all guilt, and breaks off any shame. The pain of failure vanishes. Grasp this truth of God's love. Never let it go. Stand firmly and confidently in it. Zephaniah 3:17 ministered to me as a young man wrestling with this. It helped shatter my wrong understanding of God and replaced it with a truly biblical one: *"The LORD your God is with you, he is mighty to save. He will take great delight in you, he will quiet you with his love, he will rejoice over you with singing"* (NIV, 1978). Imagine that, my God rejoices over this

rescued sinner with singing. Perhaps for me this holds a special place in my heart, because each night when I put my five children down, I would sing over them, often caressing their hair and telling them how very much I loved them. Perhaps a bit too romantic for us guys, but truth nonetheless: our Father sings love songs over us to quiet our hearts every time they condemn us. This is real love.

The Lord is your greatest cheerleader. When you fall, others may get frustrated but not God. He is gentle towards you. He speaks words of compassion, not accusation or disappointment, when you repent. He graciously helps you step back from your sin and calls you to continue your passionate pursuit of Him. His love knows no end. He scatters your sins *"as far as the east is from the west"*

(Psalm 103:12), which if you think about it, is an infinite distance.

The Father's Love

This love God has for you that can wash away every sin is truly vast. Consider the parable of the lost son in Luke 15 (sometimes called the "Prodigal Son"). The youngest son takes something that is truly valuable to his father, an inheritance, and wastes it completely. While contemplating his misery, he reflects on the possibility of at least partial forgiveness from his father. This would be better than his present predicament, so he makes his way back home.

Now consider the response of his father. Does he force him to grovel and do penance? Does he subject him to cruel punishment for his uncaring, wasteful behavior? No, none of these. Jesus said that while the son was still a great distance away, his father *"ran and embraced him and kissed him"* (15:20). The father initiates. He demonstrates far greater compassion than was expected. Though the son feels utterly unworthy, his father lavishes him with gifts, and the entire house celebrates his return with music, dancing, and feasting.

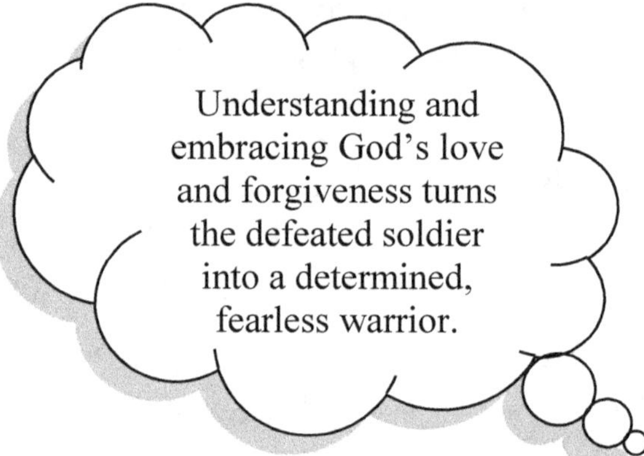

And such is the love of our heavenly Father: assertive, unexpectedly lavish, even exuberant. This is not a picture of God's love only to the penitent sinner but also to his child who repents for the seventh time.

Ready for Battle

Understanding and embracing God's love and forgiveness turns the defeated soldier into a determined, fearless warrior. Let's take David as an example. In the field tending the sheep, David had ample time to cultivate a deep understanding of God's love. *"Be gracious to me, O God, according to Your lovingkindness"* (Psalm 51:1). *"The LORD is gracious and merciful; slow to anger and great in lovingkindness"* (Psalm 145:8). *"Surely goodness and mercy shall follow me all the days of my life"* (Psalm 23:6). *"I said, 'I will confess my transgressions to the LORD;' and You forgave the guilt of my sin"* (Psalm 32:5). Understanding God's love produced a solid confidence in Him as David's protector: *"The LORD is the defense of my life; whom shall I dread"* (Psalm 27:1)? *"The LORD is my shepherd, I shall not want… I will fear no evil, for You are with me"* (Psalm 23:1, 4).

Because of this, Samuel said of David and not King Saul: *"The LORD has sought out for Himself a man after His own heart, and the LORD has appointed him as ruler over His people"* (I Samuel 13:14). Consequently, after Samuel anointed David, Scripture states, *"and the Spirit of the LORD came mightily upon David from that day forward"* (I Samuel 16:13). All this sets up what happens next in chapter 17 where David battles Goliath.

Now, Goliath was some nine and a half feet tall. "Intimidation" was his middle name. Saul and his men feared him. The Israelites broke battle formation to run from him. He terrified everyone—everyone but David, that is. David's confidence did not lie in his own strength or skill. It lay in the power of his Defender, the LORD Almighty. When the Intimidator spouted out insults and curses, David was unmoved. When his Accuser and Taunter approached, David didn't

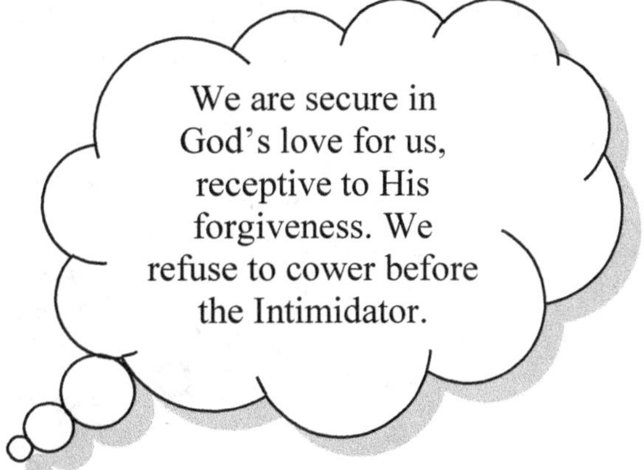

turn heel and run, he *"ran quickly toward the battle line to meet the Philistine"* (17:48). Why? Again, David was absolutely confident and secure in God's love and God's protection. As was stated in an earlier chapter, king Saul compared Goliath to himself and feared. David compared Goliath to God and was confident. The real question then is: where is your focus?

This paints an insightful picture of how we ought to fight on the front line of battle against our Accuser, Satan. We don't back down when he points out our failings. We hold the line. We are secure in God's love for us, receptive to His forgiveness. We refuse to cower before the Intimidator or break battle formation to pout in a pity party. We stand strong, eager to pursue holiness at any cost and be renewed by repentance should we fail in that pursuit. In doing this, we walk away the victor, having slain our enemy and holding high his head in our hand as a trophy of our God's great power (see I Samuel 17:54).

A Season of Tempering

God is preparing you as a young man for life's challenges. How will you face the pressures and potential failures of business, family, church, and relationships in general? The older you get, the tougher the problems.

Perhaps the greatest battle for a young man to fight is with lust. The longing to fulfill sexual desires can be nothing short of intense. Though certainly not impossible to overcome by God's grace, it can make one feel like a failure, helpless and powerless, as if victory is too elusive. While growing in Christ and in self-control, the young man must be propelled towards holiness and yet comforted by God's forgiveness, should he fail. This is a season of tempering.

Consider this illustration. The process of creating a sword is not simply taking a long piece of metal, cutting it to shape and sharpening it. Such a sword would not last in battle. The process is arduous.

After selecting the piece of metal, it must be heated up and pounded into shape. This is repeated numerous times until the exact angles are acquired. It is then sharpened, heated again to a very specific temperature, and then doused into much cooler waters. It is again sharpened, heated, and then cooled. This process "tempers" the metal, changing its chemical adhesion and strengthening it with a lasting sharp edge. It becomes very difficult to break during battle.

Young man, this is what your loving heavenly Father is doing with you right now. He is tempering you. He is forming perseverance and resolve within you. It is hard, even painful. Learn to hate all that is evil. Fight it. But should you fail, rise up with determination and step back into battle. Become the tempered warrior, strong and fierce, with eyes on the prize, holding on to what is good. This is how a righteous man may fall seven times but rise again (Proverbs 24:16).

Let the truth of this chapter be wings to you. Let it liberate you from the weight of guilt that may still burden your shoulders. Let it restore your friendship with the Father. Let it raise you to your feet a seventh time and empower you once again for warfare. Satan's infantry seeks to take you down and off the front lines, out of battle to nurse your feelings of failure. Refuse to leave the front line. Stay engaged. Wield the sword relentlessly even though it freezes in your hand. This is the heart of a warrior that embraces the full extent of God's love poured out to him. This is the heart of a victor that rests completely in the Father's forgiveness. Be resolute in this! Be determined to fight the good fight no matter how fierce the battle. Never give up. And never give in. This is the call to every Godly Man who truly desires to walk in victory. Make it yours!

BRING IT HOME!

We have talked about being "on the front lines of battle." What does this mean for you?

Has any sin or sins taken you out of the battle, causing you to lose sight of God's forgiveness?

Do you *feel* God is disappointed with you? If so, explain why.

Do you tend to have pity parties?

Briefly describe your last one: what caused it, how did it make you feel, how long did it last, what caused you to "party" so long?

What do you need to do the next time you fail in order to *stay* on the front line as a determined warrior?

Godly Men
Work Hard

You may remember I told you that when I was a boy my mother paid us kids ten cents per bag of dandelions we picked. Though the lawn looked healthier once we started pulling those weeds up by the roots, my dad thought a new lawn was in order. He did a little research and came up with a plan. Unfortunately, that plan included us four boys! We were about to learn the real meaning of hard work.

For hours a day during the summer, we helped our dad. Because he was a high school English teacher, my father took some summers "off" and focused on tackling some huge projects around our house. I was still young, not quite a teenager, so I usually busied myself with blowing up green army men, jumping obstacles with a new bike ramp, or playing wiffle ball in the nearby church courtyard. But this project of my dad's was bigger than huge. It was mammoth!

We first pulled down the willow tree in our backyard. Arghh! Then with a machine, my dad peeled back the old lawn in one foot by one foot sections. We carted each piece of old sod to the side of the house where we stacked them. These eventually got hauled off in our station wagon to a friend's field. The sodless ground then got rototilled, raked, leveled, fertilized, raked again, seeded, raked lightly again, and then got strewn with hay to keep the seed from washing away during a rainstorm. We daily watered it and raked it yet again to get rid of the hay as the new grass began to fill out our yard.

Those were some long, hard, dirty days of work. It took so long I think I lost my special curve in wiffle ball! Certainly not something my dad seemed to understand as we moved to our next project. Gratefully, it was less mammoth-sized, so we finished with time to spare in our summer vacation. A friend of mine up the street from us had a fence installed in his parents' backyard. They offered me the lumber from the old fence. I had always wanted to build a fort in our backyard, so I drew up some plans, got the "OK" from the authorities that be (as long as we were careful with the new lawn), and started measuring and sawing (no power tools at that age, we were told). The first floor stood 5 feet with a floor buttressed by 4x4s, overlaid with 1x6s. The second floor was accessed by a ladder built into the wall of the story below. The roof was topped with simple shingles left over from when my dad reroofed our house (us kids managed to escape that project—something about the possibility of falling 20 feet and plunging to our deaths—oh, well). My fort was capped with a "trap door" that led to the roof where we usually hung out, telling silly stories to our friends at night while enjoying the stars.

All in a summer's work! As I looked back years later and the fort was being torn down to make room for yet another project (this time a 14 foot by 33 foot garden), I realized my dad had instilled in me a strong work ethic. Completely accidental on my part, believe me, but quite purposeful on my dad's part. He was always a hard worker and wanted us kids to be the same. Fun had its place, but hard work was to be our focus. This was a mentality he wanted to have spill over into our school work, sports activities, and eventually our careers.

Sadly, many young men even in their twenties (and beyond) fail to grasp this very biblical concept of diligence. They are cruising through life with little responsibility as they live with mom, making just enough money to buy the next Call of Duty video game and to enjoy the hottest new movie in theaters with their friends, who are usually in a similar situation. They lack purpose and direction for their lives. Their dad, if at home, is too busy with work or perfecting his putt on the back nine. What's a young man to do?

This week we will examine what God's Word has to say about hard work and diligence. Let God instill in you, if He hasn't yet, a mindset determined to accomplish great things for His kingdom. This will certainly involve a career to support a family one day, as well as a drivenness to see His kingdom come here *"on earth as it is in heaven"* (Matthew 6:10). This should be the noble goal of every Godly Man pursuing Christ. So, let's begin.

DIG IN!

Study Section 1

READ Genesis 2:15.

Had man fallen into sin at this point?

What was God's original intention for man?

So, is work part of the curse on man?

READ Genesis 3:17-19.

How did God curse man if work was intended as something good?

The purpose of Genesis 3 then is to show us the consequences of sin in the world. One consequence was that work would be extra difficult, because the ground was cursed and our physical bodies would grow old, creating more strain for us (as of the second edition of this book, at 63, I'm becoming well acquainted with this reality). Also, working with others would be hard due to our sinful attitudes. Can you give three examples of this today? (The first is done for you.)

- Managing a store having to deal with employees who complain all the time.
-
-

READ II Thessalonians 3:6-15.

What does Paul rebuke the Thessalonians for?

What example did Paul give the Thessalonians to model?

How might a person eat if he does not work (Hint: the government can have something to do with this)?

Put Paul's "rule" in your own words.

READ I Timothy 5:8.

Describe in your own words the seriousness of not caring for and providing for your own family?

READ Proverbs 10:4 and 18:9.

"*Is brother to*" is the same as "is like." What is the result of laziness?

How might these verses be understood in the context of a student's studies?

READ Proverbs 14:23.

What is *"mere talk"*?

Can you give an example?

Have you ever talked about fixing a problem but never got around to it? What happened to the problem? Did it get worse or fix itself?

Some people love to plan to start their own business, but, if they're not careful, certain risk factors may cause them to drag their feet. Consequently, they never get it off the ground. They love *"mere talk"*. It certainly is safer. You can never fail at something you never try.

READ Proverbs 28:19.

Can you give four examples of *"empty pursuits"*? (The first one is done for you.)

- "Get rich quick" schemes.
-
-
-

READ Proverbs 12:24.

Read another way, this says, "The diligent rule; the lazy drool!" How might laziness end in *"forced labor"*? (Please be aware that slavery at that time was very different than what America experienced. Usually, one became a slave in order to pay off a debt until it was paid back in full.)

READ Proverbs 24:30-34.

Put these verses into your own words.

List five ways people can be diligent. (The first one is done for you.)

- Daily or weekly household chores.
-
-
-
-

To wrap up section 1, we have discussed that work was part of God's original creation and therefore a good thing. We are commanded to be diligent, avoid procrastination, and engage in worthwhile pursuits, especially in view of our need to provide for our family or obey our parents.

Study Section 2

READ Colossians 3:22-24.

What should an employee's attitude be toward his boss?

What does this have to say about working when the boss (or mom or dad) isn't looking?

What should our heart's motivation be then?

READ Matthew 6:33.

What should our top priority be?

List 3 things that fall into the category of "the kingdom of God." (The first one is done for you.)

- Witnessing.

-

-

List 3 things that fall into the category of "His righteousness." (The first one is done for you.)

- Working hard to support a family or provide for the future.

-

-

READ Matthew 6:19-21.

List 3 treasures that perish on earth. (The first one is done for you.)

- My new Nikes.

-

-

List 3 things that endure for eternity in heaven. (The first is done for you)

- God.

-

-

This last list of "three things" is where our heart should be and, therefore, where our top priorities and focus should be. As we work hard unto the Lord and so walk in His calling for us, we must always do so with His kingdom in proper perspective.

THINK ABOUT IT!

I grew up in the suburbs of Wilmington, Delaware in a lower middle-class neighborhood with plenty of kids my age. We loved to play together any chance we got. My friend Robbie lived a few houses up the street from me. During the summer after dinner, his dad would hit fly balls to us almost every evening. We always looked forward to this. We constantly tried to extend our play time until parents were yelling for us to come home. From after school until it was too dark to see anything, we played touch football, Indian ball, kickball, wiffle ball, basketball, or catch in our backyard. A tree down the street made for a perfect spaceship, army headquarters, or house for "Swiss Family Robinson." "Boredom" was not in our vocabulary. There was always something to do to have fun.

As I grew older, however, I needed to shift my priorities. Studies needed to take the front seat, but due to my childlike "driving skills" they were regularly tossed to the backseat—or to be more honest, into the trunk! I grew up in the public school system where accountability was non-existent until test time or book report due dates. I was a professional procrastinator, an expert at playing right up to the deadline. This created some future marital tensions that needed to be dealt with in my life, but that's another story.

A Work-Focus

At some point, teenagers need to start making this priority shift from a play-focus to a work-focus. I remember talking to a young man some time ago. He had graduated from high school and had chosen to work "full time" rather than go to college. He was living at home, working at a restaurant, and not paying any rent to his parents (not something I recommend if gainfully employed). In his conversation with me, he was complaining about how hard his work was and the numerous hours he was having to shoulder. He explained he had no social life, little time to recreate, and few hours to practice with the band he was a member of. His boss was refusing to slow down this hectic pace. I found owning my own business with employees, pastoring nearly full time, making sure I was on top of household maintenance, and keeping family at the top of my priorities list while seeking to sustain a consistent devotional life with Christ to be a brisk pace for myself, so my heart went out to this young man. Until I asked him an eye-opening question: "So, how many hours are they working you?" His reply betrayed his wrong mindset: "Thirty-five hours!"

It took a minute to pick my jaw up off the ground, but after doing so, I graciously walked him through the "finer points" of what biblical manhood and hard work looked like. At least I think I was gracious. Somewhere along the way to manhood, this principle of hard work was never allowed to take root in his life. I knew this young man fairly well and can truthfully say it had spread to his entire life, making him ineffectual both in the workplace and the kingdom of God. Life's goal had been play, to have fun. Work had truly become a four-letter word, something to be minimized or avoided altogether.

As children turn into adults, their focus needs to shift from play to hard work. This is best done gradually, not abruptly, unless the "child" is in his twenties. Strong effort in sports is a good start but only that. Much character building can result from grasping the principles inherent in most sports, but work is still a far cry from these activities. The child needs to move beyond the "I want to be football player when I grow up" mentality. Some make it in professional sports, yes. Most do not.

The goal there and anywhere in the entertainment industry can be very illusive, even delusional. For most it is a distraction from a genuine call to a career. It can appeal to our vanity and desire for men's attention and applause. I simply say, "it can." You must sort through this, but please heed the warning. We are becoming increasingly addicted to entertainment as a society.

Diligent or Lazy?

There is perhaps no greater place in a man's life where who he truly is shines through than in his work ethic. Many of Jesus' parables use work as the backdrop to make His point. In His story of the talents, those receiving five and two talents went out and "traded" (KJV) to double their original money. This word for "trade" is the typical Greek word translated "work, labor, or toil." Because they "worked" hard and gained more, the master honored them: *Well done, good and faithful servant!"* (see Matthew 25:21, 23—NIV, 1978).

But do you remember his words to the one who did nothing with his one talent? *"His master answered and said to him, 'You wicked, lazy slave!'"* (verse 26). Later, he called him that *"worthless servant"* (vs. 30—yes, I think I was very gracious in my words to that young man). Let's remember that Jesus is portraying Himself as the master. We will all give account one day for how we bided our time here on earth. Were we diligent or lazy? Were we quick to initiate or procrastinate?

I remember reading about a sign on an employee's cluttered desk: "I have job security and cannot be fired; I'm too far behind in my work!" And the infamous announcement: "The Procrastinators Anonymous meeting has been postponed till next week… we think." And one of my favorites from Proverbs: *"As the door turns on its hinges, so does the sluggard on his bed"* (26:14). Ouch! And as a teenager I had done some serious bed turning.

So, how do we acquire diligence and root out laziness?

A Biblical Mindset on Diligence

Let's get something straight from the beginning. Before the Fall, before sin had entered God's perfect creation, Adam was given work to do. This was something he could delight in, something God-ordained, even something he will find himself doing for all eternity—work. In Luke 19, a parable similar to the one about the talents, those that properly put their minas to work ruled over cities in their master's future kingdom, representative of Heaven.

This sounds like work to me! It was the curse that put a new spin on work. Much of it would be menial or arduous. Our mindset toward it, however, is another matter. A restaurant chain has played on the Thank God It's Friday (TGIF—and I use this acronym with true thankfulness to God) Syndrome that is so prevalent in our culture. The biblical viewpoint, however, says: "TGIM." I'll let you figure that out.

A Serious Challenge for Men: Diligence in Providing

Paul extends to us men a serious challenge in II Thessalonians 3:6-15. Open your Bibles to this passage right now and review it as well as your answers in the "**DIG IN!**" section. We immediately should note who this charge is given to: *"every brother"*. It is not extended to the ladies but to us men. If you are a young, married man, especially with children, working full time but struggling to pay your bills, please understand the weight of Paul's address to you and do not ask your wife to get a full-time job outside your home. Paul has commanded these younger women in Titus 2:5 to be *"workers at home"*. The word Paul uses here does not mean "when you are at home be busy working" but very clearly "be a busy homemaker", or "make your home your top priority and be busy with its responsibilities". For her to be shackled with the duties of full-time employment **and** of the home is unconscionable. Genesis 3 clearly places this responsibility for financially supporting the family squarely at our feet, men, not our wives. I am not suggesting that God is forbidding wives to work outside the home, but rather as men **we** bear the weight of this responsibility.

Hear this challenge then: get a part time job in addition to your present full-time job. Please understand, the 40-hour work week that we consider "full-time" is not a standard that Scripture has set for us, but, quite frankly, one that socialism has set as it has crept into the American political landscape. Discard it. Let it have no place in your thinking. Embrace this God-given responsibility of truly working hard and supporting your family.

Consider also the inherent challenges in other Scriptures concerning a work week. In Exodus 20:9, it says, *"Six days you shall labor and do all your work."* Working six days per week, not five, was expected. This, of course, would have included work around the house. Also, in Matthew 20:1-16 Jesus speaks of workers being hired the eleventh hour and working for one hour, totaling a twelve-hour workday. This would suggest a seventy-two-hour work week. Please understand, this should be seen as a guide and not a law, or a rule. Regardless, the forty-hour work week is not substantiated by Scripture.

Next, we should note that Paul's charge in II Thessalonians 3:6 is not a suggestion: *"Now we command you, brethren, in the name our Lord Jesus Christ."* The formula he uses here in *"we command you"* is the same as that used when healing the sick and casting out demons (Acts 3:6, 4:1-12, 16:18; Matthew 7:22). It comes as a most serious command with comparable authority. So much so, that if anyone does not heed it, the church is told not to associate with such an individual in hopes that he will become ashamed of his behavior (3:14). That's a serious challenge!

What behavior then is Paul warning us men about? The word is translated in the NIV (1978) *"idle"* and in the NASB *"leads an unruly life."* Literally, it means "irregularly, disorderly, unruly, or insufficient inclination to disciplined work in a disorderly or an irresponsible manner." Come again? Read that once more—slowly. Do you see the rebellious attitude in this laziness? Actually, it's an attitude that's part of all laziness, and Paul is acknowledging this and strongly warning against it. Those Thessalonians engaged in this behavior knew it was wrong but were refusing to change. Paul set an example for them of diligence, a model to follow that included working day and night. Men, this is the burden we bear. It is more a privilege, however, an opportunity to provide for our family and care for them.

Young, unmarried men are not exempt. Use this season of your life to prepare for your future. Proverbs 24:27 says, *"Prepare your work outside and make it ready for yourself in the field; afterwards, then, build your house."* These things were done before marriage, as the young Jewish man would bring his new bride to his newly built home (or addition to his parents' home) and not the other way around (see also Jeremiah 29:5-6 for the order of events leading up to marriage). Young men, foster this ambition for hard work and providing now. Start saving for your future. Don't wait until marriage.

Diligence in Serving in God's Kingdom

Additionally, remember that even though Paul worked day and night, he sought first the kingdom of God and busied himself planting churches. Paul says of his ministry in Thessalonica: *"For you recall, brethren, our labor and hardship, how working night and day so as not to be a burden to any of you, we proclaimed to you the gospel of God"* (2:9). Paul and his apostolic entourage were diligent both in working to provide for themselves and in proclaiming the gospel of the kingdom of God. Concerning his ministry, he states elsewhere,

"For this purpose also I labor, striving according to His power, which mightily works within" (Colossians 1:29). Please do not see Paul and those laboring with him as called to ministry but you are not. We ***all*** are called to seek first God's kingdom (Matthew 6:33), regardless of its nature: preaching, witnessing, serving the less fortunate, discipling others, giving generously, etc. Even so, dive into ministry, men. Serve wholeheartedly. For those who are married, balance work, family, and ministry. But be diligent, because Godly Men work hard!

Our mindset, therefore, should be, "I will be diligent in my work, knowing I will one day give an account for what I have done and how I have put God's kingdom first in all things." If God has called us to be married and have children, we make every effort to support them properly. I have met many grown men, well into their thirties and beyond, quitting jobs because they didn't like the boss but having no back-up job in the wings. They hate looking for work, so in a few weeks or months, after putting a few applications in to very desirable jobs and then waiting, they are forced to settle for a lesser job and worse boss. And it doesn't take long before they start missing those "wonderful days" in the former job. These men are in great need of some serious growing up.

A Godly Example

Diligence is key. Let me illustrate. My oldest daughter Kate is an absolutely beautiful, talented, godly young lady. She is so much like her mother, filled with joy and compassion, pursuing Jesus wholeheartedly. She works with the teens in our church (as of the original writing of this book) but is also a LIFE Group leader and worship dance ministry leader. She is destined to impact this generation in a huge way. Recently, she got engaged to a childhood friend she has known for most of her life. A few years back, however, this young man, Zack, had started veering off course. His studies tanked. His relationship with the Lord was severely tested. He was working a very difficult job as a part time supervisor at UPS and did not want to end up there as a career, but he was feeling he had no other alternative.

I met with Zack a couple of times per month, loving on him like a dad and speaking hope and challenge into his life circumstances and poor decisions he was making. It was really an inner issue. My wife had numerous heart-to-hearts with him, as did Kate. His family prayed, we prayed, and many others joined us, as well. We fasted. God needed to break through.

Many months later, Zack came to me a completely broken young man. Though significant change had started several months earlier, this was different. This was radical, a sharp break from his past. He implemented numerous changes. He regularly feasted on God's Word, worshiped intensely, prayed fervently, reconciled broken relationships, and became accountable. He then asked God if he should finish college. To do so, many miracles would need to line up. Every one of them did. He was faithful in his walk with Christ, faithful in his work at UPS, and faithful in his studies.

He was admittedly fearful as he headed back to school. In his first semester, however, his hard work paid off—he got straight A's at a nearby, renowned, private university. As of this writing, he will be graduating in just three months.

To do this and save up for a June wedding nine months away, he is working two part time jobs totaling about 50 hours per week, going to school full time, working with the teens in our church, having regular devotional times with the Lord, seeking Him whole-heartedly, and drumming for our worship team. Can you say, "Diligence"? Understand, my wife and I have invested 25+ years into our oldest daughter. I do ask a lot of anyone who would want her hand in marriage. But Zack has become the type of young man I want to entrust my little girl to.

What are you becoming? Is diligence being woven into the fabric of your character? Remember: *"In all labor there is profit"* (Proverbs 14:23).

Eight Successful Work Principles

As a pastor and business owner now for many years, let me share with you some thoughts on being the type of employee that gets promoted and is treasured by most businesses.

First, always give your very best, 100%. When you can, go the extra mile. Don't think: "What's in this for me?" if you do extra work. Your goal is truly to better the company. When doing jobs around your house, do the same. Strive for excellence. Pay attention to details. This comes easier for some. If it doesn't for you, work at it. If you're cutting the lawn, don't hurry through it so you can do something more fun as soon as possible. Quality of work is very important. Give it your best.

Be careful of the "hireling" (KJV) mindset. In John 10:11-13, Jesus reminds us that when the risk is high, the hireling runs, because he does not care for the employer's assets. He has not invested himself in the serious matters of the business. Instead, have an employer's mindset. The more you care about your work, your contribution to it, and the advancement of the business, the more valuable you will be to your employer.

Second, quantity of work is very important, as well. Try to work as quickly as you can to accomplish as much as you can. Have a sense of urgency. When in seminary, I too worked for UPS for a while. We were asked to be efficient. That means doing the best we can as quickly as we can, no wasted time, and whatever we did should ***never*** need to be redone.

When you work at home, at school, or at a job, do you move quickly? Or do you say, "No one else is" or "I don't get paid enough"? You cannot advance with this attitude. It's what many call "stinkin' thinkin.'" You will only become mediocre in a workplace in which others want ***your*** promotion. This sounds like a tall order. How do we do this?

Third, work as unto the Lord and not for man (Colossians 3:22-24). If laziness and procrastination are sin, then what is diligence but a virtue? If we are judged for our actions according to II Corinthians 5:10, shouldn't we strive to work hard and so honor the Lord? Man's praise is short-lived. God's honor is eternal. If we have a "work hard" button, then it should always be "on" whether our boss is looking or not. The kingdom mindset says, "I am working for the Lord more than I am working for my boss." As Christians, or Christ-bearers, God's honor is at stake here. Do people see Christ in you as you work?

Fourth, get rid of selfish ambition. This is different than godly ambition, which strives hard to accomplish God-centered goals. Selfish ambition is doing whatever it takes to promote self and self-centered goals. Don't do things that make others look bad and you look good. Don't be quick to point out fellow employee's mistakes. That's your boss's job. Even if you do it "for the boss," everyone including your boss will resent you doing it. You will be black marked.

To extract this cancerous quality of selfish ambition, a leader once told me, "Work so hard your boss gets promoted." Make it your goal to make your boss look good rather than yourself look good. If you do this, there will be no opportunity for selfish ambition. Also, praise fellow workers and bosses. Applaud their accomplishments. Help them as much as you can. Think of others more than yourself and be an excellent team player.

Fifth, don't be a complainer. Be positive and cheerful. Focus on the good around you, not the bad. I remember standing at a cash register one day while two cashiers very harshly criticized and complained about the leadership of the company. It doesn't matter how bad it is, you never complain, and especially not in front of customers. I said something to the effect, "Ladies, be careful what you're saying. Maybe some of it's true. But if I were your boss, I would either fire you right now or warn you that's what will happen the next time. Complaining is like poison. You don't want to do it!" Don't allow this poison in your life. It will leech into the workers (and customers) around you.

On a more positive note, find ways to allow the character of Christ to shine through your attitude, words, and actions. Believe it or not, most bosses and employees are attracted to kindness, joyfulness, respectful speech not punctuated with foul language, self-sacrifice in helping fellow workers, and humility. May I also encourage you to find creative ways to share the gospel with those in your workplace when time permits. Be a respectful person, and more than likely those you speak with will respect you and what you say (though they may not always ***accept*** what you say). Nevertheless, you will be seeking first the kingdom of God, and God will honor this.

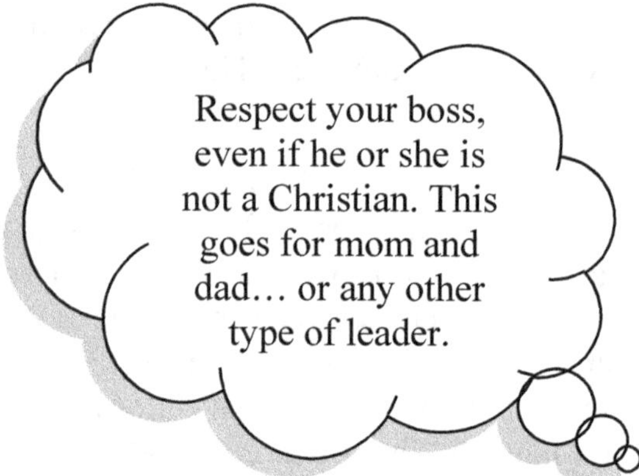

Sixth, respect your boss, even if he or she is not a Christian. This goes for mom and dad, a coach, an instructor or teacher, or any other type of leader. They deserve your respect. When my children were young, I reinforced three ways they were always to obey: immediately, completely, and cheerfully. Stomping up the stairs to take something to their room as instructed is a wrong attitude and constituted disobedience. Obey your boss with the right attitude. If you don't, you may not find yourself employed for long. If you do, that's the type of attitude your boss wants on his team and will want to promote.

Seventh, be on time. Get to work several minutes early. I tell my church leaders: early is on time and on time is late. Get to work 10-15 minutes early. Plan your morning accordingly, so you can leave in plenty of time to get there. Anticipate traffic. Most businesses don't tolerate tardiness. Many have a policy in which an employee who is late three times is automatically released—fired! Being consistently on time shows initiative and responsibility, qualities bosses want in their workers, especially leaders.

Lastly, learn to enjoy your job. Always try to go a little beyond what you're asked to do. Study the business in the off-hours, if you can. The more you know about the business, the more marketable you are in the company. If your knowledge and abilities expand, you will be able to do more jobs and increase your value and chances of promotion. This will also help you get rid of the TGIF mentality. Would a supervisor really want to promote someone, giving them more company responsibilities, if they don't like their job and are always eager to leave Friday afternoon? Now, let's consider the employee who is truly grateful to the Lord that it's Monday and gets to go back to work. Perhaps they are driven by a sense of purpose or opportunity. This is not only the type of person I would want to hire but promote. Attitudes are contagious. And this attitude is one I would want *all* my employees to catch!

Living Out the Principles at Home

Be diligent to look for opportunities to help out on a regular basis at home, employing these principles. I try to include my fifteen-year-old son, Jimmy, in repairs and maintenance projects around the house. I show him how to change the oil in our cars, replace the toilet fill valve, and the like. Together we cut our lawn weekly. Sometimes I tackle a one-man job while he is busy. Eventually, he comes out to me, asking if I need help. I'll usually tell him I've got it, so he asks if I need something to drink. He does this because he is learning to shoulder the responsibilities around the house and has a heart to serve.

If you are a young man (a teenager or older) still at home, then you should be regularly seeking opportunities to help around the house. Ask for a "Honey-Do List" (ask your dad what this is). Don't ask for pay, unless your parents insist on it (for young teens this may be the only source of income to purchase gifts for family and friends or other desired items). Spend several hours during the week and weekend tackling these tasks. Make them a high priority and not something you'll do only if you have time to get around to them.

Two summers ago, Jimmy wanted to earn some money and asked me for some ideas. We settled on lawn cutting. We made a flyer and distributed about 500 of them. The customer provided the equipment, and my son came with the hard work. He charged only $10-$15 per lawn and could cut, trim, and blow each in about an hour or so. I fielded the calls, and together we visited the potential customer and decided on a price. It was a great learning experience for him, but this past summer he wanted to work with someone and for someone. A godly man in our church has a lawn service company that he works part time, seeing he co-owns a Christian bookstore. The lawn business was getting very busy, so he hired Jimmy to work for him. My son thoroughly enjoyed this different experience as God continues to build in him proper attitudes toward hard work.

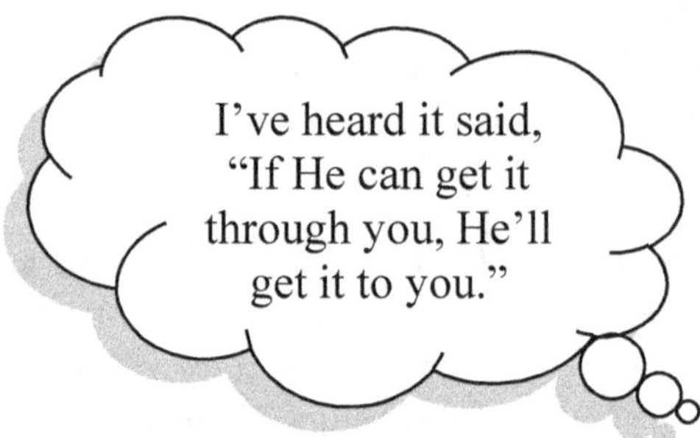

Using Your Surplus

I would like to close out this section with a word about prosperity. I will keep it brief. Deuteronomy 8:18 says, *"But you shall remember the LORD your God, for it is He who is giving you power to make wealth, that He may confirm His covenant which He swore to your fathers, as it is this day."* If you are diligent in what you put your hands to, God will extend his blessing to you with a purpose. First, He wants you to support your family. Second, He wants to bless you so your surplus can bless others. Make this your goal. This is true prosperity. I've heard it said, "If He can get it through you, He'll get it to you." If you are a generous person that loves to give to others, He will want to prosper your hard work so you can do this.

This was the practice of the early church. Many times, they sold extra properties (perhaps from an inheritance or investment) and gave the money to the apostles, who then distributed it to those who were in need (Acts 4:34-35). Paul said in Acts 20:35, *"In everything I showed you that by working hard in this manner you must help the weak and remember the words of the Lord Jesus, that He*

Himself said, 'It is more blessed to give than to receive.'" Our goal then is not to get but to give!

Today we live in a country in which its people believe they are entitled to another's wealth. This is both unbiblical and godless. Our welfare system has inadvertently produced a generation in which many have not learned this principle of hard work. The truth, though, is many work very hard but go through difficult times financially. These have been called the "worthy poor." It is but a season in their lives. They typically are worthy of our generosity. The guiding principle is this then: Godly Men work hard to provide for their families with sufficient abundance that they can be generous and give to those in real need. This is clearly what the early church in the book of Acts practiced, and this is the great privilege we have today!

Young man, let God cultivate in you a passion for hard work both in the world and in God's kingdom. Make that shift from a play-focus to a work-focus. Learn to shoulder large amounts of responsibility. Be faithful in everything your parents, your ministry leader, and your boss toss your way. Though there is no simple formula for success, the combined principles in this book, when properly applied with diligence will yield tremendous dividends. Understand this, if Satan cannot keep us from Christ, he will try to neutralize our effectiveness in Christ. So put your foot down. Say "no" to laziness. Broaden your shoulders and God will empower you to accomplish much for His kingdom.

BRING IT HOME!

If you could sum up your attitude toward work, what would it be? (Give this some thought.)

Do you have a dream for a future business that is still in the planning stage? If so, are you on schedule to start it? If not, what is holding you back?

Proverbs 28:19 speaks of "empty pursuits." Are you chasing after any? If so, list them.

What are you presently doing that exemplifies diligence? List several.

List your household chores. If you are living with your parents, boldly ask them how you are doing with them and if they should add to them (or perhaps you can make a suggestion or two).

Do you believe you have successfully made (or are making) the transition from a play-focus to a work-focus? Describe how this is evident.

What things are you struggling with by procrastinating (unfortunately, everyone, including myself, does this, even if it's seldom and in small ways)?

Just a little hint of help here: if a job(s) continually finds itself at the bottom of your "To Do List", consider bumping it up to the top. Usually, if we do not do this, we will continue to come up with sufficient reasons to not do it yet (e.g. not enough time, not that important, not very fun, extremely difficult, etc).

Of the eight principles toward being a better employee, which ones do you struggle with and need to work harder on?

What is your plan to better implement them in your life?

If you are a student not gainfully employed, how will you spend this summer?

If you are not a full-time student, are you working full time or close to it? If not, list your "reasons" here *and* make a copy of them.

In most cases it is best to substitute "excuses" for "reasons." See them as this and hand your mentor this page of "excuses" (please visualize your mentor literally taking your excuses from you so that you can no longer use them—they are now considered invalid!). Have him pray for you and hold you accountable to get full-time employment or the equivalent.

Lastly, how are you helping the less fortunate?

Godly Men
Love and Serve Others

I grew up in a family of six children: five boys and one girl. When Christmas rolled around, gifts overflowed from under the tree. Early in the morning, my siblings and I would sneak downstairs undetected by our parents to investigate. We would seek out our gifts and size them up, trying to guess what they were. One Christmas I remember getting a 007 briefcase that when a button was pressed would unfold to a rifle. It did just about everything except keep me out of trouble. I loved getting gifts. You might say I was an expert at it. What I wasn't good at, however, was giving gifts.

One particular time, I amazed myself by purchasing numerous gifts for my family about two months prior to Christmas (as opposed to the day or two beforehand). One of those presents was an unusually large bag of already popped popcorn. I hid these gifts in a suitcase in our attic. When any of my brothers were mean to me, I would threaten them, saying I wouldn't give them their gift if they continued treating me this way. This worked particularly well with my older brother for whom I had gotten the large bag of popcorn. I even showed him the present wrapped. It was huge! I had to carry it with both arms just to show him what he'd be missing out on if he wasn't extra nice to me. I remember displaying it under the tree Christmas Eve when we put most of the gifts out. It towered over all the other presents. Not knowing what it was, my older brother was excited to open it the next day. Anticipation had so manipulated his behavior toward me, I think he would have washed my feet if I'd asked him to. Between you and me, that would have been the highest form of cruel and unusual punishment imaginable, so I declined (there was a thread of compassion in my heart).

Christmas morning came, and my brother was at my beck and call. He served me like a king: breakfast, orange juice, pillows to get comfortable with, my favorite stuffed animal, all of his allowance for the next year—okay, he didn't do this, but it was on the table to talk about! Soon gift-opening time came as we gathered around the tree, sang some carols, and one by one began to open the presents. I remember my older brother opening his enormous gift from me. His eyes were large with expectation. As he ripped the wrapping, gasps filled the room. Never before had any of us seen such a bag of delectable popcorn of this size. Never! My brother immediately tore the bag and pulled out a fistful of the yellowest popcorn he'd ever seen.

The details remain a bit unclear, but what happened next has served to remind me well of my selfishness that season. My brother excitedly thrust the entire handful of popcorn into his mouth. His grin from ear to ear quickly turned to disgust. He paused with shock and then proceeded to forcefully spew everything out of his mouth. He choked and gagged. It was all over the floor and gifts in front of him. It sprayed like an outdoor hose erupts when unkinked. As the broken bits landed at my feet, I was reminded of how awful breakfast tastes the second time around. What I had thought would be the most awesome gift at Christmas (and for only twenty-five cents!) turned out to be the worst ever. In my initial disbelief I tried some. I had no idea just how bad two-month-old, stale, rancid popcorn could taste. My partial mouthful didn't spray quite as far as my brother's, but it was a good runner up. My brother sat there in disappointment. He had been duped into catering to my every need and for what? Rancid popcorn!

As I said, I learned a lesson in selfishness that season. I was a taker not a giver. When I gave, I did so with strings attached. I soon realized just how much my world revolved around me and wanted others' world to do the same. I am so grateful that as the years have passed, not only has my brother forgiven me, but God has placed people in my life to teach me and exemplify the art of crucifying self and loving and serving people. As Godly Men this is our highest calling. Paul put it this way: "Live a life of love, just as Christ loved us and gave himself up for us" (Ephesians 5:2—NIV, 1978). Love is a lifestyle, a way of living that's born from sacrifice like our Savior's. As you go through this lesson, be as honest and transparent as possible. You will find how easy it is to be led by wrong motives to try to do the right things. So, grab your Bible and pen and sit down with a glass of iced tea and some popcorn to enjoy. Allow God's Spirit to not only inform you but transform you as you read with an open heart to Him. And by the way, it wouldn't hurt to check the expiration date on that bag of popcorn in your hand!

DIG IN!

Study Section 1

READ Luke 10:25-28.
How do we gain eternal life?

Why does Jesus talk about love instead of belief here? Are they closely related? How?

Why does Jesus say we must love our neighbor if we expect to inherit eternal life? Is this a works-oriented gospel (remember Matthew 12:33 and the principle in play there on p. 12)?

Now **READ** Luke 10:29-37.
What question does the expert in the law ask next, trying to test Jesus?

What question does Jesus really answer (refer to 10:36)?

Why does Jesus change the question he answers (think about this carefully, we will talk about it later)? How does His parable emphasize this (this may be a tough question)?

List the several ways the Samaritan showed love to the injured Jewish man.

Samaritans were a group of people in Jesus' day that lived in central Israel. When the Assyrians conquered the northern kingdom of Israel in 722 B.C., they transported many Jews to distant lands they had previously conquered. Then they imported foreigners to Israel. They made these groups switch places to break the nation by breeding disunity. It's hard to communicate with people you can't understand or culturally relate to. This ensured no uprisings and continual payment of tribute. Over the centuries, the Jews and foreigners intermarried and produced the Samaritans, half-breeds who generally, though not always, embraced a mixed religion of Judaism and paganism. They were detested by most Jews, because they did not follow God as they did. This did not mean, however, that all of them did not love the one, true God.

Why is it significant then that it was a Samaritan that acted neighborly?

READ I John 3:16-18.
What is John's challenge here (in your own words)?

How did the priest and Levite in Jesus' parable violate this challenge?

READ Mark 1:40-42.
How did Jesus obey this challenge of loving His neighbor?

What prompted Him to obey it (v. 41)?

READ Luke 6:31.
Give 3 examples of this principle. (The first one is done for you.)

- Help your brother or sister do one of his/her chores.
-
-

We must understand that to truly love God with all our heart, soul, mind, and strength is equivalent to believing *in* God, which, as we have seen, is a heart commitment to Him. Also, Jesus challenges us not merely to love those near us (as some might understand the word "neighbor" to imply) but to be a neighbor even to those quite distant from us (those very different from us and hard to love—like a Samaritan for the Jews). This love for others is the fruit, or evidence, that our love for God is true and sincere (the essence of genuine faith).

Study Section 2

READ Philippians 2:3-11.
What was Jesus' attitude?

What is Paul contrasting, using the words "very nature" (NIV, 1978) or "form" (NASB) in verses 6 and 7? Why does he do this?

Why was Jesus exalted?

READ Matthew 20:24-28.
What is Jesus telling His disciples not to do?

Define "greatness" in the kingdom of God (use Matthew 18:4 as well)?

List 3 people you think are "great" and why?

-
-
-

How does the world define "greatness"?

How are these two definitions different?

Why are they different?

What was Jesus' purpose here?

READ Matthew 25:31-46.
What is the difference between the "sheep" and the "goats"?

List all the ways the "sheep" served.

-
-
-
-
-

Why does Jesus say what He does in v. 40? How are those being served like Jesus being served?

Jesus challenges us to serve others as if their needs were as important as the King's needs. Have you ever served someone only because of the important position they held? Give a personal example.

Give a personal example of when you served recently. Why did you serve?

List some reasons both good and bad that people serve.

Can you name someone you admire for how they serve?

Give an example of a way in which they have served.

Describe their attitude when they served.

Our point in this study section has been to see that greatness is not defined by anything other than a servant's heart that willingly sacrifices. Though our culture says that doing impressive things determines our greatness, God's view is quite different as Jesus' life as a servant demonstrated.

THINK ABOUT IT!

My dad was a twelfth grade English teacher at Brandywine High School. He was a very gifted teacher as well as a track and cross-country coach. He loved kids. He sacrificed much for them. When helping his students with term papers in the Spring, he would fill our station wagon every Tuesday and take them to the University of Delaware (or as some T-shirts spell it: "Dela-where?" and yes, it is a state!). He taught them the basics of research in the large library there. Students loved to hang out in his classroom after school as he would joke with them. He even won "Best Teacher of the Year" several times. The kids loved him.

A "Savior"?

When I was in tenth grade, the teachers in all the districts of our state went on strike. I remember sitting at the dinner table one evening as my dad recounted the reasons for the strike, but that it was against the law for them to do so. In good conscience and because he loved the kids and strongly felt it was his responsibility to teach them regardless, he told us he had made the decision to cross the picket line. He had prepared a letter explaining to all the teachers that he would be doing this and why. Many returned his letter with unrepeatable words scribbled in red. Anger began to heat relationships as a handful of other Christian teachers at this public school chose to side with my dad.

I remember very clearly the first day of the strike. My mom dropped my dad, my older brother, and myself off across the street from the school. Thirty to fifty teachers had already formed a line as they marched back and forth with their protest signs. Even the media had gathered for the fray. Tension was in the air. As we crossed the highway to walk the rest of the way to school, my brother and I flanked my dad to protect him. I'm not sure how much my 130 pounds could do here, but my brother weighed closer to 275 pounds and was nicknamed the "Hulk." Should a fight have broken out, he probably would have had to protect both my dad *and* me. But we proudly and confidently walked beside my dad as the picketers closed in around us. We had prayed for protection and God was answering these prayers. Though there was much anger, no one threw any punches, only sarcastic barbs like "Savior!" and "Messiah!"

Those accusations stuck with me. They revealed how the protestors thought of my dad. He couldn't rescue the situation. That was outside his control. They simply knew he was standing for what was right and it infuriated them. It's interesting they chose the words they did. My dad truly did love those kids and was willing to sacrifice whatever necessary to do his job.

The Cost of Love

This was Jesus' heart as He came to earth to rescue us from our sin. He was filled with compassion as His assailants hurled accusations against Him. Hebrews 12:2 tells us, *"who for the joy set before him endured the cross."* You and I were that *"joy set before him."* We were the ones on His heart as He gave everything. We were the ones that He loved so much. He was willing to die in our stead even though we were His enemies. This is real sacrifice. This is real love.

Day after day for six weeks we crossed the line of this angry mob and day after day my dad endured their venomous remarks. It took years for some of my dad's relationships with other teachers to become cordial again. A few were lost forever. This, however, is the cost of love. Love is sacrifice, and sacrifice implies cost. But Godly Men choose to love regardless of cost, because this is the essence and substance of the Christian life. This is who Jesus is. This is who we are to be. It is our call. It is our constant goal. It is our lifestyle.

Loving Our Neighbor

Love is the theme of the entire Bible and is at the heart of the gospel. It is God's message of reconciliation. We were His enemies. We are now His friends (John 15:15), His children (John 1:12), even His glorious bride (John 3:29). The two greatest commandments deal with loving God and loving others, or more specifically, "our neighbor." When Jesus was asked in Luke 10 who our neighbor was, His reply really

answered the question, "Who am I to be a neighbor to?" You see, "Who is my neighbor?" allows us the freedom to love whom we choose. But "Who am I to be a neighbor to?" obligates us to love all, including our enemies and those who are hard to love. But love is not bound by personal preference, nor is it limited to our cliques. It touches those who rub us the wrong way or even hurt us.

Love also reaches out to those who are socially awkward and may not be "cool" to hang out with. In my senior year of high school, I would purposefully sit down and eat lunch with different people each day to share the gospel with them. Many times, I was led to sit with those who had no one to sit with. One day I became acquainted with one of those social outcasts. His name was Allen. I had seen Allen before and understood why many people did not want to befriend or spend time with him. You see, Allen had Turrets Syndrome. When walking with him to class, he would frequently stop, reel back and let out a shriek. He called these "ticks," compulsions to act awkwardly. My heart broke for him as he commented, holding back tears of embarrassment, "Mike, I don't know how to stop this. I feel like everyone is looking at me. Do you think I'll have to live with this for the rest of my life?" I didn't know how to answer that question, but I sought instead to answer a different question of his, one he never asked but one I knew he had: "Can anyone really love me like this?"

I spent much time with Allen in school, at his home, and on the phone, sharing my testimony with him and this great love of God, who by His grace had transformed my life and could do the same for him. It wasn't long before Allen chose to stop hiding behind his hurts and come to grips with the cross. Within a year, He started coming to our church's singles ministry where he met new friends that ministered to him and loved him. God was truly changing his life as he allowed God's love to impact him through the gospel and through these new friends. This is the nature of God's love expressed through His people. If we let Him, God transforms us through it.

Love In Words

Love is the goal of everything we are about. After listing numerous Christ-like qualities, Paul concludes: *"Beyond all these things put on love, which is the perfect bond of unity"* (Colossians 3:14). Love is reflected in every godly trait. If it is not, it is not genuine or pure. If our words are harsh and hurtful, no amount of rationalizing how the person needed to be "knocked down a peg or two" (as my mom would say) will suffice and make it okay. Withholding forgiveness because the other person may become unwilling to apologize contradicts this basic principle of love. I say this because as guys we are wired to be tough and firm. However, sometimes we make quick, calculated decisions for the sake of expediency without serious consideration of people's feelings.

Now this is not to say all our decisions won't make people feel bad. There are times they will hurt others. As the saying goes, "You can please some of the people some of the time, but you can't please all the people all the time." Don't try to. But godly decisions birthed from love are both morally right and sensitive. Telling your friend you can't hang out with him this week because they didn't pick you first for the soccer game is vengeful. But telling your friend you can't hang out with him this week because you have too much schoolwork may be wise. So, let me say it again, love is our goal.

A Lesson In Forgiveness

Perhaps the greatest testimony of love is when the principle of forgiveness is walked out. It is at the heart of the gospel. Though undeserved, it is necessary. As a pastor, I find it key in the counseling I do. Many, however, have chosen to live their lives as slaves to unforgiveness. We call it bitterness. It consumes and destroys the soul. Spiritually, it eats away at us much like the consuming attraction Gollum had in **Lord of the Rings** for the one ring, his "Precious." It transformed him into a different creature, depraved and demented. Freedom from our grudges breathes life into our soul. Scripture is very clear, if we do not forgive others, God will not forgive us.

Jim and Elisabeth Elliot were missionaries to the Auca Indians in Ecuador and a great example of this principle. Though these people were considered extremely dangerous, the Elliots and others sought to evangelize them, nevertheless. In their initial contact with them, Jim and several other men were brutally killed. Elisabeth and the other missionary women strongly believed they were to continue their efforts of reaching these people with the message of the cross. Eventually, God provided inroads to these people, and many were rescued from their sin, including the man that killed Jim Elliot.

It is truly an amazing story of how Elisabeth battled through hurt and anger to forgive this man. I read they eventually travelled portions of the U.S. together, expressing the power of reconciliation through Jesus Christ. I will have to admit, it would be a tall order to forgive someone who savagely killed my wife or child, but through Christ we can do all things. It is a **must**. Forgiveness cannot be considered an option. It is an obligation. Godly Men love and willingly forgive *all* offenses no matter how deep the hurt. They do this, because this is the heart of God that He has expressed toward us.

Serving Away From the Spotlight

Perhaps the most visible way love can be expressed is in serving. Most are willing to acknowledge this, but with great reluctance. Serving is generally hard and done with little recognition. To be honest, most of us like jobs, positions, or opportunities in which we will receive attention and praise.

Let's take an example from sports. We want to be the guy that scores the touchdown or the winning basket. The truth, however, is that the greatest asset on any team is not necessarily the guy that scores the most points. It's the guy who is able to make everyone else on the team so much better. In basketball a great point guard is typically not the guy who scores a lot of points but is able to make the most assists. It's his job to feed the ball to his teammates who are open. He is able to make everyone on his team look great. In his prime, Steven Nash played for the Phoenix Suns. He was indispensable. Twice he was voted the NBA's Most Valuable Player.

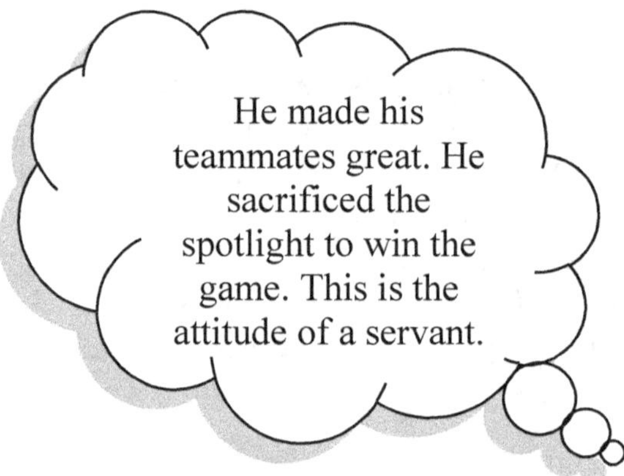

Eight times he has been an NBA All-Star. Why? Not because he scored the most points. Note this: five times he was the NBA's leader in assists. He made his teammates great. He sacrificed the spotlight to win the game. This is the attitude of a servant.

Jesus put it this way: *"Whoever wishes to become great among you shall be your servant"* (Matthew 20:26). In God's eyes, greatness is not measured by success or money or fame or awards. It is not in what we get but in what we give away. Jesus considered it his goal to serve, not to be served. Serving is rarely glamorous and often requires much personal sacrifice, but such is the life of a disciple of Jesus. Those who follow Him will eventually be like Him, even sacrificing their life for others if need be.

Five Characteristics of a Servant

So, what does it take to be a servant and be great in Christ's kingdom? Let me lay out for you five qualities of this hero in disguise.

First, he serves when it is inconvenient. Often, we are willing to help others within certain limits. We do this with God, and we do this with other people. We will serve to a point, most particularly when it is convenient for us and requires minimal sacrifice. Perhaps the best training grounds for learning these principles of servanthood for me has been as a parent. Late one night about 1 pm after a particularly exhausting day of physical labor, I was awakened by one of my children calling for me. It's these times when you want to pretend you didn't hear them, hoping they will go back to sleep.

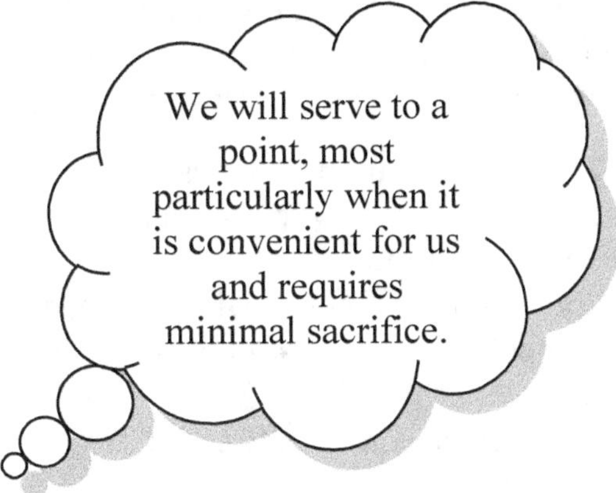

With each successive call getting louder and louder, I knew this strategy wasn't going to work, so I went in to see what the issue was. What I encountered both repulsed me and endeared me to my child. As I entered the bedroom, there she lay with vomit all over her pillow and pajamas. It had soaked her long, light brown hair and had even spilled over onto the floor. Welcome to daddy-hood! I cleaned her up as best I could, even bathing her and shampooing her hair.

No sooner had I changed the pillowcase than her sister next to her rolled over and said, "Daddy, I don't feel so good!" and proceeded to prove it—all over herself! Meredith was fully awake by now (I tend to be a light sleeper) and graciously volunteered to tag team this one. She bathed our little one while I cleaned up the mess. Half-way through this ordeal our two other girls in the next room began to heave in unison. Really? All four of our daughters—with long hair? A practical joke couldn't have been planned better. But I assure you, I was not laughing. Actually, when you truly love someone, serving even when incredibly inconvenient is not drudgery. But that is indeed the key, truly loving someone. Even though my wife and I missed out on several hours of sleep that night, we served with compassion, each of us "sleeping" between two children who took turns sharpening our servant attitudes and testing the resolve of our love for them. Because love serves even when it is inconvenient and difficult.

Second, he serves eagerly and willingly. Peter challenged his fellow elders to serve *"not because [they] must but because [they were] willing...eager to serve"* (I Peter 5:2—NIV, 1978). The question of serving in any given situation is never, "Do I want to?" but rather, "How do I best serve?" We should constantly be looking for opportunities, taking the initiative rather than waiting for mom or dad or a leader to ask us. Perhaps due to the natural calling upon a woman to be a "suitable helper," she tends to be more inclined to serve than a man. Also, those with the gift of serving tend to excel here. However, gifted or not, all of us men are called of God and obligated to serve.

When my son Jimmy notices that the trash is full, he takes it out. We have trained him to serve this way, to walk circumspectly, noticing the needs around him. Each person in our household takes turns doing dishes one evening per week. When one of us is unusually strapped with obligations like a paper that's due for a college class, others quickly volunteer to do the dishes for them, many times unnoticed. My night is Monday, and on a couple of occasions I've come home late from a meeting to find that my children have done the dishes for me.

Third, this principle is so important in the kingdom of God that ***it is a prerequisite for being a leader*** as Peter has shown us. Even the best leaders are foundationally servants. The worldly mindset thinks that the more authority one has the more others should serve him. It views this as one of the perks of leadership. But this is foreign to a kingdom mindset. Even Jesus came to serve. The concept of a spiritual "armor-bearer," a leader's protégé who serves him constantly, has been much abused in our day. It typically wreaks of brown-nosing and people-pleasing and has no place in God's kingdom. A leader's goal is to serve the people, not to have others wait on him. This is not to say we do not serve our leaders, but to say we serve them inasmuch as we serve others. He is humble and does not view himself as more important than another.

Servanthood is not merely the road to leadership any more than doing calculus is simply the pathway to engineering. Once one becomes an accomplished engineer he doesn't stop using calculus. On the contrary, he uses it all the time. Same with leadership. Serving is the platform from which leaders always lead. One doesn't stop serving once he becomes a leader. Godly leaders serve.

Before looking at the fourth quality of serving, let me ask a question: why do you serve? When I was a young married man and we had company for dinner, I found myself at times very eager to do the dishes. "Why?" I eventually asked myself. The answer I discovered after much candid soul searching was not what I was hoping to find. I realized my motivations were self-serving and not people-serving. I desired recognition. Although my wife was glad to see me volunteer, I knew my heart was wrong. As Jesus put it, I desired to *"be honored by men"* (Matthew 6:2). Consequently, I had received my reward in full. This next quality of serving challenges us to do so without a desire for man's praise.

So, I ask you again, why do you serve?

Fourth, serving must be sincere. Let me share a truth with you that may be hard to hear: for most people most of the time our motives to serve are mixed at best. Romans 12:9 says, *"Love must be sincere"* (NIV, 1978). This means it must be genuine and pure. Our English word "sincere" comes from the Latin word "sincerus," which literally means "without wax." When selling an old statue in Roman times, the owner often used melted wax to fill in the cracks from age, giving the statue the appearance that it was without defect. Nothing could have been further from the truth, however. Heat from various sources could melt this wax, and the real condition of the artwork was revealed. Any statue that had not been tampered with before selling was considered "without wax," or "sincere." What you see is not always what you get.

Today, we can fill in the cracks of our character with insincerity. When serving for personal gain or people's praise, we tell ourselves we're really doing it for noble purposes. For a long time, I told myself the reason I was helping with the dishes was to help my wife. There was truth in this, but why didn't I do it as readily when no one was over for dinner? Ouch! Such probing questions forced me to examine my real motives. I wasn't very impressed with what I concluded. My serving was insincere. I looked for a godly reason for doing the dishes and used it to fill in the cracks of my character. Outwardly it appeared noble, but inwardly it was selfish. Other improper motives for serving are financial gain, to obtain forgiveness from someone without apologizing, to get a promotion or votes, or to appear better than others. When Godly Men serve, they apply heat to their actions by asking tough questions that discern motives in order to melt away the wax of insincerity and serve out of genuine love for God and people.

Jesus' point in Matthew 6:1-4 is that those who give to the poor and serve openly to be seen by others rob themselves of future rewards. Their actions are hypocritical. Instead, serve in secret, He recommends. Do it when others aren't looking and no one can praise you. Surprise people with anonymous acts of kindness. On one occasion, after returning home with my family from a vacation, I had planned to immediately cut our lawn. It had been a while, so I was anticipating long grass and a huge job ahead of me. Much to my surprise, as we pulled into the driveway, I noticed an immaculately cut and trimmed lawn. What an incredible blessing! Our first day back was relaxing and unhurried, because a friend had anonymously served us. Although, later, I figured out who it was and very casually thanked him, he played it off as if he had no idea what I was talking about. Such is the heart of a servant, always seeking to help others, desiring nothing in return.

Fifth, we are to serve with a humble heart that refuses to complain. I remember the testimony of a well-known national Christian speaker. While in seminary, he sought out an opportunity to minister in a nearby church he was attending. When he asked the pastor what he could do ministry-wise, he was told that the greatest present need was a janitor that could clean the toilets. He thought to himself, "Whoo-hoo, my dream job! I get to sink my arms elbow deep in…in…" Okay, so his response wasn't quite so enthusiastic. Actually, he believed that this was not what he was looking for and certainly not his "gifting." He was interested in leadership positions and opportunities to teach and preach. These were not available at the time, so he declined to serve as a janitor.

Later that week, while using the men's room, he noticed the pastor coming out of one of the stalls with cleaning equipment. He asked why he was cleaning the toilets, and the pastor reminded the young seminary student that presently it was a need in the church, so he was doing it. Conviction settled upon this young man as he had complained to God that he wasn't there to clean toilets but to learn ministry. He couldn't bear the thought, however, of this older man of God continuing to serve as the church's janitor as well as spiritual leader, so he humbled himself and took on the job. At first, he was discouraged and complained, but as time went on, he realized the great need he was filling and the character of servanthood God had begun to build in him. He quit the complaining and began serving with a grateful heart. This experience revolutionized his attitude toward serving and ministry. As I said, today, God is using him mightily on a national level.

Young man of God, guard your heart against the enemy's potential foothold of complaining in your life. Recognize the negativity and deal it a death blow. Thank God frequently for opportunities to serve.

Wrapping It Up

Even when serving is inconvenient, jump in with your sleeves rolled up. Do it eagerly and willingly. Don't wait for others to ask you. Initiate, walking throughout your day with eyes wide open to the needs of those around you and serving as opportunities arise. If God has called you to leadership, don't think that serving is merely a steppingstone to that call but rather the very foundation from which you will one day lead. As you serve, watch out for self-centered motives that will undermine your efforts to carry out God's will, and be cautious of wrong attitudes that become evident in complaining.

If you can serve in these ways, you will become indispensable in the kingdom of God. You will be the type of person others will want to be around. You will be the type of person God delights to use to extend His kingdom and do great exploits. Why? Because you will be taking on the very nature of Jesus who came not to be served but to serve. This is what Godly Men do, because this is their calling—to serve. ***This*** is true greatness!

BRING IT HOME!

Who is your neighbor? List numerous examples.

How should you act toward them?

List 5 ways you can serve and what you might need to sacrifice in order to serve in each example.

-
-
-
-
-

Have you noticed any wrong motivations in serving others? If so, circle them here.

- Praise from others.
- Others recognizing what a great guy you must be for serving.
- Promotion or leadership advancement.
- To win a girl's attention or favor.
- A way of saying, "I'm sorry," without having to humble yourself and say it.
- To show you're "better" than someone else.
- To get out of doing something else that's very unpleasant to you.
- Other:____

Of the five qualities of serving listed in this chapter, which ones do you struggle with the most and why?

Ask your parents to compile a list of ways you can serve around the house (that wasn't complaining I just heard, was it? If so, list that in the previous question.). Write them here and have your mentor hold you accountable to do them.

Godly Men
Are Humble and Praise Others

Have you ever given something your best, surprised even yourself with how well it turned out, only to have someone point out its shortcomings? Not one word of praise. It can really hurt. But my real question is a little more probing: why would someone do this? What prompts them to be critical instead of praising? The answer runs very deep and reveals a significant root character issue that more of us share in than would like to admit.

A youth pastor friend of mine had been asked by his senior pastor to fill in for him while he was on vacation. He felt up to the challenge, but wondered just how the adults would receive him. The youth ministry had been growing, but the senior pastor still shared his concerns with his underling, encouraging him not to do anything that would raise eyebrows. After all, *"it is not good to have zeal without knowledge, nor to be hasty and miss the way"* (Proverbs 19:2—NIV, 1978). Caution would need to be the order of the day.

Sunday morning quickly rolled around and my friend had felt God put a strong word of challenge in his heart. Would it be over-the-top? Would he anger the elderly? No holds barred, he preached from his heart. The Spirit of God fell powerfully, convicting many of sin and calling them to wholehearted devotion. Sunday night was no different. God was doing something strangely wonderful in this church in the senior pastor's absence.

The vacation was soon over, and the church's lead pastor returned to the pulpit. He had heard a few good reports of his substitute's success. But not until after the service did the full force of the congregation's delight surface, when a group of well-meaning parishioners approached the pastor after what he believed was a powerful sermon, and said, "Pastor, you really missed it! When you were gone, the Holy Spirit moved like never before. You should definitely have our youth pastor preach more often!"

Can you say, "Ouch"? After several others approached the senior pastor during the week about my friend's impact, the relationship between these two men began to change. The head pastor became more controlling, faultfinding, and suspicious. He truly believed his youth pastor was planting doubts in people's minds about his abilities, and thereby undermining his "authority"—or should I say "popularity"? My friend was doing nothing of the sort, but the challenges and pointed questions kept coming. It wasn't long before the senior pastor asked my friend to leave against the wishes of the congregation.

Now, I realize that some young men can get rather full of themselves and think they deserve the spotlight more than the second coming of Jesus, but such was not the case here. My friend left confused and hurt. No "attaboy" or words of encouragement from his pastor, only challenge, anger, and accusation. Why? What was his offense? What was going on here beneath the surface that had undermined this relationship? The senior pastor had been "set up." Deficient character issues plus Satan's finely tuned strategies equaled defensiveness, disunity, and destruction.

It's easy to see this when it's in other people, but when it's *our* deficient character issues in the equation, it can be altogether different. How do we then recognize it in our life? What is the root problem? And how do we pull up this stubborn weed and get rid of it? As Godly Men we want to be secure enough in who we are to lavishly praise others. After all, these are the kind of men others honor, and these are the kind of men, title or no title, that people want to follow.

DIG IN!

Study Section 1

READ Proverbs 27:2.
Why should we allow others to praise us but not praise ourselves?

Does this mean we should seek out or desire others to praise us?

Why do we like praise?

The heart of the person who gives praise is quite different from the heart of the one who seeks praise.

READ Proverbs 27:21.
How does praise from others test us?

What might be some indicators that we have failed this test? (What happens? What might we do? An example is given for you.)

- We might acknowledge just how good we are.
-
-

READ John 12:42-43.
How did some leaders who believed in Jesus fail the test?

The desire to be popular can be a strong temptation. It not only feeds our pride but also pulls on our desire to belong and to be liked. This type of peer pressure can lead us to do things we may not normally do. It is very seductive. What should these leaders have done instead?

READ Proverbs 16:18.
Can you describe what kind of *"destruction"* or *"stumbling"* can occur when we become filled with pride? (The first one is done for you)

- We can lose friends, because most people dislike pride in others (though not necessarily in themselves).

-

-

READ Proverbs 26:23-28.
How does *"he who hates"* disguise himself?

A. By dressing in a silly villain costume, toting a gun that shoots vicious squids, and correcting everyone who calls him "Victor."
B. By snuggling in bed, wearing a grandma's nightgown and cap, while sporting a big nose and sharp teeth and muttering something rather random and off-the-wall like, "The better to eat you, my dear!"
C. By using flattering and charming words so no one will see the deception in his heart.
D. All of the above.
E. None of the above.
F. A and B only.
G. D and E only.

READ James 4:6.
How is this verse similar to Proverbs 16:18?

How are they different?

That last question may not be so easy to answer. The passage has us focus more on how our pride "short-circuits" God's desire to bless or help us. We must be humble to receive God's grace (Remember: God's grace is "everything that He has that we do not but desperately need").

To this point, we have observed that pride prompts us to praise ourselves or seek the praise of others and even be controlled by that desire. But such pride causes destruction and preempts the display of God's grace in our lives.

Study Section 2

READ Proverbs 18:12.
Look at the second half of this verse. What does it mean that *"humility goes before honor"* (Use a different word or phrase for "honor")?

Give an example.

Define "selfish ambition" (use a dictionary if necessary).

Selfish ambition:

How does the world view selfish ambition and honor together? (Perhaps substitute "fame" or "recognition" for the word "honor.")

Give an example.

READ Philippians 2:3.
What is God's remedy for selfish ambition?

To *"regard one another as more important than yourselves"* means to view others as more important than yourself, to think of their needs before or above your own. Describe a situation in which someone would do this.

Why might this be hard to do?

READ Romans 12:10.
What are three ways we can honor someone else above ourselves? (The first one is done for you.)

- When praised for an outstanding performance in the game, respond by talking about how well the entire team played in order to win.

-

-

READ Ephesians 4:29.
What are some examples of unwholesome talk?

-

-

-

What should our goal be in **all** our speech?

Give three examples (sorry, "three" is almost my favorite number) of this kind of wholesome speech.

-

-

-

Recount a time someone praised you. How did it make you feel? (Elaborate on your answer. Don't just write, "Good.")

Describe the power, or benefit, of praise and encouragement.

Write Ephesians 4:29 in your own words.

Due to selfish ambition the world cares little for others as it seeks recognition, promotion, or praise. It is full of pride and self-centeredness. Jesus' life was all about honoring His Father (not Himself) and serving others. We should do the same by both our actions and our words, always seeking to help and not hurt.

THINK ABOUT IT

Let me share with you a very basic principle that in my discipling others I have found vitally important: hurt people hurt people. No, that's not a typo. And I'm not given to stuttering. It means that people who carry around hurts tend to hurt other people. You've probably seen the cartoon caricature of the dad getting chewed out by the boss. When he gets home, he takes it out on his wife, who yells at the kids, who kick the dog, who chases the cat, who eats the mouse tail and all! The truth is that accumulated hurts not properly dealt with act as poison in one's heart. It can cause

unresolved anger and pride. You may wonder, "Anger, I understand, but pride? How is that?"

The Long Root of Pride

Most hurts tend to attack our sense of personal value. They can make us feel victimized, weak, and rejected. In our immaturity we react poorly. Pride rises up within us, wanting to show others that we are good, intelligent, attractive, well-liked, skilled, and yes, even "humble." To accomplish our task of lifting ourselves up before others, we often attack others to bring them down. The actual root of this issue is our insecurities as we saw in chapter two, "Godly Men Find Their Significance in Christ." This chapter before you will be an application, then, of this issue.

Our insecurities can prevent us from praising others. We long for people to admire and praise *us*. Others succeeding actually becomes competition to us. When this issue arises in women, we call it "being catty." Regardless of the term we use, it is pride, and we will need to know how to properly deal with it so we can be Godly Men who are humble and praise others.

Competing For Compliments

Jonathan was a fellow Christian college mate of mine. He had studied the Bible very seriously and had become quite a scholar, full of Bible knowledge. When others commented to me about Jonathan's vast knowledge, I tended to downplay it, usually by being critical. But I did not worry. I believed I was typically discreet in my criticism (Interesting, "Discreet criticism"? That's like government efficiency, a junior high sleepover, or a brief board meeting. These things only exist in our minds.).

I found it difficult to praise Jonathan, because I viewed him as competing with me for others' praise. Personally, I had placed too much emphasis on Bible knowledge. Scripture says that *"knowledge makes arrogant, but love edifies"* (I Corinthians 8:1). God was still needing to root out pride in my life that was fostering this competition for others' praise.

The realization of what I was doing came slowly. See, God had extensively dealt with a serious pride issue in my life several years earlier. Much changed in me. This extreme makeover blinded me, however, to other symptoms of pride that had "gone under the radar," not even a blip on the screen. Pride had masqueraded as an ability to see other people's faults very clearly, a quality I thought to be important, even godly. What a deception on my part. The unseen root of pride had produced the bad fruit of criticalness and had made it very difficult for me to genuinely praise others.

A Lesson in Humility

Let me share a humorous story about George I have found helpful in this area over the years. George had a friend much like myself, eager to receive praise but sparse in giving it. Realizing this about his friend, George decided to play with him, to help him deal with the issue, so he casually mentioned that he knew

Robin Williams.

"You're pulling my leg. There's no way you know *the* Robin Williams!" his friend shot back.

Within the hour the two were ringing the doorbell of a luxurious mansion, when Robin Williams opened the door and with great surprise remarked, "George, it's been a while! Come on in and bring your friend!"

After a few hours, they left the house and the friend sighed, "Okay, so you know Robin Williams. Big deal!"

Upon seeing no change in his friend's attitude, George offhandedly remarked, "You know, you're right. It's not quite as exciting as knowing the President."

"What? No way! Are you trying to tell me that you know the President, too?" his friend asked with obvious disdain. "Now this I have to see! Look, I'll pay for the plane tickets. Let's go to D.C."

The next day as they arrived at the White House, the President eagerly greeted the two of them: "George, it's so good to see you! Introduce me to your friend."

On the way back to the airport, George's friend dug his heels into the ground. He was not about to concede that George was a well-known, extremely likeable guy by even the most famous. Instead, he cornered George, "Look, so you've had a few lucky encounters in life and have met a few famous people, but there's absolutely no way you know the Pope."

George turned to him and asked, "So, when do you want to see him?"

This was too much, so George's friend cancelled the flights home and purchased two tickets to the Vatican in Italy. Upon arrival, George led his friend to a side entrance and knocked. A cardinal came to the door, shook George's hand, and invited him in, saying, "I'm sorry, but your friend will need to remain outside."

About an hour or so later, hundreds of people began gathering in the front. Upon investigating, the friend saw the Pope come out onto the balcony with his arm around George, waving to the enthusiastic crowd.

Sometime later, George went looking for his friend and found him passed out in the courtyard. Bringing him to, he apologized for shocking him like he had.

His friend gathered his wits and slowly replied, "It wasn't really that you knew the Pope. It was all the people that shocked me. They kept asking, 'Who's the guy with George?'"

Sorry, no refunds on that one!

But do you see? Pride can have very stubborn roots and be very difficult to deal with. You might even say it can lay you out. But as Godly Men, we must humble ourselves and be willing to praise others. In order to do this, we must first discover the cause. As I've mentioned in an earlier chapter, we cannot afford to merely pick the yellow flowers, we must dig down to pull up the weed, roots and all. If we fail to do this, we will never truly get at the real problem. The real problem here is past hurts and how we have failed to deal with them properly. So, let's do that. Let's pull up this stubborn weed by the roots.

Getting at the Root Issue

Unresolved hurts produce two problems in our hearts that we will need to correct separately: holding onto unforgiveness and believing Satan's lies. The diagram below will help us understand the issue better:

Unresolved Hurts → Unforgiveness and Believing Satan's lies → Inadequacies → 1. Criticalness
2. Withholds praise to others
3. Desires praise from others
4. Defensiveness, argumentativeness

Since unforgiveness will be addressed more thoroughly in a later chapter, I will speak to this issue only briefly.

Cancelling Their Debt

That unforgiven hurts produce anger is clearly evidenced both in Scripture and in real life. In Matthew 18, though the indebted servant is forgiven his debt, he refused to forgive the debt of another servant who owed him money. His demands were filled with anger and venom. He desired to hurt his debtor and see him imprisoned. Interestingly, this type of anger is also regularly directed towards those *not* indebted to us. As said earlier, hurt people tend to hurt people, many times in the form of criticism or the withholding of praise. Consequently, this constant overflow of hurt can affect anyone around us.

How do we rid ourselves of this? Jesus tells us that the answer is found in forgiving the one who hurt us. We cancel their debt to us. They no longer owe us anything.

Can you remember a past hurt? An offense that cut you deeply? Did you feel they owed something to you? An apology? Some sort of recompense? A reputation they took from you? A life of joy you believe they robbed you of? Then cancel their debt. They owe you nothing. Forgive them and let it go. Does this feel too hard? Does your inner demand for justice stand against you? Does the hurt seem to go too deep? Remember then the debt Christ forgave you. Your offense to Him was an infinite offense against His infinite holiness. The better you are able to understand the depth of your debt that Christ cancelled, the easier it will be for you to forgive your debtors.

Jesus concludes with a stern warning in Matthew 18:34-35, that should we choose not to forgive others, we will be handed over to the jailers to be tortured. Though this torment can take many forms, one form is certain, the bitterness inside (whether it is recognized or not) will imprison us and manifest in anger, pride, defensiveness, over-competitive-ness, etc. It's like a painful, festering wound that just won't heal.

Some years ago, I pulled a wooden trailer behind my vehicle filled with supplies and equipment for my business. While retrieving a tool one day from this trailer, I noticed a very large carpenter ant crawling on its door above my head. As I swatted it off, my finger brushed across the wood and, in doing so it, picked up a splinter the size of what looked like a small harpoon—conservatively speaking! Perhaps the shock of the moment did make it seem slightly larger than it was. Regardless, the impaling splinter went straight through my index finger. In my attempts to remove it from both sides, a piece was left inside that within a few days got infected and swollen. It was so sensitive, touching anything with it caused excruciating pain.

When people would accidentally brush up against it, even lightly, I cringed in agony as it throbbed. Only after treating the infection did the swelling go down and the remaining piece of wood eventually push itself out. To the point, unless we forgive the one who offended us, cancelling any debt we think he might owe, and allow God to heal our heart of any remaining hurt, the wound inside will only fester more, creating deeper issues for us to resolve.

Satan's Lies Can Produce Deep Inadequacies

The second problem we must deal with resulting from hurts is the subtle lies we have chosen to believe. These are from Satan, the Father of Lies, and are not easily recognized. In other words, we usually don't know that we have believed them. Look at Proverbs 26:23-28 again (and the correct answer in the Bible Study was letter "C," though I'm sure some of you were tempted to put "G"). The man filled with hatred, or lesser forms of anger, harbors deceit in his heart. Lies lie beneath the surface. Perhaps teasings from his childhood have wounded him. They have made him feel rejected. He has believed he is inadequate when compared to others. He may not think he measures up in popularity, looks, athleticism, or "being cool." But because others have praised him for his intelligence, he believes he must play this card for others to like him, value him, and accept him. This is the lie. So, when others are praised or publicly honored, it stirs up a longing in him for such attention, which he strives to attain by displaying his IQ. Smart people become his competition.

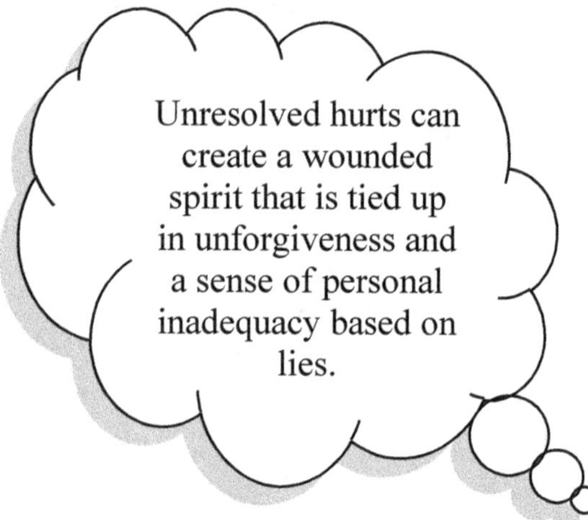

We must identify and discard these lies that we subtly believe about ourselves, if we are to be truly healed of our past hurts that have helped create this distorted view of ourselves. God does not love us or value us based on some trait we excel in. We must adopt God's perspective of our value, or worth. We cannot rely on other's opinions. Only His are true, accurate, unbiased, and constant. If we fail to do this, we will remain locked in our prison of inadequacy, struggling to give the praise to others that we ourselves long for.

So, what inadequacies might you be wrestling with? Many times, they are highlighted during times of teasing. We get easily embarrassed, even defensive, because the unhealed wound is still sensitive. Think about it. If someone like Brad Pitt or Hugh Jackman were teased about being ugly, they probably would laugh about it and perhaps join in the playful bantering. Why? Because too many people (okay, too many *ladies*) have told them they are attractive, so I'm sure they believe it. Their looks is not a sensitive issue for them. But how smart are they? How faithful or trustworthy are they? Are they well-coordinated? Athletic? Witty, or do they tell really corny jokes? I have no clue about the answers to these questions, but if either of these two falls short in any of these areas and others have hurt them with ridicule about these shortcomings, chances are they will be sensitive about them.

How do you feel you measure up to other guys? What areas in your life do you feel short-changed? The mature person can answer these questions with a rather confident and truthful, "I don't care." They really are not concerned about others' opinions of them, because they do not derive their value from what others think of them. They roll with the teasings and are secure in that singular truth that Christ loves them completely. They derive their value from this and only this. They truly do not crave or need man's praise, unlike the religious leaders of Jesus' day in John 12 who desired man's applause and affirmation over God's. What I'm really asking then is whose love are you choosing to heal your hurts? Men's or Christ's?

Let's Apply These Truths

As we can see, unresolved hurts can create a wounded spirit that is tied up in unforgiveness and a sense of personal inadequacy based on lies. These stir up a constant longing for people to praise us, applaud us, affirm us, and accept us. We compete with others for recognition, becoming critical of them instead of praising. This does not have to be so! We can be free from all of this. Let God show you right now those areas of personal sensitivity and help you forgive those who have hurt you. Cancel their debt, then acknowledge they owe you nothing; not one thing. If you find this very hard, take some time to meditate on the extent to which Christ has completely and finally forgiven you of every one of your offenses to Him.

Next, identify any lies you have chosen to believe about yourself:

- you are unlikable

- God apparently loves others more than you
- others are more important to God than you are
- you will never accomplish anything significant
- others are just better than you and therefore more valuable

Replace these lies with truths from Isaiah:

"And you will be called by a new name that the mouth of the Lord will designate…It will no longer be said to you, 'Forsaken,' nor to your land will it ever be said, 'Desolate'…for the LORD delights in you" (Isaiah 62:2-4).

"Instead of bronze I will bring [you] gold, and instead of iron I will bring [you] silver" (60:17).

"Can a woman forget her nursing child and have no compassion on the son of her womb? Even these may forget, but I will not forget you. Behold, I have inscribed you on the palms of My hands" (49:15-16).

"You will also be a crown of beauty in the hand of the LORD, and a royal diadem in the hand of your God" (62:3).

Allow yourself to be constantly reminded of God's true perspective of you. The closer you draw to Him, the more you will come to value His opinion of you over the value judgments and acceptance of others.

The Result?

As you do these things, something amazing will begin to happen. Your love for God will increase and begin to overflow into a deep and genuine love for others. Your concern will be less and less for yourself and more and more for others. You will desire to see them encouraged, loved, and commended to the point where one of your greatest joys will be to thank and praise them. You will no longer secretly long for the spotlight of honor but will desire this for others. You will do anything you can to help others excel beyond you. Others will no longer be your competition but your comrade, not vying for the attention of others (especially girls) that you desperately desire, because you won't. You'll realize you truly do not need it. It has no hold on you, does not control you, or slyly seduce you anymore. The Spirit inside of you will rejoice when others succeed. You will be free to praise others from a humbled and healed heart.

The Power of Praise

Only from this position of wholeness in Christ can we genuinely praise others with their best interests at heart. Our speech will be different. As Ephesians 4:29 says, *"Let no unwholesome word proceed from your mouth."* We will want to speak only what is helpful for others, building them up not tearing them down. I have counseled many couples who have deeply struggled in applying these principles of healing in this chapter. Consequently, their words toward their spouse are defensive, hurtful, attacking, impatient, sardonic, and accusatory. They just don't seem to "get it." My heart breaks for them. They are still imprisoned and tormented. You see, when we are freed to speak wholesome words, we will truly desire others' best no matter what it costs us, such as people's praise. We will place them ahead of ourselves and serve them with our words.

Though only Christ's love can truly heal hearts, our words can help move them in that direction. The end of verse 29 states that our edifying words *"will give **grace** to those who hear"* (emphasis added). Our words have the power to unlock the bound up, hurting heart to receive God's grace. Remember, God's grace is "everything He has that we do not but

desperately need." This is a storehouse of healing, of power, of life, and of liberty. Proverbs 18:21 declares: *"...life [is] in the power of the tongue."* So, make it your goal to praise others (not yourself) and bring life and encouragement to them with your words. Lavishly honor them in front of others. Do this then as God's healed instrument and as His instrument of healing.

"Do not merely look out for your own personal interests, but also for the interests of others" (Philippians 2:4). Find sincere, creative ways to compliment others. Have a heart-to-heart with both of your parents, thanking them for how they have loved and helped you. Put some thought into what you want to say. Don't wait for a high school graduation speech. Tell them today and frequently.

When my son, Jim, turned 16, his mother and I decided to have his friends over and celebrate. We asked them to focus on one thing they were thankful for or admired about him. We set a time limit of fifteen minutes for this. The group took thirty. It greatly encouraged him that day to know there were so many who loved him and cherished his friendship.

Seek to honor your teachers, classmates, fellow workmates, teen group members and leaders—anyone who has helped you. Seek also to put their interests ahead of your own in daily conversations. Ask them questions. Be interested in getting to know them better. Let Christ fill you with a supernatural love for others that stirs up a longing in you to see them praised, encouraged, and loved. You may

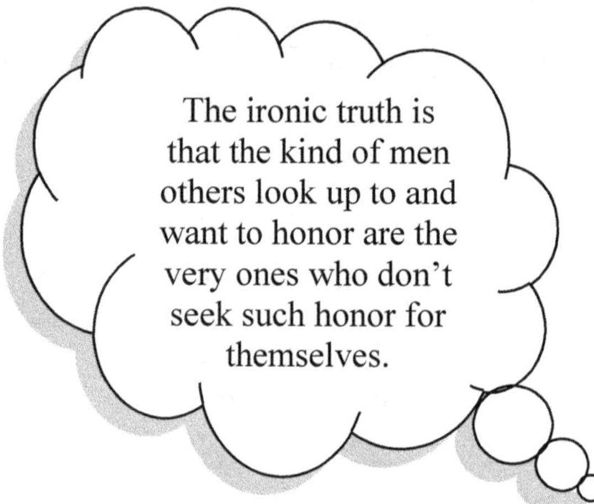

be the only person that day or that week who built them up and reignited a hope in their hearts. Remember Jesus' words, *"Treat others the same way you want them to treat you"* (Luke 6:31).

Man of God, stand up against the schemes of our Adversary. Do not allow him any longer to manipulate you with lies of inferiority. Do not permit him to slander the character of God to you, to minimize or negate the truth of God's never-ending, intense love for you. Instead, let the truth of God's love spill over in your life to others. The ironic truth is that the kind of men others look up to and want to honor are the very ones who don't seek such honor for themselves but rather lavishly praise others to see ***them*** built up. This is the heart of a Godly Man!

BRING IT HOME!

List some things that you are sensitive about, that perhaps when compared to others make you feel inadequate. Then write down any ***lies*** you believe about yourself in each of these areas. The first one is done for you ***only*** as an example.

- I am sensitive about my height. It makes me feel less grown up and that the guys taller than me are somehow better or more manly than I am (again, notice that this last sentence represents a *lie* and not the truth).

-

-

-

List people who have hurt you, humiliated you, looked down upon you, or rejected you, and you aren't sure whether you have truly forgiven them.

-

-

-

-

-

Take a moment right now and forgive each one, repeating the phrase "and I completely cancel their debt to me" after each declaration of forgiveness.

List the names of people you feel you are in competition with for others' (including girls') praise or admiration.

-

-

-

-

This week go out of your way to genuinely praise these people for something. Don't flatter them. Flattery is insincere and manipulative. It has *your* interests at heart not theirs. It seeks to gain rather than give. Find something you truly admire about them and tell them.

Make praising others a habit, regularly filling yourself up with an understanding of Christ's love for you so that it spills over to others.

Godly Men
Build Christ-Centered
Friendships

Nearly all of life is based on relationships, whether good or bad. They are central to the kingdom of God. Those extra close ones are the friends that laugh with us and act silly (even at age 63), cry with us when our pet suddenly dies, listen to us when life doesn't work out exactly as hoped, and defend us when others unjustly accuse us. But friends can also lead us down pathways of sin with their negative influences. As we will see, the friends we have play a major role in how we develop into Godly Men.

Growing up, I was blessed with a next-door neighbor my age with whom I quickly became best friends. I also had four brothers, most of whom were quite close in age to me. We did a lot together, including getting into trouble. Perhaps because my mom and dad were praying Christians, the trouble that seemed to follow us was never beyond God's deliverance, as this next story reveals.

My neighbor Gregg and I once found ourselves in an argument with one of the local bullies who loved to pick on us younger small fry. Even though there were two of us, he was twice our size and twice as mean. He made King Kong look nice. On occasion we half expected him to start swatting airplanes out of the sky. He had trapped us, and we couldn't outrun him. If we retreated in opposite directions, he would certainly pound at least one of us, and I wasn't very willing to find out which one.

Apparently, one of my brothers had seen what was developing and had gone to get my oldest brother, Ken. In the distance I saw Ken running toward us with a great sense of urgency. At this point, Gregg and I stopped looking for escape routes and started talking smack. We felt invincible. The punch line came when we told him we simply were not going to tolerate his bullying anymore, and he shot back the over-used, in-your-face retort: "Oh yeah? You and what army?"

At this, we encouraged him to turn around and see for himself. Not since then have I seen someone with more horror mixed with heart-stopping surprise in their face (except *maybe* the time we knocked down the biggest beehive I've ever seen from a tree limb, only to find out three quick facts: we were *much* closer than we'd realized, bees *hate* kids with rocks in their hands, and *really* angry bees fly a whole lot faster than I can run). Our bully wasted no time in becoming scarce and none too soon. He managed to elude my brother's outstretched arm and live to see another day. Our laughter and jeers, I am sure, helped him find his way home. In the midst of all this, Ken turned to us tikes and unexpectedly scolded us for "talking big" and stirring up our assailant's anger. He explained he may not be there the next time, and we should watch more carefully what we say. But our reality check was soon interrupted with more laughter, and this time Ken joined us.

As brothers and friends growing up together, we always had each other's back for better or for worse. There was a devotion that ran deep among us. Today, I experience that same devotion with my close friends. We are foxhole brothers, willing to take a bullet for the other or give the shirt off our back. Granted, I've outgrown the name-calling and "tough talk," but my brothers in Christ stand by my side—no matter what! Godly Men have close friends who share life with them, who spur them on in their faith, and who support them in their struggles. God created us with this desire, this need. So, what do friendships as this look like? How are they formed? Because in this world, we will face plenty of "bullies" that don't always have faces, and we will desperately need that God-sent friend *"who sticks closer than a brother"* (Proverbs 18:24).

DIG IN!

Study Section 1

Write down what a friendship is. Give this some thought. No short answers here.

READ Ecclesiastes 4:9-12.
What are some benefits of friendships?

Think of a time in which you felt lonely. Now, select some reasons you may have felt this way.

A. I bathe once a month whether I need it or not (rumor has it, this apparently is a put off for some people).
B. I break out into spontaneous singing regardless of the situation. Class time can be a little awkward.
C. I have a gift of being incredibly creative in annoying people. It's a blessing… and a curse!
D. Photobombing is my self-appointed fulltime job.
E. I get a lot of hate email. Some of it is even from other people.
F. I tend to isolate myself from my friends when I am hurting.
G. I tend to be moody and critical.
H. I am sarcastic and cut up on others excessively.
I. I do not initiate in making friends.

Who is the "third strand" probably referring to?

List some other ways that two are better than one.

READ Proverbs 17:17.
"A brother is born for adversity" means…

    A. Brothers are born to give us problems—and lots of them!
    B. Brothers are born for ***us*** to give ***them*** problems—and lots of them!
    C. Brothers are born to help us in times of trouble.

What is the significance of *"a friend loves at all times"*?

Give some examples of when we need a friend to love us (the first one is done for you).

- When we blow it and need someone to talk to and just listen to us.
-
-

READ Proverbs 18:24.
Though the love of a brother can be compassionate, the essence here is that it is duty-bound. For example, I help my younger brother out because it's the right thing to do. With this in mind, how might a friend be closer than a brother?

READ Romans 12:10.
The Greek word translated here *"be devoted"* literally means "have family love," so it refers to a close-knit love that we should see in God's family. Circle some legitimate reasons for ***not*** being *"devoted to one another in brotherly love."*

    A. The person dunked a basketball over me and embarrassed me.
    B. The person ratted on me, telling my parents I had tried to flush our cat down the toilet.

C. The person regularly does better than me on history tests.
D. The person has offended me more than seventy times seven.
E. The person does **all** of the above.
F. **Every** reason is a good reason.
G. There is **never** a good reason.

READ I Samuel 23:15-18.
King Saul has been hunting down David, thinking he is conspiring against him. David is innocent and fleeing for his life. This unjust persecution is seriously discouraging him, so Jonathan secretly visits him. What does Jonathan do?

Describe the character needed by Jonathan as the crown prince to tell David that he will be content to be second in command behind him.

READ Proverbs 27:5-6.
Give an example of *"love that is concealed."*

Give an example of *"open rebuke."*

How might an *"open rebuke"* be better than *"love that is concealed"*?

How might a friend *"wound"* us?

How do you respond when a close friend tries to help you by correcting you? (Circle at least one)

    A. I give a "your face" reply, as in, "Your face needs to stop being sarcastic!"
    B. My face *looks* sarcastic.
    C. My negative response makes *his* face look sarcastic.
    D. No one's face looks sarcastic, I just deck him—and loose face!
    E. I face the music and say, "I'm sorry!"—usually on Facebook.
    F. Other:

____

____

____

(and *please* don't use the word "face"!)

Close friends should be able to be honest with us—preferably face-to-face (okay, I promise I won't use that word again!). We need them to speak the truth in a loving way to us. If love seeks to have another person's best interests at heart, then this will include challenges from time to time.

So, in review, we have seen the importance of close friendships, supporting us during difficult times but also correcting us when we need it. Loyalty will be key here. Selflessness will be necessary. Friends help, encourage, and protect each other no matter the cost.

Study Section 2

READ Proverbs 19:22.

The word translated in the NASB "his kindness" and in the NIV (1978) "unfailing love" is the Hebrew word "hesed" and is similar to the Greek word "agape" (meaning "sacrificial love") in the New Testament. It means "covenantal love" and here is best understood as "loyalty" (see how it is compared with "faithfulness" in Proverbs 20:6). This being the case, why is it contrasted with being a liar in this verse?

Give some synonyms for "loyalty".

-
-
-

Why do you personally desire loyalty from your friends?

Give an example of a time a friend was loyal to you.

READ II Timothy 4:16.
Who demonstrated their loyalty to Paul as a friend when he faced trial the *first* time?

READ II Timothy 4:9-11.
Who *did* eventually come and be with Paul in his darkest hour (this was probably Paul's last imprisonment before his beheading)?

Find out who wrote *Acts*, which records much of Paul's missionary journeys, and write his name here: _______________. He was able to record Paul's travels so accurately, because he had spent so much time with him. They were close friends.

Do you have a friend that would stick by you in your most difficult time? If so, put his name here: _______________________.

READ Proverbs 16:28.
Have you ever gossiped before? (Don't say "yes" unless you can think of a time)

How can gossiping separate friendships?

What do you want in a friendship?

-
-
-
-
-

CAUTION: Not all friendships are good. Some can pull us down.

READ I Corinthians 15:33, Proverbs 22:24-25, and Proverbs 13:20. Summarize these verses.

Why shouldn't you be close friends with people who have bad tempers, talk crudely, or attack Christianity?

READ Matthew 7:12 and Romans 15:7.
In view of this verse, how might you be a good friend?

As we have seen, loyal friends stay with us no matter what. Among other things, however, gossip can bring division that we **_must_** avoid. We should be careful of character issues in others that could negatively impact us. But this door swings both ways. We should seek to positively impact others, too.

THINK ABOUT IT!

When I was about seven years old, my family went on a cross-country vacation that years later gave me some insights into friendships. Since my dad was a high school English teacher, he could take the summers off if he wanted to. That summer, for almost two months, we traveled to 27 states, visiting Yosemite National Park with Old Faithful, the Rocky Mountains with snowball fights in the summer, Yellowstone National Park, and the Grand Canyon to name a few. It was when we drove through the Redwood National Forest, however, that I observed firsthand something I'd never seen before: trees so huge you could drive right through them! These massive trees had manmade tunnels for cars bored straight through them. They shot several hundred feet up into the air, some as much as 350 feet. As a kid, I was completely taken by their enormous size, some weighing in at an excess of 500 tons.

Years later, I learned an intriguing fact about Redwoods: these mammoth trees are not supported by the usual root structure of most trees. Redwoods have no tap root, and their roots, only a few inches in diameter, go no deeper than 6-12 feet. What supports these trees, considered the largest in the world, when a storm of hurricane strength might hit them? Their stability is not found in how deep their roots go, but *in how wide they spread*, some 80 to 100 feet from the trunk. Additionally, we find these hulking trees close enough together so their roots intertwine with one another. To pull one Redwood down would mean pulling down a whole system of them.

Just like these Redwoods, God has called His Church to be so intertwined relationally that each believer has a vast support system that keeps them from falling. But a major problem in most American churches is that its people are very private, self-sufficient, and tend to avoid close relationships. Pastors close themselves off from the people and the people close themselves off from one another. Growing up, my family was close to only one other church family. And my dad was the worship director.

Truthfully, families can have problems they don't want anyone else to know about. Consequently, we have learned a very anemic way of living as Jesus' Church while the problems never truly get dealt with. Relationally, we are disconnected.

Now, maybe your family is different, and your church is different. Be grateful for that. But most are not. So, how do we build friendships that are biblical, stable, and provide the kind of support we all need—including pastors? Let me lay out for you ten different principles to help you build closer friendships.

1. Foxhole Brothers

I have heard it said that Jesus' Church is the only army that shoots its wounded. It is very true that we are collectively an army engaged in a very serious battle in which men's and women's lives are at stake. Our problem is that our faulty love, which is at the heart of friendships, causes us to treat one another caustically, critically, and carelessly. On the other hand, a foxhole brother is one who defends us from the enemy. The protection is mutual. We are comrades on the same side fighting the same enemy. Just as described in the beginning of this chapter, we are loyal to one another and defend each other—no matter what!

In the movie "Fireproof," the captain (Kirk Cameron) verbally chastises a "hose-stretcher" for leaving his partner during a fire. The scene is used to build the marriage theme of "never leave your partner behind." This principle is true also of foxhole brothers. We are *always* there for each other, because we *always* need each other. As in battling a fire, sometimes our lives are at stake.

We see this call to devotion in Romans 12:10, where these foxhole relationships are depicted as "family" ties. Like my brothers and I, we are always to be there for each other. Our church family is very close, too. We pray regularly for each other. We help one another when we move. We help financially when things get tight. We visit one another in the hospital (this is not just a pastor's job). An hour and a half after our weekend celebration service ends, we have to start kicking people out of the church building, because they love spending time with each other. Our singles are like big brothers and sisters to our teens, and in view of their godly character are highly sought after by parents in the discipling process. We are family. We are foxhole brothers (and sisters). We have each other's back, so we can face the fierce attacks of our enemy. As Godly Men, united we stand; there is no divided!

2. Wanted: A Godly Influence

Nature never ceases to amaze me. God has created some animals with very unique capabilities. The chameleon is able to change its color to blend in with its surroundings, utilizing a lattice of nanocrystals to accomplish this. Stretching their spacing causes different wave lengths of light to be reflected, thus changing the chameleon's color. It becomes just like its environment.

In many ways, we can tend to do the same. We become just like those around us. Word to the wise: Choose your friends carefully! Many times, we place too much confidence in ourselves. We truly believe that by befriending ungodly people and hanging out with them as Besties we will help make them godly. Rarely is this the case. Usually, the reverse is true.

At this point, some may take theological issue with this. Jesus was a friend of sinners. Consequently, in following His example, we ought to befriend the lost, so we might reach them. I absolutely agree, but how are you suggesting we do this? Jesus spent time with sinners with the express purpose of ministering to them. In I Corinthians 5, Paul says we *will* associate with those of the world but suggests (okay, commands) that we come out from among the ungodly and be separate from them in II Corinthians 6. Wisdom must be exercised as we befriend the lost to reach them. Most lack this ability to discern their spiritual strength. Many young people have allowed themselves to be blinded to their ungodly friends' negative influence on them. "Reaching out" tends more to be a rationalization for an unwise friendship.

Bottom line, God desires that we be thermostats rather than thermometers in *all* of our associations with unbelievers or immature Christians. A thermometer is quickly influenced by the atmosphere around it. It changes according to its surroundings much like a chameleon. A thermostat, however, directly affects its environment. It influences it to the degree it needs to (literally). When you are part of a group, are you the thermometer or the thermostat? If you tend to be the former, you need to exercise greater caution when reaching out to the world.

To illustrate this to an audience, I stand on the edge of a stage and ask for a volunteer, who represents the ungodly friend (I do apologize to them later) and tries to pull me down while I try to pull them up. Who wins this tug-of-war? Who has the greater advantage to influence whom? Though I tower 3-4 feet above the volunteer, I am at a greater disadvantage due to my need to bend over so far to take hold of the other person's hand. I always lose. And between you and me, I lose even if the volunteer is a girl! I hope the point is clear: though your heart may be good, the ungodly friend will tend to pull you down. Remember Scripture's caution: *"Bad company corrupts good morals"* (I Corinthians 15:33). In view of this, always be very selective of your friends.

This principle works both ways, however. Your negative influence will impact others, too. So, allow me to extend a sincere challenge to you if this is the case: be the type of godly influence your friends need from you. Do this for their sake if not yours. Cautious, caring parents will soon size up the relationship and sever the friendship to protect their son. So, be determined to pursue Christ and not the world. Jesus is that one friend that will **always** impact you for the good.

3. Friends Forever!

John came to our church and fell in love with everything about it. He was a local college professor, married with children. He truly wanted the best for his family. As I do with everyone drawn to our fellowship, I privately ask a few questions about their previous church experience. John explained they had been members of a nearby congregation for several years and had become close to its people, including the pastor. Unfortunately, John and his wife took up an offense with their pastor and in their hurt decided to move on. With love and tact, I encouraged them to go back to their pastor and make things right. This they did, and I never saw them again. A phone call three weeks later revealed the answer. In speaking with their pastor, they realized they had misunderstood the situation and harbored an offense. They walked through forgiveness, and their friendship was restored.

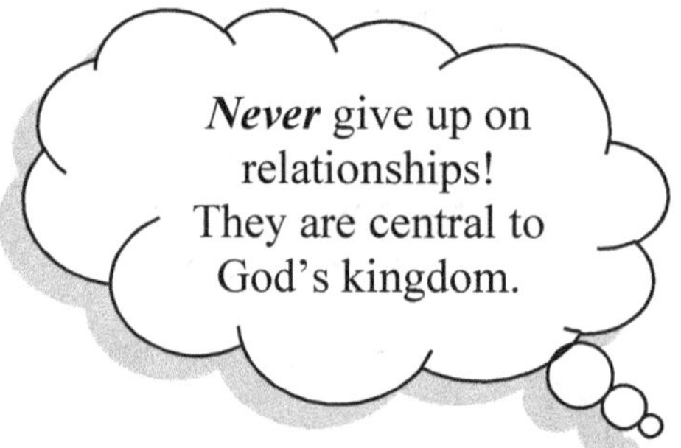

I will have to admit, we have lost a number of potential members because of this policy. But I'm okay with that. I am not in the business of "sheep stealing" but of restoration. This is a clear kingdom principle: if someone offends you, go to them privately and make it right (Matthew 18:15). Forgive or ask for forgiveness. Most Christians, however, would rather leave their church than follow this challenge, because it is hard. The result is a divided, weak church, filled with people who can't forgive or even extend the effort to find out what *really* happened. They assume their take on things is right and their actions are justified. Jesus said, "Go to them," but we turn and run to escape from them. Avoidance instead of restoration has become our default objective. We've moved on so many times, few remain close to us. We are discontented and disconnected.

In our Foundations Class for those new to our church, I tell people up front that I will offend them at some time. It is not my intention, but it will happen. I urge them to allow me the opportunity to ask for forgiveness. I conclude the session with this challenge: *Never* give up on relationships! They are central to God's kingdom, so *always* walk through conflict seeking restoration. Do this humbly. Do it in love. Giving up is *never* an option. Do you have an open-ended conflict in one of your friendships? Go to them. Seek reconciliation. Do all you can do. If they refuse to be reconciled, let that be on them and not you; *"forgiving each other, just as God in Christ also has forgiven you"* (Ephesians 4:32). Make it your goal. Be friends forever!

4. Focus on Them

I was a squirrelly kid. Not much to admire and lots to be embarrassed about. One such embarrassing confession is that when a new friend would come to my house, I felt obligated they get to know me. To do this, I marched them over to our family trophy case and showed them the ones that were mine, usually with a little self-aggrandizing story. Can you spell i-n-a-d-e-q-u-a-c-i-e-s? I was relationally challenged. Building friendships was all about me. I am so grateful that by the power of the cross we can be changed—rescued, really. And how I needed it!

Relationships done Christ's way seek to put others first. Paul says *"with humility of mind regard one another as more important than yourselves"* (Philippians 2:3). We are to give more consideration to others than to ourselves. Our goal should be to put them first. Consider others' needs as more important than your own. In verse 4, he continues: *"do not merely look out for your own personal interests, but also for the interests of others."* Find out the interests of others. To do this, I've learned to be a questions-asker and an active listener. This means asking questions about what the person is saying. This shows engagement in the conversation and interest in learning more about them. Make this your goal.

My wife, Meredith, has written a book entitled *Friends to the End*, in which she lists numerous questions you can ask to get to know someone better. The following are some of them:

- What are your favorite movies or books and why?
- How long have you been a Christian? What led up to your conversion?
- What was (is) your family like growing up?
- What person has influenced you the most and how?
- What are your dreams and goals for the future?
- What is the most significant thing you have accomplished in your life?
- What is your favorite passage of Scripture and why?
- What is the Lord teaching you in your Quiet Times?

Remember, make *them* your focus!

5. Friends Sacrifice For Each Other

As a sophomore in high school, I picked up the guitar and began practicing. I enjoyed playing it as well as singing. Two years later, I began shopping around for a new guitar. At the same time, however, I was saving money for college. This created a dilemma. So, after several months, I was still unsure about buying a guitar. A very close friend, Bob, realized this and came over to my house with one of his several guitars. I pulled out my extremely cheap, little guitar to play with him. He apologized that he didn't have time to play and that that wasn't why he had come over. He extended the guitar to me and said, "I want you to have this!" This was no ordinary guitar. It was probably his finest one, a 12-string Takamine made by Martin. It was beautiful. I was speechless.

Some 35 years later, I still have this guitar, and it still sounds amazing. This friend of mine was willing to sacrifice his best for me, because this is what friends do. Jesus said to His disciples: *"Greater love has no one than this that one lay down his life for his friends"* (John 15:13). Jesus' death on the cross for us was the ultimate sacrifice. He gave His very best. And to what end? That we might become His friend. Friendship is not weighed on the worldly scales of acquisition. It does not ask, "What's in it for me? What am I getting from this?" Instead, it chooses not to turn self-ward. It does not seek its own. It turns outward, seeking the benefit of others. Friends, like Bob, find it *"more blessed to give than to receive"* (Acts 20:35).

This also means that we seek to excel in perceiving others' needs. Sometimes our own needs blind us to the needs of others. Honestly, my wife mentors me in this area. One day before boarding our plane, I stopped by a small store and purchased some Mentos to chew on. It helps to equalize the pressure on the inner ear during take-off. When I sat down, I asked my wife if she would like one. She graciously declined and pulled out several packs of gum and offered a pack to each of our children. The thought of meeting my wife's need only occurred to me as I was pulling a Mento out for myself. I offered her one to be gracious. My wife, however, thought of *all* of our needs when making her purchase. She constantly considers the needs of others. Maybe this is the reason she has so many friends.

6. Apparently Transparent

Guys seem to have an innate fear of appearing weak. Consequently, it's easy for us to wear facades and come across better or stronger than we really are. The root issue here is our inadequacies. We feel others are more adequate or better at something than we are. This causes us to compete, perhaps unknowingly, with other guys. We feel a strong need to appear better than we are for fear that others may find out our weaknesses. And if you're anything like me, there are plenty of them. So, we try to hide them. Friends, however, are willing to bear their weaknesses. They are transparent.

Us guys can spend some "friendship" time together and walk away knowing the detailed reasons why the Heat lost to the Spurs in the 2014 NBA Championship; who has the best chances of winning the next Super Bowl; what companies are a sure bet on the stock market and why; and what tomorrow's weather report is, which of course will determine when we will cut the lawn, trim the bushes, and watch the football game. Yet,

we fail to know that our guy "friend" just received word that his father passed away, that his wife is pregnant with child number four, and that he recently received an artificial arm implant. However, we knew *something* was different when we shook his hand this time!

Am I far off? We can lack transparency, guarding our emotions, because we are fearful of sharing what we believe will be perceived as a weakness. About the only emotion we express is our outrage with a ref's bad calls or our parents' "bad" decisions. We need to stop concerning ourselves with how others may perceive us when we share our struggles, our sins, our disappointments, and our hurts. James 5:16 says, *"Confess your sins to one other."* We would be amazed at how others will open up after we become transparent about *our* sins or weaknesses. They will do it because they perceive it to be safe. So, let's be humble and transparent. Build trust with one another. This is the essence of real friendship.

7. Share Life Together

As I've said, our church family is very close. We are always in each other's homes. Birthday parties are turned into church-wide events. Beach excursions are planned small, but half the church ends up getting invited. We build sandcastles together (okay, us dads built them separately, and it turned into a competition). A pass-the-mic time during a weekend celebration service for Mothers' or Fathers' Day turns into a tear-jerking testimonial session. We laugh together, cry together, pray together, play together, eat together, fast together. We're close. We share life together. We're friends!

The Bible paints a very clear picture of what the Church is supposed to look like, and friendships are at the center of it. Should you read through Acts 2:42-47, you can't help but notice how close everyone was. Words like *"continually devoting," "everyone," "sharing," "all those who had believed," "all things in common," "as anyone might have need," "together,"* and *"house to house"* speak of a vibrant, close community of believers. They shared life together. They were friends.

The biblical injunction to "practice hospitality" is not only a qualification for elders (Titus 1:8) but a general admonition given to all (Romans 12:13). This makes it clear that God wants His people to use their homes as a place for building close friendships and doing ministry. It is crucial. Every household will do this a little differently. It is not uncommon for me to come downstairs on a

Saturday morning to find that one or more young men or young ladies have spent the night and are either sleeping on our family room floor or having their Quiet Time. We are particular about who spends the night, but our children (ages 16-25 at the time of the first edition of this book) love having friends over and ministering to them. They end up doing everything with us for the day. And, yes, that includes chores. They share life with us, because we are friends.

8. Be a Life-Giver

"A soothing tongue is a tree of life" (Proverbs 15:4a).

"Death and life are in the power of the tongue, and those who love it will eat its fruit" (Proverbs 18:21).

I have heard it said that we should give words of praise and encouragement ten times more than words of correction or rebuke. Bosses in the workplace who practice this principle have employees that thrive under their leadership. Charles Schwab once said: "I have yet to find the man, however great or exalted his station, who did not do better work and put forth greater effort under a spirit of approval than he would ever do under a spirit of criticism." And he also said: "I consider my ability to arouse enthusiasm among the men the greatest asset I possess, and the way to develop the best that is in a man is by appreciation and encouragement" (Dale Carnegie, **How to Win Friends and Influence People**, pp. 36-37). I think Charles Schwab got it right: heavy on the praise and appreciation and light on the criticism.

When we praise and encourage people, we breathe life into them. If they are discouraged, our words of hope inspire them. Have you ever been so down you wanted to give up? Shortly after I had given my life to Christ at 14, I began to experience knee problems. Being a wrestler and distance runner at the time, this was bad news. As I shared earlier, in a wrestling tournament, I broke cartilage in my right knee. This was followed by four months on crutches with a set of bewildered doctors experimenting on my knee.

After surgery, rehabilitation was very slow and discouraging. My life of sports began ebbing away. Dreams died. My heart sank. At one low point, I asked my mom why God was allowing all this to happen. The words she shared with me were uplifting and faith-infusing, and the Scripture she read to me soon became my life verse: *"And we know that God causes all things to work together for good to those who love God"* (Romans 8:28). Within the next few years, God began showing me why He had allowed this. My life-driven focus on sports needed an extreme change. God was calling me to be a pastor. He needed to remove some rotted wood in my life in order to build a surer foundation for what He was calling me to. That word of encouragement from my mother spoke life into my soul and healing to my heart. God is good that way.

In your conversations with your friends, always focus on building them up with words of praise and appreciation, of hope and encouragement. Be an agent of God's grace. Speak words that empower. Be a life-giver!

9. Speak the Truth in Love

Let me say again that praise is extremely important, and correction should take more of a backseat. However, Proverbs does say, *"Better is open rebuke than love that is concealed"* (27:5) and *"faithful are the wounds of a friend"* (27:6). There is a place for correction. As much as we should praise and honor our friends, there comes a time in which we need to *"wound."* When I was a teenager and had knee surgery, the doctor made a two-inch long incision in order to remove the broken cartilage. That wound was neces-sary to accomplish a much-needed goal. As wounds do, it healed, and I was able to walk and run again a few weeks later. So, how do we bring needed correction to our friends in a way that heals and helps?

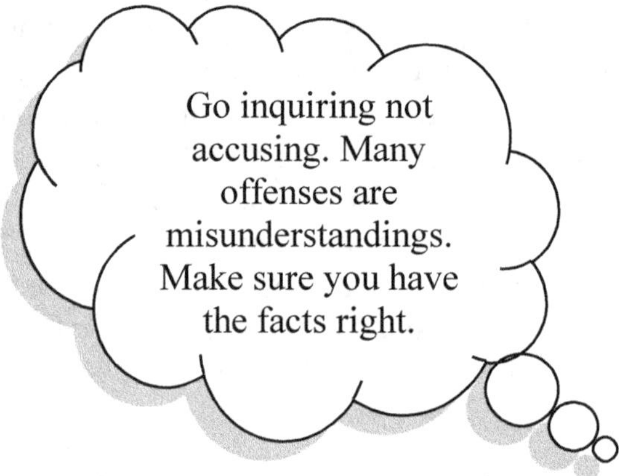

First, check your heart. What's the real motivation(s) for correcting your friend? Are you hurt or angry with him? You may be rebuking him to get back at him. This is revenge. Check that attitude at the door! Your sole goal is to **help him**. You must be completely honest with yourself here. Get rid of any anger. Do not let hurt motivate you. If your genuine desire is to help your friend deal with an issue in his life, it will determine the words you use and the attitude you express when you correct him.

Second, speak the truth in love (Ephesians 4:15). Choose your words carefully. Don't use sarcasm, a tell-tale sign you are angry with him. Don't exaggerate; he will think you are blowing the whole thing out of proportion. If you can begin with something positive, such as something you appreciate about him, this will make it a little easier for him to hear the correction. As it's been said, "Just a spoonful of sugar helps the medicine go down."

Third, go inquiring not accusing. Many offenses are misunderstandings. This is common in friendships. Make sure you have the facts right. Ask him. Allow him to explain what he meant, if he said something that hurt you.

And lastly, allow him to own his mistakes (or sins) and apologize. Follow this up with an affirmation of your love and friendship. Pray together if you can. Again, remember this is all to help him not to "get it off your chest" or vent. If the problem is relational breakdown, seek to restore it.

My close friend, Mike, was struggling in his relationships with other people. I regularly sought to encourage him, but several times I needed to pull him aside and bring loving correction. At first, he would be defensive, but in time he stopped "kicking dust up in the air." He always thanked me and expressed appreciation for taking the risk of correcting him. He knew I had his best interests at heart. He knew I loved him. And why not, we are friends.

Another good friend of mine, Steven, is an up-and-coming leader in our church. On occasion I have had to graciously speak into his life. He has ***always*** responded gratefully: "Thank you for saying what you did. I needed that. Thank you for caring enough to help me rather than punish me with words or say nothing at all. I just didn't grow up with this. Thank you!" Even the "wounds" of a friend can heal, bring redirection, and give hope.

10. Get Rid of Offensive Behavior
Perhaps a little story can help illustrate this last principle for us.

The overbearing dictator of a very small country came to realize that his people were not purchasing the new stamps with his portrait. Upset by this, he visited his postmaster, who explained that the stamps tended to not stick.

"This is ridiculous," said the outraged dictator. "Watch this!" He then grabbed a stamp, licked it, and stuck it to an envelope. "See?" he said. "It sticks fine!"

After a few moments, the postmaster shook his head and replied, "No wonder! They've been spitting on the wrong side!"

Truth be told, much like this dictator, we sometimes acquire behaviors that are offensive to people: pride, defensiveness, argumentativeness, criticalness, or selfishness—just to name a few. Granted, most people are too gracious to spit in our face, but that doesn't mean we don't deserve it sometimes! Because we love people, we should humble ourselves and cry out to God to change us.

On several occasions, someone has needed to point something out in my life that I had never seen before. This type of issue is called a "blind spot." Even when pointed out by others, these issues tend to be difficult for us to change and to assess personal growth. You will need to trust others' input here. At times, I have asked close friends, my wife, or my older children to be candid with me and speak into my life, showing me any offensive areas or how I communicated in certain situations. When several people were seeing the same thing, I began to get a clue. It has provided breakthrough numerous times. So, swallow any pride. Be humble and teachable. That is the recipe for transformation.

"Abhor what is evil; cling to what is good" (Romans 12:10). If you make this your ambition, you will become the type of person people love to spend time with. Don't allow your actions or words to repel people. If you truly love others, you endeavor to cling to the good and allow Christ to live through you. Your friends will be grateful you do!

Because love never fails (I Corinthians 13:8), friendships should endure every rough road. We never give up on each other. Whether the fault lies with us or our friends, we make things right. This honors Christ. We are not faultfinding but fault-forgiving. We are humble and willing to share our weaknesses, as well as own our mistakes and sins, and apologize as needed. We defend and sacrifice for each other. We are more interested in them than ourselves. We avoid negative influences and always seek to have a positive impact on those close to us. We do all of this because this is the stuff of friendships. Satan's goal is division, but Christ's goal is unity. So, be prepared to fight for your friendships. This is a battlefield where the enemy *must* be defeated, because this is the very heart of the kingdom of Christ. And Godly Men fight for the heart of God!

BRING IT HOME!

Describe what you do with your friends. List as many activities as you can.

Tell of a time you encouraged a friend in the Lord like Jonathan did for David (see I Samuel 23:15-18).

Has a friend recently corrected or challenged you?

On what issue?

How did you respond?

How are you changing?

Do you have a close friend with whom you can share your struggles and weaknesses?

If your answer to the above question is no, then write a reason for this to the best of your knowledge. Is it something you can change? (Have your mentor help you here.)

Is this close friend also a "Luke" who would stick by your side in your darkest hour? At some point this week, tell this close friend how much you appreciate him.

Let's take some time to assess how we are doing in the 10 principles of friendship.

1) Are you a foxhole brother to someone? List their name(s) here:

2) Are you a godly influence on your friends? Are you a thermometer or a thermostat? (Think through all your friendships before answering.)

3) Is there a grudge you have with a friend or that a friend has with you? If so, are you working it out? If you are not working it out, describe how you will (have your mentor give input here and hold you accountable for follow-through).

4) Do you initiate friendships or just let them happen? Write down some questions from the lesson that you will ask some of your friends this week. (Have your mentor hold you accountable on this.)

5) Give an example of a recent sacrifice you made for a friend (and letting him borrow one of your six gaming controllers can't count).

6) Apart from a family member, write down the name of someone you confide in.

7) List some activities you do to "share life together" with your friends.

8) Have you encouraged anyone this past week? What did you say? If not, think of a friend you can build up. Who is it, and what could you say? (Again, have your mentor follow up with you on this)

9) Recount the last time you had to bring correction to a friend. Was it loving? Beneficial (for them)?

10)   As you read through the lesson on offensive behavior, did the Holy Spirit show you anything you need to change? If so, write it down here and have your mentor pray with you about it.

REMEMBER: to **_have_** a friend, you must **_be_** a friend and practice these 10 principles!

Godly Men
Are Driven by a Sense of
Divine Destiny

S O, what do you want to do when you grow up?"

Has anyone ever asked you this question? If so, how did you answer them? Especially for us guys, there is an undercurrent desire to do something of significance, to make a splash in the world around us. Granted, some of this is the outward workings of some insecurities we are wrestling with, that others view us as important or even popular. But selfish ambitions aside, God has placed deep within the heart of every godly young man a yearning to be used by Him and fulfill his divine destiny. Whether we walk fully in this destiny or not depends on how we yield to God's Spirit preparing us and leading us.

Growing up, I would answer the above question by saying, "I want to be a professional baseball player and one day be in the World Series and hit that Grand Slam that wins it all for the team." Or that I'd like to be a professional football player that makes that spectacular clutch catch in the end zone in the final seconds of the Super Bowl to win it. I wanted to do something of tremendous significance, at least in my eyes at the time.

This changed, however, two years after I had given my heart to Christ at age 14. That summer I had a life-changing experience with the Spirit of God that put a fire in my heart for personal spiritual growth and evangelism. I was a junior in the public school system. God opened opportunities for me to share the gospel every day. This was exciting. I loved it. That same year I began asking this question again about what I wanted to do with my life. Since I had been playing the guitar in my spare time and singing in the school chorus, I thought I would be part of a Christian rock band and evangelize. This "vision" excited me. I thought for sure God had finally revealed to me what I was destined for. The songs I began to write, however, were the kind that only a mom would say, "Oh, that's so nice!"

As God began extracting some selfish ambition from my personal dreams for the future, I began to realize how desperately in need I was of an "extreme makeover" in this department—less of me and more of Him. The dreams of thousands in the audience gave way to more Christ-centered personal ministry, regardless of an audience.

All of us, as we pursue God and His kingdom, must go through a refining of sorts that places our focus squarely on Jesus and off ourselves. As He becomes our consuming passion, we exchange our self-centered desires and dreams for Christ-centered, kingdom-focused ones. Though you may not be called to be a pastor, you absolutely *are* called to minister. This is something to be gladly embraced. We do not shrink back from the call of Christ, but as Godly Men we step into this divinely orchestrated destiny with anticipation and faith, knowing that God truly has great things in store for all who follow Him.

DIG IN!

Study Section 1

READ Ephesians 2:1-10.
Give four descriptions of yourself before you came to Christ from this passage. (The first is done for you)

- I was dead in my sins.

-
-
-

Describe what you think it means to be *"dead in your… sins."*

According to 2:4-6, what does God do for those who believe in Christ?

-
-
-

Why?

God doesn't save us, or rescue us from our slavery to sin, just so we can go to heaven. According to 2:10, what is His purpose?

That God has a plan for us, that is, good works which He has prepared ahead of time for us to do, is an absolutely awesome concept. God must, however, do something *in* us in order for us to accomplish all of these good works. Paul uses the term "workmanship" to describe God's work in us. What does "workmanship" mean to you?

Does God have good works prepared for you to do?

What does the truth that God has prepared these good works in advance for you to do communicate to you?

What do you think some of these might be? (Think in terms of your immediate future and more distant future)

READ Jeremiah 1:4-8.
When did God call Jeremiah—first prophetically, then actually?

Why did Jeremiah emphasize that he was only a "youth"?

What was God's take on this? (See verses 7-8)

Is age ever an excuse for not doing what God wants us to do *now*?

READ Judges 6:12-16.
What objections did Gideon have with the angel's decree? List them.

Nevertheless, what did the angel say Gideon would accomplish? What good works would he walk in?

READ Exodus 3:9-12; 4:1-10, 13.
What did God call Moses to do?

What objections did Moses have (even if they are a bit exaggerated here)? Circle the best answers.

A. "I'm no one special. Why are you asking *me* to do this?"
B. "What if no one takes me seriously? After all, I *was* raised Egyptian not Hebrew."
C. "I'm not a good speaker. I failed Public Speaking 101, remember?"
D. "Can't someone else do this? I'm sure there's a gajillion people here more qualified for this job. Hire them!"
E. "I can't! I'm highly allergic to flies, frogs, gnats, the *dark*… Should I go on?"
F. All of the above.
G. None of the above—especially on Tuesdays.
H. A, B, C, and D (well, kind of) but definitely *not* E.
I. A, B, C, D, E, F, G, and H but not I.

Now **READ** Acts 7:22.
What is Stephen's assessment (inspired by the Holy Spirit) of Moses?

Then why do you think Moses felt the way he did about himself in Exodus 3 and 4?

READ Acts 7:23-30.
How old was Moses when he killed the Egyptian and fled into the Midianite desert?

How old was Moses when he stood before the burning bush and was called to deliver the Israelites out of Egypt?

Contrast Moses' attitude toward himself at these two times. Why the difference?

How did God use Moses' new occupation in the Midianite desert to prepare him for leading Israel in the desert for 40 years? (For a hint, read Genesis 46:34, Exodus 3:1, and Numbers 12:3.)

READ I Samuel 13:13-14 (Samuel is speaking to King Saul) and 16:1, 6-13. What was the most important thing to the Lord in choosing a King?

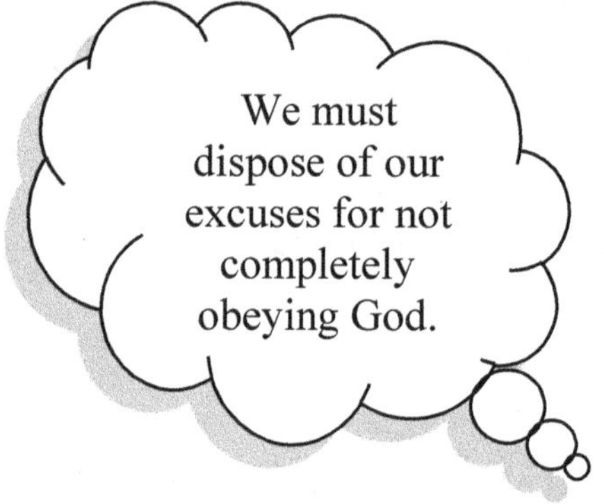

Contrast the character of King Saul and David.

During the sacrifice and feast, where was David?

The greatest prophet and greatest king of the Old Testament were both shepherds before fulfilling their calling. Why? (Circle one.)

    A. Shepherding was where the big bucks were.
    B. They just loved that fresh morning aroma of musty, wet wool.
    C. God loves practical jokes.
    D. It built plenty of needed character for future leadership.

List some potential types of character you think shepherding could build into someone.

We have seen that God had good works for Jeremiah, Gideon, Moses, and David to walk in. Because of their sin nature, however, they each needed character development. This took time. It will for each of us, as well. We must dispose of our excuses for not completely obeying God and move forward with *His* agenda in *His* timeframe, if we are to do this and walk in our divine destiny.

Study Section 2

READ Genesis 50:20.
Joseph, as second in command in Egypt next to Pharaoh, is speaking to his brothers. Can you recall some of the things his brothers did to him to try to harm him? If not, look it up (Genesis 37) and list them here.

Can you remember any other "bad things" that happened to Joseph?

How did God turn these things around to serve His purposes?

Can you remember any "bad things" that happened in David's life? List some here.

How do you think God used them for David?

READ Romans 8:28.
What does this verse say about how God watches out for you?

READ Jeremiah 29:11.
The context of this verse is God's discipline of the kingdom of Judah with 70 years of exile in Babylon. Jeremiah is in Israel and has sent a letter to those exiles. Describe God's plans for these people.

Are God's plans for you good?

Now, pause for a moment and think about your last answer. Do you really believe this? If so, why?

Circle any of the following attitudes, if any, you have had recently.

A. I got angry with God about how something didn't work out the way I had hoped and prayed.
B. I've gotten jealous about some other guys being more popular, better looking, stronger, smarter, funnier, or even godlier than me.
C. I am disappointed in general.
D. I feel depressed about how my life is going right now.
E. If I were God, I would change some of the circumstances in my life.
F. I feel God is distant from me.

Honesty with your feelings is important. ***They do not, however, always accurately reflect the truth.*** If you have struggled with any of the above attitudes or some similar to them, perhaps they are indicating a measure of hurt that you have towards God. Remember, He is in your corner and has your best interests at heart, regardless of what your emotions may tell you at times. ***Choose to embrace the truth!***

READ II Timothy 2:20-21.
List some *"vessels"* of honorable purposes in a person's life. (The first is done for you.)

- A strong desire to evangelize.
-
-
-

List some *"vessels"* of dishonorable purposes in a person's life. (The first is done for you)

- Holding a grudge against someone.
-
-
-

How do we become holy and useful to the Master?

This has been a longer study than most of the others, so let's conclude with this last verse.

READ Deuteronomy 7:17-24.
Israel's divine destiny was to inherit the Promised Land, the land of Canaan. How hard was this going to be?

Why wasn't God going to allow them to conquer the land all at once?

Who was going to drive out these nations (vs. 22)?

Would Israel need to fight?

Apply these verses to walking in God's plans for you. How will this be accomplished?

In conclusion, we can say that God used the difficulties in Joseph's life to prepare him for his God-given destiny. So then, were these struggles "bad" or "good"? Joseph determined to have the vantage point of God and saw His hand in them. What could have been seen as "bad" and thwarting the plans of God, were really "good," advancing God's sovereign purposes. This is God's promise to all of us who follow Jesus fully. But we *must* allow God to do some "house cleaning" in us to prepare us. And as we yield to His will, He will many times lead us gradually, step by step into this calling. So, we *must* be patient in this process.

THINK ABOUT IT!

As a boy, I loved my summers, especially if they included finding buried "treasure." My grandparents' cottage in Primehook Beach held many activities to keep us kids entertained during summer family vacations: creating pathways and forts in the marsh reeds, packing our mouths with an unending supply of large red raspberries, sand shark fishing, frog gigging in the marsh, catching small sand eels at low tide on the sandbar, walking on the beach to collect seashells, and occasional treasure hunting. One such hunt turned into a dig between the cottage and the beach. We thought for sure that the metal box we began to uncover was a pirate's treasure. We were excited. Further digging, however, proved us wrong—unless you consider the contents of a septic tank treasure!

A Lesson From the Original Blue Bloods
Not *all* treasures are well hidden, however—like the horseshoe crab. After our frequent swims in the Delaware Bay, we had to wash the oil off our bodies before entering the cottage per our mother's orders. Great care had to be exercised during these swims, because horseshoe crabs abounded and the last thing you wanted to do was step on one of those guy's barbed tails and track blood into the cottage. God rest your soul! These ugly crabs were everywhere you went on the beach. I think they were more prevalent than the washed-up seaweed and

beer cans that littered the shore. On occasion, my brothers and I would turn one over to see its numerous legs kick helplessly and its tail swish back and forth, trying to get itself right-side up (don't worry, it always managed to).

Little did I realize back then the amazing design and worth of these nuisance creatures. The Delaware Bay was very polluted, and with pollution comes toxins and high potential for infection. Not to worry though, these unique crabs had specialized blue blood that in the presence of E. coli bacteria, viruses or fungi would clot and isolate the contaminant to fight off infection. Their blood is now used in the drug industry to test for the presence of bacteria. A quart of this blue blood goes for $15,000. As kids, we **had** discovered a treasure but never realized it(www.IFLscience.com/plants-and-animals/how-horseshoe-crab-blood-saves-millions-lives, *How Horseshoe Crab Blood Saves Millions of Lives* by Stephen Luntz, September, 2014).

Just as God amazingly designed the horseshoe crab with valuable, specific purposes both for itself and mankind in general, so God's special design of you as His child has ultimate purposes of great worth. In fact, design implies destiny. Your Creator has deposited an incredible treasure within you and around you. He gave you a certain personality, specific gifts and talents, and peculiar (I mean, "particular") siblings, unusual parents (though I choose to see it the other way around), close friends, specialized character-forming circumstances (the list could go on) for very definite purposes. Good purposes. God's purposes!

You have been fashioned in life by God's good intentions to prepare you with a divine destiny to accomplish His awesome purposes in your generation. His purposes for you are those good works

described in Ephesians 2:10, which God prepared in advance for you to walk in. They are the "work of service" spiritual leadership is called to help train you for (Ephesians 4:12). A powerful eulogy over David's life is revealed in Acts 13:36:

"For David, after he had served the purpose of God in his own generation, fell asleep." May this be your heart's desire: that you might be found absolutely faithful in God's calling on your life and accomplish all he created in advance for you to do. Later in Acts, Paul even says that God "determined *their* appointed times and the boundaries of their habitation, that they would seek God…" (Acts 17:26-27). God had you born in the perfect place and the ideal generation for you to seek and serve Him.

A Strong Foundation

The story is told of a contractor who was asked to assess a woman's garage in order to build an addition above it. As the lady pointed to where she wanted the stairs, the contractor had his head down, seemingly disinterested in the woman's instructions. Somewhat perturbed, she pointed to the garage's ceiling about where she wanted the bathroom. At this the contractor mumbled, "I see," and continued looking down. The frustrated woman then pointed out where she wanted each window, only to have the contractor say, "Okay," and keep staring quizzically at the floor. Irate because of his aloof behavior, she said, "Maybe you don't understand! I want all of these things up ***here***," pointing to the ceiling. At this the builder replied, "No ma'am, I don't think ***you*** understand. It doesn't matter ***what*** you want up there if your foundation down ***here*** is not strong enough!"

I'm sure you get the point. If our foundation is faulty, the ministry built upon it will eventually come tumbling down. It won't be able to hold the weight of responsibility, the burden that ***any*** ministry, small or great, places upon it. This foundation is our passion, or love, for Christ, resulting from the gospel transforming us as we are rescued from the kingdom of darkness and brought into the kingdom of light. Character, tested and refined, is then built upon this foundation. This will many times mean much trial and heartache, as God is weaving into the fabric of our character a "Life Message". This is not a sermon but a testimony, an accumulation of truths and life experiences, themes of God's grace displayed in our life. It will be unique to us. From this "Life Message" will flow our calling, countless opportunities to minister from God's workmanship throughout our life as the diagram below portrays:

Ministry

Life Message

Character

Foundation of Christ

To really grasp this truth, let's see how it played out in the lives of some men of God in the Bible.

Moses' Humility

Moses was raised by Pharaoh's daughter. He was schooled in all the ways of the Egyptians, no doubt including the complex mathematical formulas needed to build the great cities and pyramids of his nation. He was well educated. At age 40 he became envisioned with a nobler plan than pursuing the duties and luxuries of a prince of Egypt. He attempted to step into the role of Israel's deliverer. He sought to become the self-appointed Savior of a nation in slavery. This ended, however, in epic failure. In his attempts to rescue a Hebrew slave from the antagonism of his Egyptian task master, Moses ended up killing the Egyptian. This really put a damper on his plans!

The next day Moses discovered that what he had done had become known. Pharaoh was angry and wanted to kill him, but Hebrews 11:27 says, *"By faith he left Egypt, not fearing the wrath of the king."* Why then did Moses flee Egypt to live in the desert of Midian for the next 40 years? It wasn't because he feared the king would kill him, though Exodus 2:14 does say he was afraid. Why? Why flee in fear? I think it's fair to say that Moses' dreams of being Israel's hero were beginning to topple. Who would want a murderer to be their deliverer? His need to flee effectively closed the door at the time on all aspirations to set his people free from Egyptian bondage either by the swift sword or the long arm of politics. He feared he had failed beyond recovery. Such are the consequences of self-filled dreams.

We must choose to embrace all that God has for us to do, but we must proceed with caution. Pride is ever so subtle. It's not hard to conclude that if I do something great for God, I will become great. This was Moses' downfall. His wounded pride caused him to flee Egypt in failure. As Proverbs 16:18 states, *"Pride goes before destruction, a haughty spirit before stumbling."* We must ask ourselves a sobering question: Am I truly wanting to do something of significance for God's kingdom or am I just wanting to be significant? Pride mixed with some noble motives can become our undoing as it was for Moses.

But all was not lost for Moses, because as you know, he ***did*** become Israel's deliverer. Observe that at age 40 ***he*** viewed himself as ready for the task and God did not, and at age 80 ***God*** viewed him as ready for the task but he did not. Also, within that first year of the Exodus (when Moses was 80) it states in Numbers 12:3 that *"the man Moses was very humble, more than any man who was on the face of the earth."* How? For 40 years on the backside of the Midianite desert, Moses learned true humility, an absolute prerequisite for the task of leading some two million Hebrews out of Egypt to the Promised Land. He worked as a shepherd, a profession that as an Egyptian he absolutely despised (see Genesis 46:34). He traded the luxuries of the Egyptian palaces for the arduous living of the desert. Everything that exalted him as a person of importance by age 40 was permanently stripped away. When God eventually called him from the burning bush, he still believed his abilities were in the tank. But then after seeing the mighty power of God displayed shortly afterward in the first few plagues, his focus shifted, and he found his significance in God's perspective rather than in his faulty view of himself.

Had Moses been allowed to deliver Israel at age 40, one can only imagine the destruction that could have resulted from his faulty foundation. For example, after Israel sinned by creating a golden calf to worship, God told Moses He was going to destroy them all and wanted to start a new nation through Moses. How this would have pacified his pride! Can you imagine his response? "Now, Lord, I think you're onto something here! Who needs these stubborn people anyway? They'll just hinder your awesome plans. But if I father a nation—now ***that's*** brilliant!" Instead, Moses defended Israel to God. He pleaded that ***his*** own name be blotted out of the Book of Life rather than theirs. Moses acted as the good shepherd that he needed to be, defending his flock. All of this, of course, God did to test Moses' heart to see what was really inside.

The same test will need to be applied to ourselves. What's in ***your*** heart? Are you allowing God to build humility into your foundation? How teachable are you? Do you get defensive easily? Do you say or do things to impress others? Is there something inside you that longs for people's recognition and praise? How offended are you when someone else gets the credit for something you did? Do you tend to be critical of others' mistakes while ignoring or downplaying your own? We need to ask ourselves these tough questions to sift our hearts and discard the refuse: *"As grain is shaken in a sieve, but not a kernel will fall to the ground"* (Amos 9:9). We do this because God is building in us a life message, character that has been tested and tempered by hardships and struggle.

David's Devotion

King David is also an excellent example of God preparing a person for future ministry. He was the youngest of eight boys—the runt of the litter, so to speak—and no doubt got stuck with the most menial of tasks, like tending the sheep while all the others got to attend Samuel's feast in Bethlehem. God had told Samuel to go to this town to anoint the future king of Israel, whom the Lord would reveal to him. Jesse, David's father, had become the host for the occasion. Since God had said "no" to the older sons, the spotlight fell on David. Called from the field where he no doubt spent much of his time cultivating a worshipper's heart, David was prophetically anointed King. Thus began a long journey of initial success followed by numerous trials, as he was accused of being a conspirator of the throne.

Those years that eventually led up to his coronation as King over Judah helped build in David his life message. The painful refining fires that burned away the dross of compromise instilled in David a purer heart after God. When no one else could rescue, God stepped in as David's Rescuer. From these times of testing, David wrote a number of psalms that reflect both his present anguish and his firm faith in God's future deliverance. When confronted with the advance of his persistent adversaries, he declared, *"How long will my enemy triumph over me?... My foes will rejoice when I fall. But I trust in your unfailing love, my heart rejoices in your salvation"* (Psalm 13:2-5). And thus, a foundation was laid that enabled David to become a King who stood as a standard of righteousness and wholehearted commitment to the Lord for subsequent Kings.

Deep devotion to Christ is necessary for each of us if we are to remain on course. Temptations can quickly seduce us otherwise, and the pain of trials can soon weary us. Compromise awaits those whose strength falters and faith fails. Life messages come at high cost and cannot be short-changed. Our devotion anchors us to Christ and enables us to sail high above life's treacherous waters, to *"run and not get tired... walk and not become weary"* (Isaiah 40:31).

Daniel's Faithfulness

Lastly, Daniel stands as the consummate prophetic politician who submitted to character formation trials and thereby rose to platforms of service and ministry from which he impacted a King and possibly an entire empire. Snatched away from an easy life of wealth and security in Israel, he was brought to Babylon as a youth, perhaps no older than yourself, and subjected to the rigors of a foreign culture, trained to be a Magi. Having lost family and fortune, he did not accuse God of an injustice but sought to make the most of this difficult opportunity to advance God's kingdom. Yes, it was an opportunity. The Lord used Him at every level of promotion throughout his 65 years of service as a statesman/prophet.

The forging of Daniel's character is not as easily seen as Moses' or David's, but at the end of his service during the first year of King Cyrus (and Darius), he was set to be promoted to a position just under the king. The other high-ranking officials grew jealous and sought to sabotage Daniel's career but couldn't. He was completely competent in his governmental duties: *"They could find no ground of accusation or evidence of corruption, inasmuch as he was faithful, and no negligence or corruption was to be found in him"* (Daniel 6:4). I'm sure that when Daniel died and stood before Jesus, he was told, "Well done, good and faithful servant" with an emphasis on "faithful"!

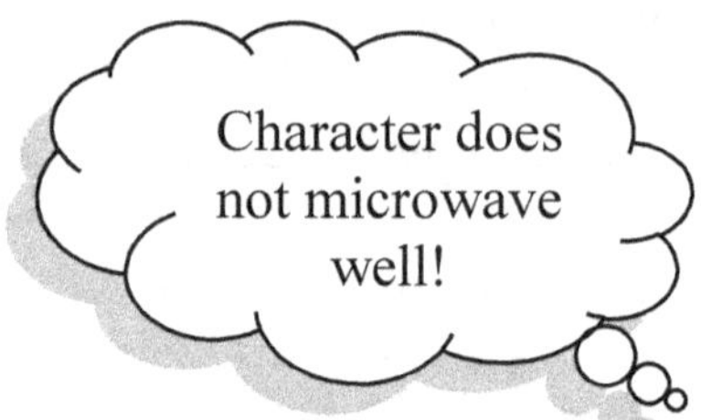

In business, faithfulness can be a deal-breaker for the employee who is overseeing a project and the entrepreneur seeking to obtain another account. Businesses want faithfulness. Though employers value how intelligent or gifted you are, if you're not faithful, you will not retain your job for long. Faithfulness is a highly esteemed character quality. If you lack it, such as in lateness for work or in completion of a job, lack of follow-through due to procrastination or forgetfulness (which can be eased by proper attention to administration, like day planners), or simply laziness, not wanting to do what you need to do, you become a liability to the company you work for.

Daniel crossed his t's and dotted his i's in all of these ways and more. He was a man whose life message so honored God and upheld truth that his boss, King Nebuchadnezzar of Babylonia, finally declared toward the end of his reign, *"I blessed the Most High and praised and honored Him who lives forever; for His dominion is an everlasting dominion, and His kingdom endures from generation to generation"* (Daniel 4:34). And King Darius the Mede later declared: *"I make a decree that in all the dominion of my kingdom men are to fear and tremble before the God of Daniel; for He is the living God and enduring forever, and His kingdom is one which will not be destroyed, and His dominion will be forever"* (Daniel 6:26). I get the feeling Daniel took his calling from God very seriously, fully trusted that the Lord would take his present, unpleasant circumstances and turn them around for good, and lived a life totally and radically sold out to God and His kingdom purposes.

Remember that cutting short one's training to jump into the fray of rescuing the galaxy or simply saving the world is the stuff of Hollywood not reality. Last I checked, Star Wars and Luke Skywalker were still in the fantasy section. No, training is crucial. Building a proper foundation is essential. There are no short cuts. Character does not microwave well! Some character-building processes can last for years—40 in Moses' case. Should we actively wait this process out and bend to our Master's will, He will faithfully form us and fashion us, ground us and grind us to sharpen us and unsheathe us so we become that holy instrument of honor, *"useful to the Master, prepared for every good work"* (II Timothy 2:21). So, let Him build in you the humility of Moses, the faith and devotion of David, and the faithfulness of Daniel—just to start. But know this, too, that with this character, God will supply you with everything needed to fulfill your divine destiny as a world-changer.

The Next Level

"Blessed be the LORD, my rock, who trains my hands for war, and my fingers for battle" (Psalm 144:1). The words of David reveal an insight that God's providential circumstances in his life were not accidental but very purposeful. They helped impart to him the necessary battle skills to become the type of King Israel needed. As God did with David, so He will do for you. Fundamentally, God must build in you a pure and sincere devotion to Him, such that you would

never forsake your First Love (Revelation 2:4). Upon this, He will establish solid, tested character that speaks a life message of God's grace to the world. Finally, He will develop in you and fine tune the necessary *disciplines, skills, spiritual gifts, knowledge, etc.* that you will need to accomplish those good works that He has prepared in advance for you to do. Remember, you are his workmanship (Ephesians 2:10).

Needed Disciplines

Although each of us are called to invest and multiply our "talents" in diverse ways and, thereby, impact this generation differently than the next person, we all must use the same method to accomplish this—truth! Truth does not simply seek to inform but to transform. It changes us. In fact, apart from God's truth there is no transformation. Apart from the gospel there is no salvation. Only God's truth sets us free. It teaches us, rebukes us, corrects us, and trains us in righteousness, *"so that the man of God may be adequate, equipped for every good work"* (II Timothy 3:16-17). This is the job of Scripture as God's breathed Word. It is not just for pastors to be equipped by it, but for *all* of us. Take it upon yourself to study it, meditate upon it, memorize it, and utilize it for your *"every good work."*

There are no exceptions to this principle. No one can fully walk in their *"work of service"* (Ephesians 4:12) apart from the equipping of God's Word. As discussed in an earlier chapter, let it percolate deep into your heart. Let it thoroughly renew your mind (Romans 12:2). Let it sharpen and shape your divine destiny in Christ. Only as you do this can you be properly trained.

So then, as you find the Word of God transforming you and equipping you, now immerse yourself in the disciplines of prayer and worship. These will set your focus on the real source of anything you will accomplish in His kingdom. As men, there is the unfortunate tendency to be self-reliant. Frequently, this means walking in our own strength and abilities. We can rightly respond quickly to opportunities to help, to minister, or to speak an appropriate word but bypass a personal heart's cry for God's strength, wisdom, or

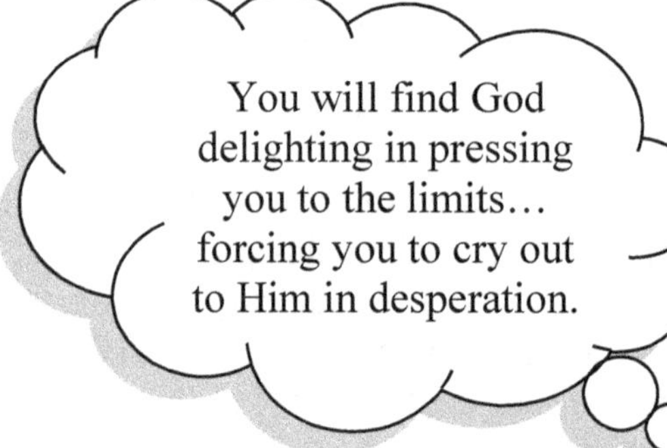

anointing. Prayer and worship are crucial. You will find no substitute. Worship humbles your heart before the Almighty Creator. Prayer ushers you before His throne of grace. And grace is the answer to releasing everything in this chapter, and even this book, into your life.

You will find God delighting in pressing you to the limits of who you are and what you can do, forcing you to cry out to Him in desperation. It is here in your place of personal weakness, in the thoughts of "I can't" and in your fears of failure, that God's power is made perfect. It is here on your knees, you will truly know God's grace that is sufficient (II Corinthians 12:9). You cannot help but be won by such a display of God's majesty, endeared by His affection for you. It humbles you and emboldens you at the same time. God's grace will teach you that though you can't, He can—through you. In prayer and worship, you will learn to embrace this paradox, to live in the tension of "I am weak but He is strong—in me and through me." Simply put, prayer and worship permit us to tap into God's amazing grace, by which we experience His divine purpose for our lives.

Skill and Gift Formation
To these spiritual disciplines you will need to allow God to add the necessary training in skills and giftings. For Moses, much of this came in his first 40 years: *"Moses was educated in all the learning of the Egyptians and he was a man of power in words and deeds"* (Acts 7:22). For David and Daniel, much of their special skill sets were acquired after their foundational character development. Either way, skill development, education, knowledge and wisdom, and growth in spiritual gifts are all necessary for you to minister effectively. And all of you, not just pastors, are called to this. You will be amazed at the different avenues God uses to do this for you.

If you are presently in school, God will use this for future ministry purposes. While taking an upper-level math course my senior year in high school, my attitude soured as I contemplated the use of math for future ministry. Since I saw no need for it, my math performance plummeted. Though today I don't use this level of math in ministry, I do use the concepts of logic that all math utilizes. Understand that God applies all He imparts to you for your future. Nothing is wasted. Your education will impact you in ways you may not see now, so don't let your attitude sour. Stay the course!

Though owning a business had never been my dream, God has had me do this for multiple reasons (not the least of which was to support my family while getting our church started). Today, I am grateful for what I have learned in working with employees and dealing with used car managers. The lessons have proven invaluable for ministry. God uses our education, work experience, and everyday circumstances to form the necessary abilities we will need to walk in the *"good works, which God prepared beforehand"* (Ephesians 2:10).

Seeing Life From God's Vantage Point

Let me conclude with a word about perspective. My second daughter, Julianna, hates sand. She hates sand between her fingers and her toes. She hates sand in her car. She hates the feel of sand on her skin. She "freaks out" if sand gets in her hair or in her clothes. I think she comes close to a nervous break at the mention of the word "sand." One problem, though—our family loves the beach. We live 45 minutes from the ocean and frequently vacation there. For Julianna, going for a walk on the beach with a friend or family member is a serious labor of love. She would prefer to view it from the safety of our condo's porch and splash in the water of the nearby pool. Truly, for her, "sand" is a four-letter word.

I am grateful that not all of God's creatures treat sand this way. The irritation of sand is not always a bad thing. For example, though sand particles are irritants for oysters, they neither avoid them nor do they merely expel them. As the grain enters the oyster's shell, it immediately begins to be coated with nacre, the same substance that lines the inside of the shell. Over time, the build-up of nacre around the sand grain becomes thick, round, and very smooth. The end result is a beautiful pearl.

In the same way, God permits difficult circumstances in our lives that can really irritate us. Typically, we avoid them, reject them, or if forced to live with them, do so very grudgingly. To illustrate, in the past I have had a love-hate relationship with my paint touch up business. I loved how it could provide for my family but hated the time needed for it that could have been "better" spent tending the church I had started. I hated the exhaustion I felt at the end of a long, humid, 95° summer day, only to lead a meeting in the evening. And God chose for us to do this in Orlando, Florida, the humidity capital of the world, for what reason again? So, the attitude went.

Eventually, I got a clue that God's perspective of this business was a lot bigger than mine. And a whole lot more positive. Over time, I began to see how the business was sharpening certain abilities and helping crucify a lot of "me" in my ministry. I began to thank him for the irritating "sand" and to pray that the "pearls" He was forming in me would somehow be precious and honoring to Him.

Realize that not all "bad things" are necessarily "bad." For this reason, James challenges you to "consider it all joy, my brethren, when you encounter various trials" (1:2). What struggles are you facing today? What enemy opposes you? What obstacle is blocking your way: Personal sin issues? Insecurities? Pride? Lack of finances? No open doors? Hurts from the past? Fears of the future? None of these should overwhelm you, because none of them are too big for God to remove or turn to your advantage. A closed door, for example, may require more effort on your part to push open, or it is God's way of redirecting you. Is God building muscle or spiritual discernment in you?

Remember: *"And we know that God causes all things to work together for good to those who love God, to those who are called according to His purpose"* (Romans 8:28).

God has good works prepared for you to do. To accomplish this, He must mold you and shape you by a variety of circumstances, so that as you learn to walk through them, applying biblical principles, you are capable of doing all He has called you to do. You are His workmanship. This is a process—sometimes long and hard. Welcome His hammer and chisel as he sculpts His work. Maintain a right perspective. You may be tempted to give up, to compromise, or to take short cuts. Don't! You may feel too weary or discouraged by failure at times. But you were destined for such a time as this. Trust God to see you through. *"Will the clay say to the potter, 'What are you doing?'"* (Isaiah 45:9). Stay the course!

Are You Up to the Challenge?

The world is in desperate need of rescuing. God is enlisting all who will entrust themselves fully to Him as He "trains their hands for war," as He equips them for the battle of ministry, to go behind enemy lines, pillage the enemy's camp, and rescue those enslaved to sin, those taken captive to do Satan's will (II Timothy 2:26). Are you up to the challenge? Can you endure the rigors of training? God's Men say, "Yes!" and throw themselves into the purposes of God.

They do not back down, slow down, or shut down. They *never* give up, but always show up and step up. This is not a time for untempered, untrained, and unyielded men to step into the spotlight to satisfy personal desires for "fulfillment" or to do great things to make themselves great. Heroes are not defined here by the length of men's applause but by the breadth of their sacrifice, not set on a stage before thousands but commanding the audience of but One, knowing that it is only His opinion that matters no matter what others' opinions may be.

This is not an invitation to the fainthearted or those who choose not to count the cost now only to turn back later. This is a clarion call to all who would take Christ's yoke upon themselves, to be molded into the simple form of a servant who seeks not his own will, his own pleasures, or his own grand dreams. He seeks **only** the will of Him who sacrificed everything for our good, for our deliverance from the Enemy's snares, that He might use that which He has fashioned in the furnace of affliction for His great glory and for His ultimate purpose of rescuing this lost, broken world. Are you willing to enlist for this mission? This may not be for all men, just Godly Men who are willing to allow the Father to prepare them in the present to release them into their divine destiny.

BRING IT HOME!

To your knowledge, what is God doing or needing to do in your heart as His workmanship to prepare you for the good works He desires you to walk in?

Do you see your age as a barrier to serving God?

What trials or hard circumstances are you facing right now?

Are you struggling to see God's good purposes in some of these incidents in your life? If so, which ones? Talk about these with your mentor. Please understand that many times God chooses not to reveal His purposes for our struggles. You will need to trust Him for each one.

What dreams have you had for your future? List as many as you can here.

Now cross off those that at present you believe focus too much on you and selfish ambition. Be as honest as you can. Talk to your mentor about this list. If you crossed off most or all, begin to pray for *God's* vision for your life to grip your heart. If while doing this lesson and discussing it with your mentor, you believe God is beginning to birth a new vision for your life, write it here:

What "pearls" do you see forming in your life as a result of the "sand" of those trials you listed above?

Can you see how these "pearls" might be used for future ministry? If so, explain.

Epilogue: The Sword Ceremony

When does a boy become a man? Many cultures have different types of ceremonies to usher their sons into manhood. The Vanuatu of the South Pacific have their teen boys dive 100 feet from a platform, bungee style (except using vines), "tap their heads on the ground," and hopefully live to tell about it. The boys from the Hamar tribe of Ethiopia must run across the backs of a long row of steer without falling. Forget marriage, children, or manhood for that matter, should they fail. No Nike super performance-enhanced treadwear permitted! For the less daring and perhaps more sensible, there is the Bar Mitzvah. Here a Jewish boy turning thirteen celebrates this rite of passage as he is now considered a "son of commandment." That is, being a man, he is held personally accountable for observing the law, is eligible to publicly read from the Torah (the first five books of the Bible), and can legally marry and own property. This celebration usually takes the form of a special meal or party. Personally, I'd rather have a party than dive 100 feet and walk away with permanent brain damage!

A Proper Ceremony

What rite of passage do we have for *our* sons? At what age do we consider them men and treat them so? When they get their driver's license at 16? Graduate from high school at 18? Reach the legal drinking age of 21? Graduate from college at 22? Most men I've talked to truly have no idea when they became a man. Some still wonder if they've even reached that milestone. I would like to close out this study in godly manhood by helping us dads define that moment for our sons and form a ceremony that would facilitate that giant step into manhood for them. Though it will not define them (only Christ can do that as He builds His character in them), it will help to call them and significantly transition them to it as we shall see.

In raising four daughters before my son, I've had ample opportunity to think about this subject. For each of my daughters when they turned 16, I took them on a special date to an expensive restaurant of their choice. At some point in the course of the meal, I began sharing with them why I was so very proud of them, giving some specific examples from their lives. I then told them I would like to be the keeper and protector of their heart until that special someone came along and married them. I gave each a purity ring and asked her to covenant with me that she would remain pure and allow me to help guard her heart. These have been very special daddy-daughter occasions, but not something that would be suitable to call my son to manhood. Plus, he's never worn a ring and has no intentions of ever wearing one, except a wedding ring. That symbol just doesn't say "virile" to him. So, what would?

A Purposeful Ceremony

Before I tell you what I did with my son, let me share three reasons why I believe a ceremony for this purpose is important.

First, it is a call to remember the past. When the Israelites had weathered their 40-year wandering in the desert, they came to a decisive moment before the Jordan River. They remembered Moses' parting of the Red Sea just ***after*** leaving their land of slavery. Now, God was wanting another memorable act that would be indelibly marked in their minds just ***before*** entering and conquering the Promised Land. To do this, He stopped the flow of the Jordan several miles upstream. With the ark of the covenant representing God's presence and leading the way, the Israelites crossed over. But before the waters rushed back into place, they had retrieved 12 large stones with which they built a memorial of the occasion at what became their military headquarters in Canaan—Gilgal (Joshua 4:19-24). Here, regardless of the difficulty of these battles (remember, warriors die even in victories), when they returned from their campaigns they were reminded by these stones of the promise and power of God to bring them successfully into this new land.

Memorials are important. Both the Passover in the Old Testament and the Lord's Supper in the New are pictures of God's amazing grace in rescuing us from slavery and setting us free in His new kingdom. The word "remember" is used 16 times in Deuteronomy, and the phrase "do not forget" appears nine times. Not too long ago, my wife returned with some of our daughters and friends from a much anticipated trip to England. They took no fewer than 1,300 pictures during their visit. Can you say "overkill"? Needless to say, they have **never** forgotten this adventure—not one moment! God uses memorials, like pictures, to seal events in our memories that will always remind us of the displays of His grace.

Second, it is a call to embrace the present. If you recall from the introduction, I Corinthians 16:13-14 gives five commands to the church, the middle of which is a single word literally translated, "Be a man!" Hopefully, this study has helped you begin your quest of true, biblical manhood. To be a man means to be full of courage, to cheerfully take on necessary responsibilities, to remain strong in moments when others may be weak, to stand firm in resolve and conviction where God does, and to choose to respond lovingly when hurt has been tossed our way. These are Paul's directives to the Corinthians, and these, among others, are the challenges we need to extend to our sons as we call them in the present to godly manhood. In this ceremonial call to my son, I felt compelled to reiterate the theme of purity that I had spoken about to my daughters. Though it is a serious battle for men, it is one I believed my son could walk victoriously in by God's strength.

Third, it is a call to step into the future. We need to challenge our sons to embark on the journey of discovering their purpose. Along this journey they will encounter numerous opportunities to serve, and so to allow their gifts, talents, and passions to surface. As the last chapter highlighted, we do not want to raise a generation that walks aimlessly in life, uncertain of what they were placed on earth to accomplish.

A Planned Ceremony

In view of these three important factors in calling my son into manhood, I chose to give him a sword instead of a ring. Not only is a sword a masculine symbol, but it conveys the aspects of battle and purity I wanted. On the plaque that now holds my son's sword, I had engraved, "Defender of Purity." It speaks to the dual challenge of both defending the purity of his sisters in Christ and his own. In formulating the ceremony, I asked three other dads to join me in calling their 16- or 17-year-old sons to manhood. Each dad believed his son was ready for this crowning moment to leave behind childish ways and embrace the stage set before them of new responsibilities and challenges.

Each son was bought a sword different from the others; some engraved on the plaque, some on the sword. There is a local Flea Market where a vendor sold a wide assortment of swords and knives ranging from $50-$100. This price range is usually for display swords. Real battle-ready swords are typically quite a bit more expensive. Similar swords can also be purchased online.

The dads met several weeks before the event to discuss the itinerary, the cost of the dinner ($10 per person), and an outline of what we would want to say in our challenge to our son. I have included this below, as well as the challenge I gave to my son, Jim, to help you in formulating your own ceremony.

We met at my house at 5 PM on the appointed day. For the next hour we all played an outdoor game while one of the dads cooked the steaks and others prepared the side dishes. During this time, us dads left our kids outside playing while we retrieved the swords from our vehicles. At this point none of our sons had seen their sword, so we laid them covered on a 6' fold-up table in my family room where we were to hold the ceremony.

After our steak dinner, each dad stood at the front of the room to deliver his charge as his son stood a few feet to his right. Each charge lasted about eight minutes, followed by the sword presentation and the group of men praying over the young man (about five minutes), with a time deference given to the dad to lead the way in prayer. Many powerful, even tear-filled prayers were prayed, and several prophetic words came forth with godly insight and deep conviction. We closed out our evening with a movie that focused on loyalty in battle and principle in life.

It was indeed a memory-building event. The ceremony was filmed, and numerous pictures were taken (this was insisted on by the moms and siblings that were not present). To this day, each son proudly displays his sword in his bedroom ("Gilgal") as a daily reminder of his call to purity and godly manhood. Personally, I have noticed a difference in each of these five young men since our time together (almost a year ago). They have stepped up to the charge, have become even more diligent in their studies, and have taken more seriously their responsibilities and quest to go deeper with Christ as Godly Men and Defenders of Purity.

Sword Ceremony Agenda

Arrive at 5 PM

5:00-6:00 – Games (cooking/grilling dinner)
        Corn Hole
        Redneck Golf

6:00-6:45 – Dinner ($10/person)
        NY Strip steak (16 oz.)
        Baked potatoes
        Corn on the cob
        String beans
        Dessert (ice cream)
        Drink (coffee, soda, water)

6:45-8:00 – Sword Ceremony (Video-taped. See next page.)

8:00-10:00 – Movie (Eat dessert at this time.)

Sword Ceremony

The following is a reproduction of what I handed out to each dad in preparation for their challenge to their son.

(Approximately 10-15 minutes each, including prayer. This will be videotaped.)

(***Please*** take the time to thoroughly think through and pray about what you want to say and write it down, at least in outline form.)

1. Share some fond memories of your son, perhaps a funny one and a serious one that captures your son's character.
2. A word of encouragement—reflect on the positive qualities you see in your son. Perhaps share a recent story to illustrate.
3. Read a Scripture that you believe God has laid on your heart that captures the charge you will give to your son.
4. The Charge—speak into your son's life. Call him to manhood. Be positive. Be prophetic (forthtelling, and perhaps foretelling, should God so lead you). Include the charge to defend his purity, as well as the purity of his sisters in Christ around him and embrace the call to godly manhood that you are now placing upon him. Reveal his potential.
5. Presentation of the sword.
6. Pray over your son. Then other men may pray over your son (short).
7. Take pictures of father and son with sword.

Jim's Challenge

(What follows is my eight-minute challenge to my son, Jim. Please understand, it is a glimpse into a father's heart for his son that seeks to express his intense joy and commendation for him. Consequently, it is heavy on the praise as our charges to our sons should be.)

We still have video footage of a Christmas morning when you were two or three years old, Jim. As the camera pans the room while your mother and sisters are sharing, you are in the background constantly sliding down a large box. You had taken something so boring as a box and managed to entertain yourself and have so much fun that you had forgotten about the actual present that had been inside.

You've grown up now, as tall as your dad! I know you've had fun as a child, but you are turning the page to a new chapter in your life. This chapter, called adulthood, is already upon you, Jim. I remember not too long ago, we had divided the lawn cutting, but you were able to start about 45 minutes before me. You finished your half and then began to work on my part until the whole job was done. I told you that you didn't need to, but you insisted this was what you wanted to do. So, you ended up doing all of yours and a large part of mine. You did this because this is the quality of giving and serving and compassion that you have allowed God to build in you. These are the qualities of a Godly Man. Jim, today I need you to know, you are a man!

A few months ago for your birthday, I had the teens take 15 minutes to share some things about you that they admire and respect. They chose not to follow my directions, and instead shared for *30 minutes*! So, what I'm about to say are not just my thoughts, they are shared by all of your peers, as well.

Jim, you're a hard worker. I've *never* heard you complain about cutting the lawn, even though you come in each week covered in dirt and cut grass. You are focused on and diligent in your studies. You desire to excel and do your very best. I suppose in part you enjoy the competition in class and on tests. Your hard work tells me that you are destined to do *great* things!

You are so faithful and *persistent*. What other word better describes a young man who has his mind set on a goal and proposes a plan that doesn't quite set well with his father, but he asks over and over and over with slight modifications if it could work now until that father finally says, "Now that might work"? *Persistence*! For the last several years you have had daily Quiet Times. Granted, no Captain Crunch until your "5 Things" were done was added motivation, but today you are faithful to seek Jesus early each morning, because you love Him and desire to walk closely with Him.

In Daniel 6, wicked government officials sought to sabotage Daniel's character for personal gain, but they couldn't. *"They could find no ground of accusation or evidence of corruption, inasmuch as he was faithful, and no negligence or corruption was to be found in him"* (v. 4). Jim, you too are a man of integrity. You hate compromise and are completely trustworthy in all you do.

You are also sensitive to other people's needs and feelings. I'm sure having four sisters and a mother like you have has greatly benefited you here. You take after your mother in how you love people. Never forget, for strength to be truly strong it must always have a tender side.

You also are attentive to detail: your room is spotless, your dresser drawers are *wonderfully* organized, and everything has its place in your room and closet—sorry, Buddy, that one's on me! Jim, the Lord's Grace is upon you. I am seeing it poured out upon you in two stages.

First, *"he who is faithful in a very little thing is faithful also in much"* (Luke

16:10). We see this demonstrated in Joseph's life: *"Now his master saw that the LORD was with him and how the LORD caused all that he did to prosper in his hand. So, Joseph found favor in his sight…and all that he owned he put in his charge…the LORD blessed the Egyptian's house on account of Joseph"* (Genesis 39:4-5). Be faithful in **all** God places upon your shoulders, Son. He will bless you with greater things and make you a blessing to all.

In your life, faithfulness will be the seeds of anointed and successful ministry, **the second stage** God will bring you into. *"Elijah said to Elisha, 'Ask what I shall do for you before I am taken from you.' And Elisha said, 'Please, let a double portion of your spirit be upon me'"* (II Kings 2:9).

As Elisha **longed** for the anointing of God for the new ministry that lay before him and **received** it in greater measure than anticipated, so you will **long** for that greater anointing. So, be faithful in all He entrusts to you, then walk in His anointing, in His timing, and in the call He places upon you.

Son, today is a very special day. ***Today***, I call you to be a Defender of Purity, both in yourself and the young ladies around you, to defend that which is holy

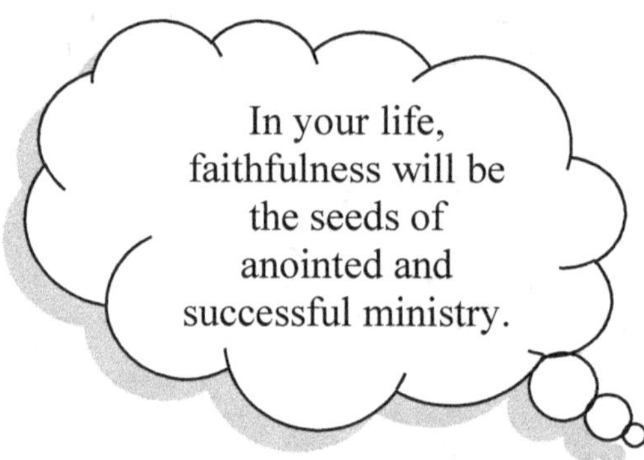

and sacred, to protect honor and dignity, to allow no place to our Enemy, the Devil, and to champion that high calling of Virtue. ***Today***, I call you to continue your progress in your journey in Christ's character, to push past ***every*** obstacle, and to shine His light in this dark world so others may see Jesus in you. ***Today***, I call you to new levels of purpose and ministry and strength, to walk in your God-given, God-anointed calling that seeks Jesus and His kingdom first and others second. ***Today***, I call you to bear the mantle of leadership opportunities with zeal and passion. ***Today***, I call you to that Great Calling—Manhood!

Jim, I need you to know that I could not be prouder of you! All of these things I convey to you today, you are already walking in. It may not ***feel*** like it at times, but you have impacted many around you. You are an excellent example of steel and velvet, of strength and compassion. Your mother and sisters adore you. They feel safe with you around. They feel protected. One day I'm sure you will get married, and that special woman in your life will feel the same way. She too will adore you!

I've hung this plaque in my study for many years. It says, "If a man is honest with others and with himself… If he receives gratefully and gives quietly… If he is gentle enough to feel and strong enough to show his feelings… If he is slow to see the faults of others but quick to discover their goodness… If he is cheerful in difficult times and modest in success… If he does his best to be true to his beliefs… Then he is truly an admirable man." Jim, you are an admirable man!

To illustrate what I am saying, I give you this symbol of Manhood as a Defender of Purity—a sword! Slay the enemy, Jim. Conquer for Christ's kingdom!

A Final Challenge

Allow me to leave you with one last word. Remember that we presently live in a society that does all it can to either erase the distinctions between men and women or hyper-inflate the realities of such differences, appealing to macho-ism or sexual attractions. The world flounders in understanding right and wrong. Confusion abounds. God's Word alone is our moral compass. It faithfully points due north. Never be ashamed, men, to hold it up as our standard for truth. Stand resolved *never* to back down in the face of ridicule, *never* to concede to the lies espoused by the "experts" as facts, *never* to yield ground to the assault of that darkness around us, and *never* to give in or give up when countenanced by what seems like overwhelming temptation. Godly Men stand firm, poised for battle, swords tempered and sharpened, armor fitted and in place, minds keen, and spirits fierce, knowing their struggle is not against the men and women of this world lost in sin but against the evil, spiritual warriors of darkness behind them.

Always make it your goal to live a surrendered life, yielded to the king's commands. Take seriously the charge to change this world, rescuing those enslaved to sin and addicted to self. Only the gospel of our Lord Jesus Christ has the power to open hearts, change minds, break chains, and bring salvation. You are and always will be His servants. Give yourself to His call. Listen for it. Long for it. Live for it. And, yes, even die for it! And there will be awaiting you a crown of righteousness your Savior will bestow upon you in that final day with these words: *"Well done, good and faithful servant! You have been faithful with a few things; I will put you in charge of many things. Come and share your master's happiness!"* (Matthew 25:21—NIV, 1978).

God bless you in your pursuit of Him, Man of God!

Author's Invitation

If you found this discipleship manual helpful, I would love to hear from you! The purpose of this workbook is to help the church effectively mentor the next generation by raising up young men who are passionate for Christ and unashamed to live out their faith in a way that profoundly impacts those around them. To help further this purpose or simply because you enjoyed this book, could you:

1. **Give a review**. Do so on Amazon. This greatly influences others to experience the same help and transformation you have. Then spread the word!

2. **Check out my author web page and sign up on my email list,** if you have not already, to get a FREEBIE and regular updates about the release of upcoming books and to receive articles, fun activities for kids, and other awesome stuff! Check it out here:
www.powerlineprod.com/forging-godly-men

3. **Email me** at:
Pastormike@powerlinecc.com

4. And did I mention **give a review**? Thanks!

The Noland Kids Adventure Series

After moving into a newly inherited house, the Noland kids discover clues to a supposed treasure hidden by their great-great-grandfather. But when town rumors and some spiteful neighbors suggest foul play was involved, Caleb and David set out on a quest to prove otherwise.

With unexpected dangers looming large and threatening their mission, can the Noland kids discover the mysterious treasure, or whatever lies at the end of their treacherous venture, before time runs out and all is lost?

The parents of twelve-year-old Lens Kabambi have gone missing in their search for a lost city. The Noland kids, Caleb, David, and Lizzy, now eight years older since their last adventure, suspend their missions trip in the Congo to help find them. But dangers lurk around every corner and the quest seems doomed from the start.

With incredible odds stacked against them and an unexpected enemy endangering their search, the Noland kids must uncover the dusty clues to this ancient city and discover its long, lost light in order to rescue Lens' parents… and themselves!

In search of their father who has gone missing, the Noland kids travel to Vietnam's world-famous Phong Nha cave system but find themselves in a whole new world vastly different from their own and on the brink of disaster.

Enmeshed in a deep history of distrust and feud, three tribal leaders guard their land, traditions, and possessions with a jealous eye and a misplaced focus. But can the Nolands shine truth in this maze of dark, twisted lies and find a way out before these primitive civilizations self-destruct?

At a camp on a Caribbean island with forty orphans, the Noland kids discover a two-century-old riddle that leads to something more than a pirate's treasure and realize that life is not always Paradise.

The dark, mysterious history of Paradise Cove is complexly entwined with its foreboding future. So, Caleb, David, and Lizzy must unravel the hidden (and, yes, at times very dangerous) secrets of this little tropical island before utter evil is unleashed and the lives of these orphans, and more, are lost!

About the Author

Pastor and author Mike Curtis offers dads a valuable tool to mentor their sons in his discipleship manual ***Forging Godly Men***. He is also the author of the popular **Noland Kids Adventure Series**. Growing up in a sports-focused family that loved camping, exploring, and all things adventure, Mike dove into teen ministry in his early twenties to creatively bring the Good News to a distracted and struggling generation.

He is married to the popular homeschooling author and speaker Meredith Curtis. They live in Lake Mary, Florida and have five children and eight grandchildren. As a homeschool conference speaker and pastor of Powerline Church, his passion is sharing life-giving principles from God's Word that impact and transform others.

In his spare time, he loves to watch adventure movies like The Lord of the Rings and The Hobbit trilogies with his family and friends, and on occasion has been found sacrificing for those he loves by watching a Hallmark romance. He can also be found indulging in books on apologetics, theology, and leadership, in addition to some aggressive ping pong matches during discipleship time with young men. And next to a good steak, Mike's favorite dish is beef tongue!

His desire is to use his books to mentor the next generation, sharing Christ and biblical principles of character in relevant and enjoyable adventure stories and practical studies.

www.ingramcontent.com/pod-product-compliance
Lightning Source LLC
Chambersburg PA
CBHW081925120726
47997CB00010B/3038